Joyce Cary's Trilogies

Books by Hazard Adams

Fiction
The Horses of Instruction
The Truth About Dragons

Nonfiction
The Academic Tribes

Criticism
Blake and Yeats: The Contrary Vision
William Blake: A Reading of the Shorter Poems
The Contexts of Poetry
The Interests of Criticism
Lady Gregory
Philosophy of the Literary Symbolic
Joyce Cary's Trilogies: Pursuit of the Particular Real

Books edited by Hazard Adams

Poems by Robert Simeon Adams
Poetry: An Introductory Anthology
Fiction As Process (with Carl Hartman)
William Blake: Jerusalem, Selected Poems and Prose
Critical Theory Since Plato

Joyce Cary's Trilogies
Pursuit of the Particular Real

Hazard Adams

A Florida State University Book
University Presses of Florida
Tallahassee

Quotations from Joyce Cary's novels are made by permission of
Curtis, Brown, Ltd., on behalf of the Joyce Cary estate and by permission of Harper & Row, Publishers, Inc.

Herself Surprised, © Joyce Cary, 1941; *To Be a Pilgrim*, © Joyce
Cary, 1942; *The Horse's Mouth*, © Joyce Cary, 1944. Copyright © 1957
by Arthur Lucius Michael Cary and David Alexander Ogilvie.

Prisoner of Grace, © Joyce Cary, 1952; *Except the Lord*, © Joyce
Cary, 1953; *Not Honour More*, © Joyce Cary, 1955.

for Carl Hartman

Contents

Preface

"Pursuit" in the title of this book is not Joyce Cary's but my effort to enunciate a particularity that, however elusive to critical discourse, Cary has successfully embodied in his two trilogies. I have written this book, first, because I believe that these best works of Cary are not nearly well enough known or highly enough regarded by serious readers of prose fiction, and I want to celebrate them, and, second, because Cary's work raises important questions for the study of narrative in a relatively pure form. I am writing to serious readers, not merely to other academic critics, though I find it appropriate to engage the issues that have become common in the published criticism of Cary's work, as well as more general issues about which there has been recent theorizing, but not with Cary's work in the forefront. From the time of Wayne Booth's *The Rhetoric of Fiction* (1961), which gives only the briefest mention to Cary, through numerous theoretical studies of narrative like Scholes and Kellogg's *The Nature of Narrative*, to Gerard Genette's *Narrative Discourse* and the recent spate of writing on the subject, much of it dull, mechanical, and repetitive, Cary's name rarely if ever appears—in spite of the fact that Cary took what Booth calls the "unreliable narrator" very far in a special direction. He took it too far, perhaps, to be attractive to a Chicago-based criticism which since the time of Ronald S. Crane's famous essay on *Tom Jones* has been much interested in the plots of prose fiction. But he may not have been politically radical enough to interest those who work under the domination of continental critical movements. Cary is a very English novelist in a tradition of English Protestantism and English Liberalism.

Cary expressed his views of politics and art in several books of nonfiction and essays. Almost all who have written at any length about him have employed this material to demonstrate that they are the views explicit or implicit in his novels. (On occasion there has been real disagreement about their value and even about what they are.) The general tendency has been to emphasize the abstract ideas Cary professes and to be content with them as explications of his novels. After noting this critical tendency in his good brief introduction to Cary, R. W. Noble (p. 106) states that Cary's basic metaphysical ideas are "implicit in his best novels and explicit in his least satisfactory. He is a novelist who is most successful in works in which the coherent and original expression of true perceptions, emotions, and sensations subsumes the communication of metaphysical truths." I believe Cary would have agreed with this remark, if it is understood to mean that the "metaphysics" of a novel is never properly abstract but always properly consubstantial with the novel's radical particularity, which is what constitutes its way of constructing the world.

Cary criticism seems to be trapped in circularity. The circle moves from various abstract ideas found in his nonfiction, to novel, back to those ideas, and it has now expanded about as far as it can. A good deal of repetition is attributable to Cary if one remains in this circle or at this level of abstraction, and a good deal of repetition goes along with it in the criticism of his work. It has occurred in spite of the one overriding abstract idea in Cary that implicitly rejects the abstracting approach—the importance of the continued presence of the particular and unique in any artistic creation. Cary's allegiance to this principle rarely wavers in his best work. It provides, however, merely the beginning of a way to discuss the novels, enabling us to proceed toward grasping (but never finally articulating) the particularity of his trilogies.

Cary's commitment to the particular is for him a matter of being true to what the art of prose fiction is. His way came to him only after a long period of self-training. But Cary liked very much to theorize, and he tended to read his own work too schematically. I don't mean that he always did so. Indeed, he made many interesting statements about his work; and some of his schematizing discussions have a considerable *critical* interest for us. However, an argument can be made that Cary talked too freely about his work, and that the prefaces to the Carfax edition were a mistake (as interesting as some are). They seem to have led readers to relax their vigilance and adopt a narrower or more distant reading of the novels than they should have. If one were to make this argument, however, one might want also to note that the prefaces were written at a time when, given the reviews he had received, Cary had good reason to think it necessary to provide a primer. It would be foolish, of course, to disregard the prefaces, but neither does one want to take all that they say for granted.

My aim is to recognize the particularity that makes Cary's two trilogies the rich works that they are. But critical discourse is abstractive and allegorizing in spite of all efforts to make it something else. (Sometimes it actually does become something else, and that can sometimes be worse.) What I hope to achieve is a growing nearness to the works, culminating in my last chapter in the presentation of a critical language adequate to the task of maintaining that nearness, so that the works are here again in a more intense way. At this point it may be of interest to offer Cary's own notion of the critic's task, without assuming that all Cary criticism should follow it: "Nor indeed did [Boileau] understand his business as a critic, which was not to make laws, but to discover them—to explore the structure of each work by itself and show, if possible, where it succeeded and why and where it failed; not to define from outside but to clarify from within" (*SE*, 141).

There have been good books on Cary to which one is inevitably indebted. I have not hesitated to call on them for help or, from time to time, to quarrel with them. No book yet, however, gives itself to a rigorous analysis of the language of Cary's speculative thought before making critical use of it or finds a way to approach as close as I think is possible to the particularity of the novels. One of the reasons for this has been that in even the best criticism of Cary there has been little theoretical self-consciousness. Some of the most well known criticism of Cary has been, perhaps for this reason, misleading. The Cary presented by Malcolm Foster in his biography (1968) could not, it seems to me, have written the trilogies. Cary's ethical stance has been seriously misread and erroneously judged in Robert Bloom's study (1962) and his view keeps reappearing in less extreme forms. Thus, even after twenty years it requires systematic refutation. Barbara Fisher's study (1980), though helpful in its early, more general chapters, is quite untrustworthy in its particular interpretations, allegorizing the characters of the trilogies unmercifully, and by tenuous chains of reasoning based on naïve principles arriving at ruthlessly abstract readings. I shall not pause to quarrel with her on specific points. All but the last chapter of my book was written before hers came into my hands, and in any case to answer her whenever we disagree would take far too long. It must suffice to say (except for remarks I make in the last chapter) that I approach Cary in an entirely different way and believe that her way leads to a false picture of the two trilogies, though a different one from Bloom's. The most recent book on Cary, Cornelia Cook's *Joyce Cary: Liberal Principles* (1981), also became available after my work was virtually complete. In a few places, I have been able to take account of it. Her interest is in how Cary's political (and ethical) liberalism is embodied in his texts. Her gaze is mainly on Tom Wilcher and Chester Nimmo, among the characters of the two trilogies, and her concern risks restricting her to a more abstracted interpretation than is my aim. Much Cary criticism has turned on the issues Bloom raised, and a surprising amount of criticism in general still harbors such notions, not new when he wrote but gathered together in Wayne Booth's *The Rhetoric of Fiction* in the previous year. The issues raised there are still present in about the same shape today, and I shall not ignore them but rather attempt to treat them as I pass on to a study of the particular.

My first three chapters constitute the passing through. They begin with an abstract view of Cary's thought and the two trilogies under the rubric of notions of the real, the symbolic, and freedom. At the outset I take some time to straighten out a few persistent confusions in common readings of the key terms of Cary's own critical and philosophical discourse. There follow efforts to engage in a critical discourse of my own that can focus gradually on the particulars of the trilogies. Finally, there is a conclusion which is a renewal of a preface to reading by way of return to the abstract, but this time a set of critical categories for the study of fictive narrative derived from an observation of what it has seemed necessary to do in the preceding chapters. Constructed after those chapters were written, it contains a somewhat barbaric vocabulary that I have not imposed by hindsight, because to do so would clog up discussion. I have been advised by more than one astute reader of my manuscript to place this last, and last written, chapter first. My ground for not doing so is its purely theoretical nature. I hope I shall be forgiven by my theoretically oriented colleagues if I declare that theory best generates itself, for me at least, *in* the process of criticism and that criticism does not necessarily come in the act of theorizing. Thus my theoretical chapter remains, good advice to the contrary, at the end in the position in which I wrote it. Those who want their theory first, rather than where I discovered it, can easily turn to chapter 6 and read it at once.

Preface

This book actually began with my writing an essay on Cary designed to be part of my recent *Philosophy of the Literary Symbolic*. However, the essay, which constitutes Chapter Two here, soon grew beyond my concerns at the time into questions of narrative. *Philosophy of the Literary Symbolic* and that chapter were written with the help of a Guggenheim Fellowship. I therefore again gratefully acknowledge the assistance of the Guggenheim Foundation, which helped me set forth on the rest of the task.

I am indebted to Professor Andrew Wright, whose book on Cary remains an excellent introduction, and to Winifred Davin for important help early in my work, to Professors James B. Meriwether and James Gindin for their most helpful reading of my manuscript, to the Bodleian Library, the libraries of the University of California and the University of Washington, and to two groups of students at the University of California, Irvine, who discussed Cary's trilogies with me. More recently members of the colloquium in theory at the University of Washington very helpfully discussed a version of chapter 6. Unpublished materials are quoted from the Osborn Collection of Joyce Cary Papers in the Bodleian Library of Oxford University by permission of Winifred Davin, executrix of Joyce Cary's literary estate. I am particularly grateful to Mary Gazlay for typing and generally editing the manuscript.

This book is dedicated to Carl Hartman. Years ago he and I, as colleagues on the staff of *Epoch*, discussed stories submitted to it. From those discussions I learned more about the criticism of prose fiction than I have since, and I think I have learned at least something since.

Abbreviations Used in the Text

The text of Cary's novels used is, except for *Except the Lord*, the Carfax edition. However, there are many obvious errors in that edition, and I have silently corrected some of them by referring to the American editions published by Harper and Row.

Books by Joyce Cary

AR: *Art and Reality: Ways of the Creative Process*. New York: Harper & Brothers, 1958.

CAF: *The Case for African Freedom and Other Writings on Africa*. Austin: University of Texas Press, 1962.

EL: *Except the Lord*. London: Michael Joseph, 1953.

HM: *The Horse's Mouth* (Carfax edition). London: Michael Joseph, 1951.

HS: *Herself Surprised* (Carfax edition). London: Michael Joseph, 1951.

NHM: *Not Honour More* (Carfax edition). London: Michael Joseph, 1966.

OC: Unpublished material in the Osborn Collection of the Bodleian Library, Oxford University.

PG: *Prisoner of Grace* (Carfax edition). London: Michael Joseph, 1954.

PM: *Power in Men*, Introduction by Hazard Adams. Seattle: University of Washington Press, 1963.

SE: *Selected Essays*, ed. A. G. Bishop, Introduction by Dame Helen Gardner. London: Michael Joseph, 1976.

TBP: *To Be a Pilgrim* (Carfax edition). London: Michael Joseph, 1951.

Other Books and Articles on Cary's Work Cited by Author in the Text

Bloom, Robert. *The Indeterminate World: A Study of the Novels of Joyce Cary*. Philadelphia: University of Pennsylvania Press, 1962.

Brawer, Judith. "The Triumph of Defeat: A Study of Joyce Cary's First Trilogy." *Texas Studies in Literature and Language* 10 (Winter 1969): 625–34.

Bridge, Thomas James. "Objective Reality in *The Horse's Mouth*." Master's thesis, Ohio State University, 1964.

Cook, Cornelia. *Joyce Cary: Liberal Principles*. London: Vision Press, 1981.

Echeruo, Michael J. C. *Joyce Cary and the Dimensions of Order*. London and Basingstoke: The Macmillan Press, 1979.

Fisher, Barbara. *Joyce Cary: The Writer and His Theme*. Gerrard's Cross: Colin Smythe, 1980.

Foster, Malcolm. *Joyce Cary: A Biography*. Boston: Houghton, Mifflin, 1968.

Garrett, George. "The Major Poetry of Joyce Cary." *Modern Fiction Studies* 9 (Autumn 1963): 245–56.

Hall, James. *The Tragic Comedians: Seven British Novelists*. Bloomington: Indiana University Press, 1963.

Hoffman, Charles G. *Joyce Cary: The Comedy of Freedom*. Pittsburgh: University of Pittsburgh Press, 1964.

Larsen, Golden. *The Dark Descent: Social Change and Moral Responsibility in the Novels of Joyce Cary*. London: Michael Joseph, 1965.

Mahood, M. M. *Joyce Cary's Africa*. London: Methuen, 1964.

Mitchell, Giles. *The Art Theme in Joyce Cary's First Trilogy*. The Hague: Mouton, 1971.

Noble, R. W. *Joyce Cary*. Edinburgh: Oliver and Boyd, 1973.

Söderskog, Ingvar. *Joyce Cary's "Hard Conceptual Labour": A Structural Analysis of* To Be a Pilgrim. Göteborg: Aeta Universitatis Gotheburgensis, 1977.

Stockholder, Fred. "The Triple Vision in Joyce Cary's First Trilogy." *Modern Fiction Studies* 9 (Autumn 1963): 231–44.

Teeling, John, S. J. "Joyce Cary's Moral World." *Modern Fiction Studies* 9 (Autumn 1963): 276–83.

Wolkenfeld, Jack. *Joyce Cary, The Developing Style*. New York: New York University Press, 1968.

Wright, Andrew. *Joyce Cary: A Preface to His Novels*. London: Chatto and Windus, 1958.

1
The Abstract Real

I begin with consideration of one of Cary's words that frequently
enters discussions of Cary at an early stage, often in a confusing
and sometimes in a confused way. For Cary, "real" is usually a
noun. It contains persons, places, things, ideas that have gotten to
the stage of expression, and ideas still on the way. It is very, very
large—too large to be of much use as a critical term or a philosophical term. The "real" is also very powerful, in the sense that it is always *here*, something for human power to confront. One is likely to
understand it in the way that one comes to grasp the ubiquity of
fate in Hardy or the enveloping fog in Dickens's *Bleak House*. Except
that it is rarely mentioned by name in the novels; it is present only
in its many separate unique instances. In Cary's nonfiction, by contrast, it is the product of Cary's speculation, something built up as
an abstraction. Yet as an abstraction it has a dubious life of its own,
and it is voracious, enveloping other words almost as fast as Cary
offers them to it. It is not something sought but never found; that
would be "being," a term Cary employs a few times, but not with
the enthusiasm that he expends to make "real" a noun. The stubborn "nounness" of "real"—there are "reals" in Cary, like Blake's
spaces—strikes me as a deliberate form of emphasis which, even in
the writing of Cary that comes closest to philosophy, seems to be
trying to make abstractions into particulars. "Every class is individual," Blake held against Reynolds in his annotations to the third
discourse, and Cary, who read Blake carefully, probably agreed. I
believe he regarded his major abstraction as a giant form grown
from experiences of particular othernesses. He would have liked it
to have the force of a thing. Jack Wolkenfeld (p. 111) is correct to
remark that "Cary . . . denies the existence of abstractions except
for the strange, the often dangerous and contradictory existence
they have in real people in real situations." In *Power in Men* (p. 52)

Cary writes, "Tradition, patriotism, the ideas of national honour have immense power; so also do ideas common to humanity— brotherhood, equality; but they are real only in the acts of individual men," and (p. 88) "what is certain in the average is merely probability in the individual." Cary has not too much respect for probability. The whole of his approach might well be summed up in a remark he makes in *Power in Men* (p. 124), where, with respect to a matter he is discussing, he says, "Abstractly this difference is trifling; in practice it is real and profound."

Before he was finished the noun "real" was crammed full of all that is available to intuition. There is something left on the other side of it called "being," but "being" strikes one here as an afterthought, while in a philosopher's work one knows that if it is mentioned it is central even in its absence. "Being" appears in *Art and Reality* to be the product of an obeisance to philosophy itself and to a momentary desire for metaphysical neatness. As far as I can see, it has no status at all in the novels, whereas all that fills up the noun "real" is very, very present there, and is quite enough.

If one needs a large critical frame to put around the novels, the "real" is it, but it is more a proscenium arch than a frame, because one looks through it. From a distance necessary to get a general impression through the arch, the design one sees is quite large and only a design. Early Cary criticism, and much of the late, has seen the "real" of the speculative prose in the novels, not so often the "reals" that make it up. This has been quite all right and perhaps even necessary. This chapter does almost the same thing, but it also insists that as we get farther away into an abstract notion of the "real," the particular "reals" of the novels tend to get lost. Criticism must return to them. Blake had his heroic figure Los going around making "spaces" as a contrary to abstract Newtonian space, because particular experience is lost in that space.

Sometimes in the speculative writing—that is, chiefly *Power in Men, Art and Reality*, and some of the essays—Cary appears to be speaking of a metaphysical real or an epistemological objectivity, but he is not a philosopher, though clearly he enjoyed speculation. Although he engages philosophical notions in these works—Kant's thing-in-itself and categorical imperative, Croce's intuition—one soon realizes that his interest is that of a novelist in experience, and the "real" is *really* whatever any character comes up against, including that character's own selfhood, the intransigent and the unpredictable in the world.

2

Behind the "real" there is, as I have mentioned, "being." This is absolute truth, which we cannot know. Although Cary rejects the Kantian thing-in-itself, he allows it in through the back door in a remark in *Art and Reality*: ". . . immediately life takes place in the subconscious, before it is known to reflection; and its sources, the active nature of being itself, are completely beyond the human imagination" (*AR*, 116). This tends to make Cary's "real" an attribute of "being," which is an absence, but in his trilogies one doesn't find this "being" as an absence. It is ignored. Rather, one discovers a reversal, because the "real" is so fundamentally present in the forms of all that opposes the individual human will that there is no room for it except as an attribute of the "real." Unless it is God. But God, too, becomes for Cary a presence.

Let me ask again, what is this "real" of Cary's speculative writing? One other mention of "being" is necessary. He speaks of "matter" as "certain fixed characteristics of being"; it presents us with a "whole framework of reality" (*AR*, 6). This "real" is physical law, which we defy at our peril. But though the "real" contains physical law, it is much more. Cary says simply that it is the world as it is, the world in its own quality. It is the world independent of the perceiver, but Cary does not intend this to mean that he defines it in terms of Locke's primary qualities of experience, though it would include those qualities, did they exist outside of Locke's fictive construction. Cary does not engage that venerable question of the subject and the object, though he uses both terms. Indeed, he calls the "real" the objective world, but it is not a world objective merely because measurable, though it includes this aspect of things and physical laws. As Jack Wolkenfeld points out (p. 758), Cary objects to Hegel because he feels that Hegel doesn't take into account a physical reality that "affects the needs and feelings of men." Cary's "real" always involves an individual, but is not there by virtue only of the individual. It is at the same time always a particular here and now, not simply *for* an individual but involving the individual. Further, the individual belongs to this "real," while yet he is apart from it. This is the first and most important of a series of five paradoxes which I shall attempt to isolate and by means of which I hope we can understand the trilogies from the abstracted distance the paradoxes create.

Cary describes the "real" in a number of ways. The "real" is dynamic, a temporal process; yet it has within it fixed characteristics. There is, for example, a "universal real" of feelings, which I take to

3

mean an unchanging human nature. There is a "universal moral real" that accompanies the consistencies of physical fact (laws) and of human feelings. Mainly, though, Cary fills up the "real" with attributes: freedom, liberty, power, family love and responsibility, the good, ambition, loss, bitterness, danger, cruelty, anxiety, injustice, disease, evil. The "real" includes the "facts." The above are "facts" that Cary specifically identifies with the "real." Another fact is that of human "machinery," which is the individual's own physical being. It can be a part of the real as *other*, part of a real placed over against one's freedom. It can also be the vehicle of freedom. A subparadox here is Cary's insistence that "liberty cannot exist without determinism or determinism without liberty" (*OC*, Box 202), that "the freedom of man absolutely depends on the determinism of matter for its own exercise" (*OC*, Box 232). The alternative is chaos as chaos.

Events constitute the real. They are the "actual." Cary sometimes calls things in novels "actual," that is, particular; but mainly the "actual" is what makes up society, the sum of events at any time. Events, simply as events, are a chaos full of chance and injustice. There is a lot of determinism in events because of physical laws and human machinery (but that does not make them less a chaos in sum). Ideas as events are only partly determined. Cary invokes the idea of human freedom here, always pushing back against the real as determined event. One notices that the real itself is insufficiently formed, despite its laws, at least for the human imagination, which sets out to do something with it, rather than merely to react passively to it. (I shall have more to say about this in chapter 2.)

But there is a problem here, because this pushing back against the real, which is freedom itself in Cary, sometimes looks very much like possession—not quite demonic possession, but almost— and thus free only from the rational. It is perhaps captured by a sort of instinct. One sometimes wonders how close Cary's notion of freedom comes to the quality that Plato worried about in poets and rhapsodes.

The second of Cary's paradoxes is that even a determined event is unique. The basic real is a machine or a bundle of laws, but it is also a "living whole," being infused with the products of a freedom acting over against it. Though the sun rises daily according to physical law, and each day as mechanism is the same, as event it is unique. This uniqueness is the result of the free individual's involvement with the real.

4

The fundamental relation of individual and real is grounded in "intuition." Cary quarrels with Croce over the nature of intuition, and that quarrel I discuss in the next chapter. Here I want only to show how Cary uses the term and draws from it a third paradox. Intuition, as Cary uses the word in *Art and Reality*, seems to be feeling working directly upon events at a pre-verbal or pre-symbolic level. Intuition is the power of an individual (as separate from the real) to reconnect with the real. In one's effort to express an intuition (about which more in chapter 2) one achieves sympathy with other minds and things which constitute part of the real. Intuitions are ways of "checking" our abstract notions of the real against reality itself.

This emphasis on "checking" against the real is one reason Cary rejects Croce's argument:

> I have to admit that for all Croce's brilliant argument, I think his theory fails to meet the facts. I suspect also that it has been disastrous to artists who have attempted to believe that all intuition is expression, all expression art. For if intuition is expression, how does the artist know anything but his expression? He is cut off from reality by his own act. (*SE*, 135)

In all of this, feeling plays a role that dominates reason and method. It is the "ultimate motive power of man's action" (*OC*, Box 200). So one can see that Cary does not think of contact with the "real" merely in the language of verification according to science, though he does not reject such methods. But it is clear that feeling is a means of checking one's fictive constructs (scientific or mythical) by correspondence to the real. The paradox, our third, is that intuition is the first step by which we proceed to make the fictions that require checking by feeling, which is intuition's ground. The reason for this paradox, which is of a circular nature, is that for Cary there is a gap between intuition and expression. Expression culminates in the symbol, which involves a certain coherence while at the same time it runs the risk of losing correspondence achieved in the intuition. Expression seems to be intuition thematized via technique, producing the symbol.

The symbol is a sign by means of which we fix and communicate the real of intuition. At least we try to. The gap between intuition and expression via these signs causes a certain loss of the intuition or, perhaps, a distorting elaboration, whether aesthetic or conceptual. This expressed symbol is what constitutes the social or cultural world in which we live, the humanly created social structure at any given time, which is combined with the "real," but in fact becomes part of the real that the individual in his freedom faces. But it is always *in process* like Blake's London, eternally building and decaying. Thus we live in part in a dream of the future, a remembrance of the past. Dreams of the future can go wrong, of course, and remembrance can be sentimental. All these are the risks of symbolic constructions that are essentially "as if," including scientific constructions:

> [W]hat scientists do is to dissect the living body of the world and examine one cell or organ *as if* it could work alone and by itself. And the *as if* is achieved by an effort of the imagination, representing to the scientist's mind, a situation which does not or could not exist. (*OC*, Box 200)

The fourth paradox is that suggested by the notion of a "total environment," partly "real," partly symbolic, based on an "as if," that can go wrong and needs to be checked by intuition against the "real," but also, wrong as it may be, can become part of the real by the persistence of its wrongness in society. This becomes a total "real," inasmuch as the individual comes up against the symbolic beliefs of others, no matter how fanciful. A total "real" at any given time can be infused with varying degrees of good and evil. Because there is a "universal moral real" available to intuition, we can know such worlds directly in their goodness and evil and act upon that intuition to create a new symbolic order. One can then claim that nature affects the symbolic, which has to come up against it, and the symbolic can affect the real by its simple presence in nature. This is not exactly the way Oscar Wilde had it in *The Decay of Lying* when he said that nature imitates art as much as art imitates nature, but it is close. Cary will have little to do with the idea of imitation, while Wilde was still trying to demolish it.

Finally, there is something we call "meaning," which is a characteristic of life, though meaning often seems to dissolve in the chaos of event. "Trollope found in life what we all find, a mass of detail without meaning, of useless cruelty, stupid evil, blind fate, fools doing accidental good, and well-meaning saints doing immense evil." For this reason Cary declares that "to copy life would be to produce nonsense" (*SE*, 150). Meaning is a product of art, which Cary defines very broadly as any submission of intuition to expression and the symbol. The fifth paradox is that meaning is clearly meant to be a return to the "real," a deepening of our sense of it, in a coherent shape that in its coherence nevertheless maintains a correspondence by means of feeling: "The reader is often aware of learning more about the world from a book than he gets from actual experience, not only because in the book he is prepared to find significance in events that mean nothing in life, but because those events in the book are related to each other in a coherent valuation which sets them in ordered relation of importance, and this can reveal to him in what had seemed the mere confusion of his daily affairs new orders of meaning" (*AR*, 137). Cary sees as very difficult this effort to return to the real via the expression of a symbolic structure. We, too, see it as difficult as we try to follow his arguments in the speculative writing. With all the obstacles, how can we possibly ever return to the "real"? No one, let alone Cary in his novels, says it is easy!

Moreover, this problem is intensified by Cary's concern with the necessity of communication among individuals via the feeling:

1. "Only art can convey both the fact and the feeling about the fact, for it works in the medium of common sympathies" (*AR*, 10).
2. "The symbol, in short, like the concept . . . is also the enemy of the intuition" (*AR*, 84).
3. "Wittgenstein has said that everyone has his own world. I should rather say that men are together in feeling, in sympathy, but alone in mind" (*SE*, 157).

Clearly it is art, in Cary's very broad sense of all symbolic expression, that is supposed to be the vehicle of sympathetic identification. But may not art, by Cary's own argument, or part of it at least, be creating as many difficulties for communion as it overcomes, as many false "as ifs" as true ones? Is not the artist dissatisfied with the "real," clashing with it and even, therefore, with those to whom he is supposed to be communicating? Cary's novels, at least, seem to answer "yes" to these questions without giving up the possibility of a fortunate success, and so there is darkness beneath Cary's optimism. He fears for what man may do with his imagination.

The five paradoxes I have mentioned are not all explicitly stated as paradoxes by Cary, but a study of the vocabulary he employs— being, matter, the real, the actual, facts, events, intuition, expression, symbol, art, meaning—leads us to them when we attempt to bring an abstract order to his speculative thought. But this thought is hardly rigorous in its use of these words. They come and go, enlarge and contract. Past a certain point one is imposing a conceptual neatness at a higher level that is not present at the lower where Cary is working. Furthermore, one senses that even Cary's lower level is not the level on which he is really thinking, that he is thinking in specific events that expand into the abstract quasimetaphysical vocabulary with which I have been coping. Even here the words seem more like creatures in a fiction, strange Blakean creatures with powers of sudden expansion and contraction in a hierarchical world. One might at this point think of one of Gulley Jimson's ideas for a painting—a presentation of God as a huge human form with people moving about and fighting in his stomach, causing a cosmic gastric disturbance (*HS*, 206). One senses, too, that Cary's speculative vocabulary is evolved as meaning from his novels or the experience of making them. They seem like abstractions from intransigent living forms with which he had to cope. His *Art and Reality* seems to draw its power from certain spots of time that engender, in the course of speculation on them, the more abstract vocabulary. The two are, in fact, intermeshed; but one senses the priority of the particular events:

> I remember one of my children, as a baby of about fourteen months, sitting in its pram watching a newspaper on the grass close by. There was a breeze along the ground and the newspaper was moving. Sometimes the top page swelled up and fluttered; sometimes two or three pages were moved and seemed to struggle together; sometimes the whole paper rose up on one side and flapped awkwardly for a few feet before tumbling down again. The child did not know that this object was a newspaper moved by the wind. It was watching with intense absorbed curiosity a creature entirely new to its experience, and through the child's eyes I had a pure intuition of the newspaper as object, as an individual thing at a specific moment. (*AR*, 31–32)

This precedes a charming description of a young child's drawing of a swan that I shall discuss in chapter 2.

Cary returns to events like this frequently in his writing as if, indeed, they were a special sort of Wordsworthian remembrance—intellectual food. They are, to employ Eliseo Vivas's term, "insistences." They are ground for abstraction into *existences* or meanings. One of these remembrances of an old brokenhearted French painter appears in *The Horse's Mouth* and is thought upon abstractly in *Art and Reality* and elsewhere. In some writers one might think of these things as illustrations, but with Cary they are sources. The process in this is revealed when Cary recalls the source of one of his own stories in an event that occurred on a sightseeing tour around Manhattan Island (*AR*, 127–28). What Cary made of this he goes on to describe in some detail, but this description is itself of an activity, and the generalizations about creativity emerge *from* it. This is about as complete a contrast to the philosophical analysis of intuition and expression in Croce's *Aesthetic* as it can be, and it is not surprising that Cary says of Croce's theory: "But this is not at all the way it seems to an artist or a writer!" (*AR*, 2). For Cary, previous philosophers and artists are part of a reality one comes up against. I don't mean by this to adopt Harold Bloom's ingenious theory of misprision or creative swerve, though one can say, I think, that there is a good bit of individualistic interpretation of others in Cary's writing, but not for the psychological reasons Bloom would proffer.

One part of the real that Cary read very seriously was William Blake, and his inspiration by Blake is a matter of personal record, as an unpublished letter to the Blake Society, written in 1956, indicates:

> I have been a devotee of Blake since my nonage. I still possess the two volumes of the Ellis edition which I used at College, heavily annotated. He is for me the only philosopher, the only great poet, who had a real understanding of the nature of the world as seen by an artist, that is to say, the world of the individual, unique person, the unique thing. The world, of course, is as much a unity as a collection of individualities, that is the fundamental problem for all systematic philosophers, as it is for religion. And for Blake its unity is that of a character, a harmony of particulars.
>
> What every artist needs is both a general idea of the world and a strong sense of the individual, whether in person or thing, and Blake, of all artist-poets, had both in the highest intensity. No one conveys more sharply the unique quality of the particular thing or event, no one is more consistently aware of the world character in which all particulars have universal significance and all events relate to final causes. No one more completely despised on one hand the worm's eye view of the materialist, and on the other, more successfully escaped the dazzled myopia of the idealist philosopher or transcendental poet confounding the limitless novelty of concrete living existence in some empty abstraction called spirit or the absolute, destitute of form or significant action. For him the thinghood of reality was as immediate as its energetic soul, its person; he knew them both in their eternal and pungent quality. (*OC*, Box 233)

This is an adulatory letter and there is no reason to think Cary did not mean every word of it. In the thirteenth chapter of *The Horse's*

Mouth, Gulley Jimson recalls an important moment early in his career when he "took Blake's Job drawings out of somebody's bookshelf and peeped into them and shut them up again. Like a chap who's fallen down the cellar steps and knocked his skull in and opens a window too quick, on something too big" (*HM*, 63). Apparently, Cary himself put Blake away for a time. His early, privately printed and embarrassingly bad *Verse* (1908) shows some influence of Blake's youthful *Poetical Sketches* (both books seem to have been suppressed by their authors), but the many years between *Verse* and publication of *The Horse's Mouth* do not reveal an obvious Blakean influence. For Jimson, Blake's influence emerged as he moved from his "lyric" to his "epic" phase, following Blake's own pattern of development. For Cary, Blake's influence emerged as he moved from the African novels to the more spacious trilogies, where he developed his themes most fully.

Still, it is possible to go at the very considerable connection to Blake in the wrong way and give it the wrong emphasis. For example, to call Hickson in *The Horse's Mouth* "Bromion and Theotormon, both patron of the arts and defender of order," as Fred Stockholder does (p. 241), seems abstract and unproductive, merely grinding Cary exceedingly rough. Cary and Blake do not agree in all things, as for example the relation of soul and body, Cary's mind and machine. In any case, it would be far too abstract to treat all of Cary's novels as strictly Blakean. In the two trilogies, outside of *The Horse's Mouth*, Blake is mentioned but once. Sara Monday in *Herself Surprised* does so, but only because Jimson speaks of him frequently. Sara's sense of Blake is rather dim, and when she does refer to him, she feels she must identify him to us as "a poet about a hundred years ago" (*HS*, 121) whom Jimson was always reading. Even in *The Horse's Mouth*, Blake's role can be made too literal and less playful than it is. Both "The Mental Traveller" and *Milton* have been considered bases for the structure of *The Horse's Mouth*, and Cary's own working notes have a lot about Blake in them. There is among them even an elaborate scribbled chart which purports to organize events of *The Horse's Mouth* in parallel columns according to the cyclical process of "The Mental Traveller." I cannot decipher every word of the chart, but I can read most of it—enough to see that the chart didn't work out for Cary except in an exceedingly rudimentary way as an early plan for his novel. Its relevance is limited for the most part to chapter 13. Indeed, several of his notes on Blake, like many of the notes for his heavily revised novels, are speculations and ideas not actually carried out in the text as we have it and often not even in earlier drafts. Cary once made a list of nicknames Jimson might use for Blake, but only one is finally employed: "Blake. The prophetic. The crackerjack. Old Hammer and Tongs. Los. Old Rampant. Old Randipole. Old trouble the waters. Old shoot the moon. Old Billyache. Old catch 'em alive. Old Adam. The two eyed stance. Old middlestump" (*OC*, Box 82). And a good thing, too.

At an early stage he considered a possibility that is too mechanical and that he doesn't use: "? if one could find 300 linked quotations from Blake to run through the book, with argument and the pictures, Gulley investigating. He has the book, Blake in his pocket, but some pages missing. He uses it as a sorter" (*OC*, Box 82). He writes elsewhere: "Quotations must be organized and follow train of feeling independent of the scene, i.e., the train of pictures" (*OC*, Box 82). There is even ground to think that the well-known chapter 13, which is constituted by Jimson's history of his artistic development, with parts of "The Mental Traveller" as commentary, is something of a mistake. We know it was a late interpolation into the text. I shall return to this matter in later chapters; here it is important to get clear in what ways Cary did respond to Blake, whose image has loomed large in Cary scholarship. And here it is necessary to confess that in spite of what has gone before, there is going to be quite a lot of Blake in this book, though I do not intend to look at Cary through Blake.

For Cary, as we have seen, there is a crisis of the "real." The "real" is *there* in Cary in a way different from the presence of the real in Blake. It is not true, as some seem to think, that Blake fails to recognize the existence of a separate real. The question is what *status* he gives to it. He gives it very little, because what is supremely important to him is the creation out of it of an ever-new culture, society, and the moral real. A Blake devotee may balk here, remembering that Blake always employed the word "moral" in a derogatory sense. Blake's notion of morality is not based on an "abstract real" of moral law, but on a radically protestant notion of individual inspiration, enthusiasm, and responsibility through love. Blake is so radically protestant that, as Jimson says of his friend Mr. Plant, he is "against all churches, especially the Protestant" (*HM*, 46); the activity implied here is the shaping of the world of matter into cultural form. The figure in Blake's long poems who thinks that the world of matter shapes man becomes Satan, while those who recognize a world to be shaped become identified with Jesus.

Jesus acted not according to law but according to imagination. In

Blake, the ultimate real is the ethical world made from what is given to man, and that given, Blake diminishes in authority; it is only a potentiality for ethical action. Blake's four degrees of vision are levels of humanly shaped reality. The lowest is externality as Lockean primary material and Newtonian law—single vision. Its moral parallel is the law of an external, hidden, avenging sky-god. This vision is real, in a sense, but its existence is a sign of moral and imaginative passivity, which creates only the abstract. One has to rise up to a higher level of vision in order to apprehend anything truly solid to the senses, for matter is abstract and ephemeral. Solidity is the work of imagination. When one begins to do this, one comes into the realm of *relationships* (of natural objects and animals) and finally into a human society. Relationships of love are imaginative and moral, the highest form of the real.

Blake seems to posit for man a radical freedom for the imagination. He is an optimist and prophesies (that is to say, imagines) a free, classless culture. It is true that he speaks of the "stubborn structure of the language," which would appear to be an obstacle to creation; but for him this is a recalcitrance holding immense possibilities—a thereness for use and making. Words are potentially human forms, by which Blake means, among other things, that they make and contain their meanings rather than signify difference. This optimism about language, so foreign to so many today, is only one aspect of his enthusiasm, which is connected closely with the tradition of religious "enthusiasm" in his age. Of course, the word "religious" is a negative word in Blake, connected as it is with organization into churches and the abstract moral law, but certainly the ground of Blake's whole vision lies in great part in enthusiasm, a religious movement that emphasized feeling over law and has been defined by Walter E. Houghton as a "standard of judgment which may be called moral optimism" (*The Victorian Frame of Mind* [New Haven: Yale University Press, 1957], p. 297).

Cary describes himself as an optimist for man. He said on several occasions that he thought the opportunities for progress were immense. At the same time, Helen Gardner was certainly right to observe that the Cary she knew had a tragic aspect beneath a gallant exterior. He himself recalls in one of his last essays that as a young liberal he "overlooked the enormous power of evil working incessantly to destroy happiness and peace anywhere in the world" (*SE*, 246). And he speculated about the future ironically:

> It is quite certain that in twenty-five years the present day [1956] will seem even more remote than 1900 does now. For the revolution of

the free mind goes faster as that mind invents new tools. We live, literally, in the creation, and every year there are more creative imaginations at work. And more, much more, for them to feed on. The world grows more tense, more dangerous, but also infinitely richer in experience. There is no more happiness, perhaps less, but very much more intensity of living, more occupation for the mind and the senses. (*SE*, 247)

By any Blakean standard, Cary is a pessimist, though an exuberant one. This is not to claim that Blake was a sentimental, blinded optimist, only that the pressures Cary speaks of were not as significant for Blake, perhaps not as severe in Blake's time. Cary, himself, admired Blake's toughness and tended to imagine him in the modern context of tension he describes:

Point of Blake is his depth and adequacy—close to the ground. His acceptance of *evil as real*. Through creation, generation to regeneration. The stoic English view but he enters into freedom and individuality through experience. (*OC*, Box 82)

Cary is probably the only person ever to connect Blake and stoicism. Surely he clothes Blake in something more characteristic of himself, if Helen Gardner is right. Further, Blake always treated the word "evil" as error to be overcome in visionary creativity at a higher level. For Cary it is ineradicably present in the "real," which is always there and always a stumbling block. It is there, regardless of man. What culture achieves is as much in spite of it as with it. This accounts for Cary's choosing Blake's pessimistic vision of the cyclical world, "The Mental Traveller," to use in *The Horse's Mouth* and why it seems so universally illustrative of his world.

Blake's poem can be regarded as a vision of what Cary might have called the "abstract real." In tone and stance it is exceedingly distant, a quality it shares with several of the other poems from the so-called Pickering Manuscript but does not share with the rest of Blake's work. What Gulley Jimson tries to do with Blake's only diagrammatic poem is to individualize it radically and to offer an interpretation (if that is what I may call it) that stresses its variety of individual application. There is exuberance in this, but like most of Jimson's talk it is a sort of whistling in the dark. In the light of it, it seems possible to imagine Jimson as a projection of the last Blakean, who in a supreme effort turns Blake's enthusiasm into a discipline of self-protection and getting on.

Cary, on the other hand, whistles in the dark to a different tune.

Jimson whistles to try to maintain his own creative powers in action. He has enough difficulty doing that without taking on the problems of the rest of society. He is well aware of them, as I believe the titles of his epic paintings make clear; but for the sake of his activity and sanity he deliberately ignores them or builds ironic attitudes toward them, treating them as part of the inevitable intransigence of the "real."

Cary takes a larger view. It is larger even than the view Jimson deliberately suppresses in order to function as a type of artist. It is larger in the sense that Cary can encompass Jimson's attitude in a view of the relation of individual to real that covers a greater range—from optimism to a vision of the darkness. It is this moral encompassment, not the so-called indeterminacy of his world, that characterizes Cary's work in the two trilogies and offers an identification with Blake while at the same time asserting its own modernity.

But, as I have said, the Blake connection can be overdone. I suspect that, as with so many English writers, the precedent of Wordsworth is as important, though Cary nowhere to my knowledge mentions it. The connection lies in the importance of memory, not only to Cary in his own speculative writing, where specific events or scenes are recounted as "germs" for ideas or stories, but also to some of Cary's characters, especially to Tom Wilcher and Chester Nimmo. Indeed, *Except the Lord*, a portion of Nimmo's memoirs, is organized around spots of time. They are unlike Wordsworth's in certain important ways, as we shall see, but they perform a similar task.

All this is to say that if we stand back too far and too long, a lot of blurring takes place even for the farsighted. We have to look more closely. Gradually we shall do that, but for two more chapters, though closer, we shall still be at a distance and concerned with larger structures.

2
Intuition and the Symbolic
First Trilogy

Blake contributed, along with the British empiricists, Kant, and Croce (some aspects of these negatively), to Cary's theory of the symbolic, which is really his view of the artist's employment of language. This, in turn, though not possessing astonishing originality, stands in Cary's *Art and Reality* and in the manuscripts of numerous lectures and essays as a summary of and a somewhat unique twist to a tradition of thought about the literary use of language that dates back to the sources of the old distinction between symbol and allegory. Cary continues to emphasize the romantic notion of the artist's struggle with his linguistic medium; he offers his own idea of symbolic form, of the relation of intuition to expression, and a cyclical view of the birth, death, and possible rebirth of symbols in the culture. Clearly a personal testament, *Art and Reality* nevertheless represents or synthesizes a number of artistic attitudes emerging as the tradition of *symbolisme* culminates. One senses also that in the main character of *The Horse's Mouth* a certain summing up occurs.

The two books are very close together in their preoccupations. *Art and Reality* (1958), written painfully as Cary was dying of a progressive paralysis, is in many ways a commentary on the aesthetic themes of the novel and the epistemological concerns of the whole *First Trilogy*. The task before us is to move from one to the other, to analyze Cary's theory of symbols, and to see what light it throws on the *First Trilogy*'s construction. In order to do this I shall refer not only to the final published version of *Art and Reality*, but also to passages from earlier published and unpublished lectures and drafts of parts of the book. Cary had a limited number of theoretical statements to make, and he made them with varying degrees of explicitness in different contexts. *Art and Reality* sometimes does, sometimes doesn't, contain the clearest statement to be found on specific points.

I begin with an examination of Cary's notion of the relation between intuition and expression. These terms were presented to Cary by his reading of Benedetto Croce's *Aesthetic*. Croce attempted to hold intuition and expression together; Cary insists on their separation. It is not easy, however, to tell precisely where the difference between his view and Croce's lies, particularly in the light of Croce's own introduction of the separate term "externalization" to account for the material medium. Cary's discussion is also difficult, as R. W. Noble (p. 104) has observed, because of "his inconsistent use of fundamental terms such as 'intuition,' 'idea,' 'fact,' 'feeling,' 'theme,' 'concept,' and 'meaning.'" In his short book Noble does not attempt to sort these terms out. I hope I have clarified some of them (as much as they can be clarified) in the previous chapter. The question had become one of whether intuitions had to be formalized linguistically or in some other symbolic form in order to be accorded the status of intuitions. In a lecture called "What Does Art Create?" Cary argues that a man can never, even to himself, express all his feelings (intuitions?), being for the most part alone with them. The objectivity of the symbol creates a profound gap in communication:

> You may say with Croce and other idealists that the experience becomes part of the child; it enters into him as intuition before he can know it; that the world, in short, only exists in states of mind. But we need not trouble about arguments intended to avoid dualism, a purely philosophic and logical problem to which we can and must find answers. All I am declaring now is something which is, in fact, acknowledged by Croce in another part of his aesthetic, that the work of art, as a thing, a composition of symbols, is a deliberate construction created by the artist to communicate his ideas, out of a material, an experience, which stands to be examined.
>
> I do not mind if some Crocean likes to argue that this material is already expressed, is already a mass of precepts. The important point is that somewhere in the act of creation this gap occurs, that somewhere the artist, like the child, looks outward upon an objective world of experience and asks himself, "What does it mean?" I perfectly agree that this experience has, in the first place, been direct. It has been felt; but for the artist's purpose it must be contemplated. (*OC*, Box 249)

Cary appreciates Croce's desire to maintain the directness of the artist's experience as against the abstractness of all other forms of thought, but he is unwilling to accept a position in which the artist is not regarded as "vividly aware of standing outside and away from the material which he has to use" (*OC*, Box 232). Croce keeps subject and object together, as a good idealist should, but Cary thinks he does it at the expense of truth to human experience. And it is not, after all, merely a matter of the artist's point of view being different from and logically independent of that of the philosophers. Cary argues this point more vehemently in a typescript than in *Art and Reality* itself:

> Croce will say that by dividing intuition or expression one is cutting up the world or, as he puts it, someone "dividing the seamless robe of the universe." I do not agree. To say that intuition is only known in the expression is in fact a much worse division. It is to cut off expression from life and from reality. It is committing the same dangerous fault as Kant's statement that one cannot know the thing in itself, but only phenomena. That judgment was a disaster for philosophy and perhaps for Europe. Croce's judgment could be a disaster for art. And Croce has less excuse. Kant's intuition was probably something like this. God is beyond my imagination. I know him only in his works, his appearances. Therefore I cannot know the thing itself. But Croce was dealing with daily and handy experiences. (*OC*, Box 232)

Cary returns to this point often, perhaps trying to assure himself that he has been fair to Croce, whom he admires but must, in his role as artist, combat. He considers, perhaps with Croce's idea of "externalization" in mind, that he may have misunderstood Croce's meaning:

> Croce may not mean by the expression an actually symbolic expression, but merely form in the sense of meaning. That is to say, if he means that immediate intuition of beauty is not known unless it has the form of its appropriate emotion, he is obviously right, but it seems to me that in that case he is stating a tautology. An intuition that does not have a distinctive form is not an intuition. What we mean by intuition is a formal experience, and the point, the vital important point with which Croce is dealing is the artist's relation to reality. (*OC*, Box 238)

By "actually symbolic expression" Cary means what Croce calls "externalization" via a medium and technique. He again accuses Croce of ignoring "primary experience," but he has not cleared up the problem, for there is no vocabulary available to him to differentiate the "forms" of pure emotion or feeling that he mentions above. This is one of the reasons—the main one finally—why Croce himself does not want to discuss intuitions except *as* expressions. Expressions are symbolic formalizations, and there is a possible language to categorize these forms. Cary acknowledges this, but then refuses to accept that the form must be verbal or in some sense an internal representation:

> It would still be possible to say that the intuition as formal experience is only known to the artist by some verbal symbol. For instance, that he does not recognize and classify even to himself the experience of beauty or ugliness without the word, without some formal expression. . . . But all the evidence is the other way, all the evidence points not only to the significance of intuition without verbal analysis, of knowledge and even of reason without words. Children, before they can speak, certainly acquire knowledge, and reason upon it. (*OC*, Box 238)

Here Cary faces the inevitable formal vagueness of preverbal intuitions, if they exist. We may recall here on the one hand the futility of I. A. Richards's chart of squiggly lines (in *Principles of Literary Criticism*) meant to delineate impulses or emotions, and on the other John Crowe Ransom's remark in his well-known essay "Criticism as Pure Speculation": "[F]eelings are grossly inarticulate if we try to abstract them and take their testimony in their own language." Yet Cary is right in arguing that children are able to reason in a rudimentary way before they can speak. The question remains whether this power is not so rudimentary and so limited that it hardly qualifies for status until its acts are given symbolic form.

It appears to me that the disagreement between Cary and Croce is finally over what status in existence each is willing to give to whatever it is that comes first in the artistic process. According to Cary, the artist begins with some "general idea" (*AR*, 86). Croce would probably have rejected this neoclassical bit of language and argued that the utter vagueness of the term, the inadequacy of any other terms, and the elusiveness of this idea as an objectifiable thing finally require that we assign it no status apart from its formalization in word, note, or shape. Even Cary comes near to acknowledging this when he writes that the artist is

> not merely expressing an intuition, he is continually discovering new possibilities in his own work, now become objective to him,

and realising them. The whole process is one of exploration as well as expression. (*AR*, 86)

Indeed, if this statement were more central to *Art and Reality*, much of the difficulty of accepting Cary's argument would disappear. Through the argument with Croce Cary obviously wants to preserve the author's sense of the objectivity and otherness of the work as it is in progress, an existence which requires that the author address himself to it. In the process the object gains a progressively more independent life and takes a greater hand, so to speak, in its completion. As this occurs, the original intuition is lost or at least translated into other terms.

Croce, of course, argues against the existence of mute inglorious Miltons. For him, intuitions have no status except as expressions. Expression for him, however, is not external but internal in language or in the painter's internal eye or the musician's ear. Externalization, which is the application of techniques and materials, follows. Cary will not have this, either. If Croce's gap is between expression and externalization, Cary denies that gap and places expression and externalization together, separating this entity from intuition. He insists that exploration and discovery take place in technical externalization, while Croce is driven to see externalization as a mimesis in a foreign medium of an already established internal expression.

Cary tries to avoid this difference by making all expression the effort to externalize and objectify, indeed "translate" (*AR*, 27) into a medium an original intuition. This intuition, elusive as it may be, still has an existence of some sort, and is always lost to some extent in expression. For Cary, it seems to follow that in this process something else is often found. He sees this situation as a torment to the artist because of his inability to hold on to the original intuition; it has also its occasional, ironic rewards.

Can Cary then continue to proclaim in these terms that art really expresses "direct knowledge of the world" (*AR*, 2)? Such acquaintance, he holds, can be of "things," "characters," and "appearances." But what can "appearance" mean except to imply that there is a thing in itself beyond appearance? Here Cary's unknowable "being," mentioned in chapter 1, rears up to plague his argument. Perhaps he would hold in the classic way that there are false appearances and true appearances, and that the artist must distinguish among them, that artistry is the technique of distinguishing among them. In *The Horse's Mouth*, Jimson refers to one of these successes as the kick of the foal before its birth (*HM*, 43). The artistic act in Cary comes as a result of the kick. Extension of the metaphor, however, would give Cary trouble, since the kick is apparently the intuition and is yet merely an "appearance"—better, a prophecy—though certainly a true one, of the foal, which really appears only when it is born. But Cary argues that the process of art or the giving birth inevitably distorts or, as he says, "translates" the intuition. By Jimson's metaphor, extended, it would seem that the work of art is more real than the intuition, that is, a more complete appearance than the partial appearance implicit in the kick. This may be unfair, but it does reveal if not an inconsistency in Cary then a real difficulty with which he is concerned and which requires further exploration. I shall eventually claim that Jimson in Cary's novel has an involvement with his partly created forms that *Art and Reality* doesn't ever quite do justice to, even though Cary recognizes there that the process from intuition to completed object tends to take over, and is discovery, exploration, and revelation in itself.

The original intuition that begins the process is highly "evanescent" (*AR*, 30) in the grown, educated man, who unlike the child has a sophisticated world of symbols surrounding him. Every intuition is invaded by that symbolic world. Exploration and revelation require work and education, training in technique. (Cary's paradox of education as both destroyer and sophisticator of intuition I shall discuss shortly.) The painter, for example,

> has somehow to translate an intuition from real objects into a formal and ideal arrangement of colours and shapes, which will still, mysteriously, fix and convey his sense of the unique quality, the magic of these objects in their own private existence. That is to say, he has a job that requires thought, skill, and a lot of experience. (*AR*, 4)

The writer's somewhat different problem is that he

> does not use a raw material; he uses words that already carry an emotional meaning. He produces his whole of meaning, this total symbolic form, from a material that consists of words which are themselves primitive works of art, probably the earliest of all, and which carry already symbolic meaning. (*OC*, Box 232)

We can see why with this view Cary does not want intuitions in themselves to be linguistic, for if they were, there could never be in his system a completely fresh, original intuition, only new combinations, like combinations of ideas in the old theory of the association of ideas.

The first of the two passages above may seem to express a variety of naïve imitation that takes us back past Kant. The writer imitates in another form his sense impression. There is little suggestion in the passage that the human intuitive power is either constitutive in itself or directly in touch with objects. At this point in his discussion Cary introduces something that at first seems like a Kantian manifold of sensation, upon which the intuition operates as a synthetic power. The world is there to be intuited only as a "wild confusion of events from which we have to select what we think significant for ourselves" (*AR*, 5). The "wild confusion" seems to contain objects that can be directly intuited as independent forms. Just as in Cary's belief "any work of art must embody only a narrow part of the author's meaning" (*OC*, Box 232), so the intuitive power orders only some of the "wild confusion." At the same time, as we saw in chapter 1, Cary insists that this "wild confusion" does have laws and that our intuitive powers ignore them at their peril. For example, one cannot affront gravity, which is a permanent part of the "real." Yet these laws do not in themselves make the world into a place of *human* coherence. They provide only the substratum for *meaningful* reality, which must be *humanly* constructed (though, as we saw in chapter 1, there are things that are *humanly* constant). So what Cary is talking about here is not really a Kantian manifold; nor is he even introducing an epistemological question in the usual sense. Instead, Cary has moved out of the real of epistemology into an area we might call social or cultural symbolism, where for him art *does* play a constitutive role. The social or cultural reality is, of course, also subject to basic laws, and human nature itself presents us with "certain constants." A further complication is that human nature and society are themselves part of the "wild confusion"; yet human nature, because free to possess imagination, is, as the artist is with his materials, always in conflict with that fundamental reality:

> So we have a reality consisting of permanent and highly obstinate facts, and permanent and highly obstinate human nature. And human nature is always in conflict with material facts, although men are themselves most curious combinations of fact and feeling, and actually require the machinery of their organism to realise their emotions, their desires and ambitions. (*AR*, 6)

On the surface, Cary seems here to be matching up the world of "highly obstinate facts"—the basic given—with the world of the Lockean bifurcation of subject and object, the clock world of Deism that Blake ridicules. As in preromantic and early romantic writers and theorists, fact would seem to become the province of science with feeling alone left to the artist. If this were the whole story, we could dismiss Cary's notions as mere repetition of earlier romantic ones, though perhaps more confused and more desperate. His language is slippery, but he does not leave only feeling to the artist. He insists that the nature of art is to keep fact and feeling together. Fact alone is mere brute reality like gravity; fact alone presents no "meaning," which Cary always defines in human terms. This "meaning" must be *constructed* in such a way that fact is not affronted: "It may be said that all works of art, all ideas of life, all philosophies are 'As if,' but I am suggesting that they can be checked with an objective reality" (*AR*, 7).

It is true that Cary sounds like Edmund Burke when he writes:

> Man can't change the elemental characters. If you could, the world would probably vanish into nothing. But because of their very permanence, you can assemble them into new forms. (*AR*, 7)

In his *Philosophical Inquiry into the Origin of Our Ideas of the Sublime and Beautiful*, Burke remarked that the mind can create nothing new, but instead merely assembles ideas into new combinations. But Cary doesn't really say that. He isn't assuming the existence of Burke's ideas of sense. He sees man building "meaning" in his languages upon a chaos of mechanics, including things like gravity. How can a chaos be also mechanical? By chaos Cary means the "real" without human meaning: A machine in itself has no human meaning and is, though explainable by scientific analysis, a chaos until it is given its ethical place by the imagination. Moreover (and this is a version of the first paradox of the previous chapter),

> The creative soul needs the machine, as the living world needs a fixed character, or it could not exist at all. It would be merely an idea. But by a paradox we have to accept, part of this fixed character is the free mind, the creative imagination, in everlasting conflict with facts, including its own machinery, its own tools. (*AR*, 7)

The conflict is given the order of human meaning by art, defined initially in *Art and Reality* as all expression and communication whatever. All meaning is personally created. In Cary's view, as we have seen, though we are not alone in feeling, we are alone in mind and therefore compelled to "form our own ideas of things" (*AR*, 9–10). Here Cary goes back beyond Kant to David Hume:

> We are almost entirely cut off from each other in mind, entirely independent in thought, and so we have to learn everything for ourselves. Hume pointed this out in his *Enquiry Concerning Human Understanding*, published in 1748, and no philosopher since has found an adequate answer to him. (*AR*, 9)

Cary's problem is that he has no terminology to stand on between that of the British empiricists and the German idealists. He would create two sorts of truth. One is a sort of absolute truth but very rudimentary—knowledge of the brute reality, of which gravity is an example. This truth is what one might once have thought science would ultimately or ideally turn by accumulation into a complete account of reality. However, Cary seems to feel that this truth is finally not completable as a system—a fully mechanical account—at least by man. Even completable it would have no meaning, in Cary's sense, and would remain paradoxically a chaos. It must be completed only in human or ethical terms—involve human meaning, even as it is acknowledged that human beings are in conflict with manifestations of fact. Another and ultimately more important truth, then, results from the individual's attempt to mediate between himself and brute fact or between the individual as separate from that fact and the individual as "part of it as created" (*AR*, 14). This truth is always a truth created or reached by the solitary mind. It is not meaning unless it is made or achieved. In Cary's view, for reasons we shall come to, it must also constantly be remade or rewon. It is constructed, if in verbal form, with symbols virtually all of which have previously established significances and are therefore stubborn matter with which to work. Cary remarks that modern philosophers have come to discover "what poets have known and complained of two thousand years ago: the inadequacy, the vagueness of words" (*AR*, 16).

> [T]he logical positivists, having abolished representation and system building from philosophy, have said, "Let us find out exactly what philosophy consists of. Let us throw out every thing, which is not the pure stuff of philosophy," and have been left like the artists with nothing but the bare materials of expression, the word. (*OC*, Box 238)

As a result they have attempted to invent a system of more adequate—that is, less vague and capricious—symbols, but the ones that do not shift and change produce only expressions of "quantity and dimension, relation and probability" (*AR*, 16) and thus are drained of meaning.

I have already indicated that for Cary meaning is human. In meaning, quality and value are always implicit. As Gulley Jimson says to Lady Beeder, "Sit down and ask yourself what's it all about?" (*HM*, 153). For Jimson, and for Cary, as long as one defines art broadly, this is art. Lady Beeder's acts in water color don't do it very well. It is not easy to do it well. Symbols expressive of value are very difficult to control, seem to insist on lives of their own, become objects that themselves require ordering, and die, sometimes to be reborn. If we go farther with Cary into the meaning of "meaning" we arrive, as we have seen, at the word "moral": Cary tends to use the word "moral" as a general term descriptive of meaning. We know that by it he does not refer to moral codes of behavior or belief, but to that which is involved in the search to answer the question, "What's it all about?" In a passage that was canceled from *Art and Reality* but expresses directly a notion put not quite so directly in the text, he writes:

> All writers are moralists. It is impossible to organize experience without a moral standpoint. What are called amoral writers are in fact moral dissenters. (*OC*, Box 231)

However, moral values are never externally real as given. They are internal and emanate from individual discovery. In a passage edited out of *Power in Men* when it was condensed for publication but clearly reflective of his views, Cary wrote:

> Although moral values like courage, generosity, truthfulness are constant, they are realised always in new actions. They can no more provide a standard than the aesthetic value can give a permanent law for critics by which new kinds of art can be judged. (*OC*, Box 202)

In Cary's system even the word "morality" must be reborn into new meaning. Meaning, which is moral, is *created*—one creates meaning—but, of course, it must take account of the basic stubborn given reality; thus one can talk about "the permanent moral reality of nature" (*OC*, Box 231). "The function of the great artist is to reveal in the actual chaos of the world a meaning not discordant with the reality which underlies that chaos" (*OC*, Box 232).

There are some difficulties here, for Cary introduces the term "beauty" at this point and mixes it up with the problem of the meaning of morality. On the one hand Cary argues that the writer has something he wants to say and that, in the case of Flaubert's *Madame Bovary*, for example, the effect is moral. On the other hand he accepts one "very true thing" that Kant perceived: "that beauty does not need to have anything to do with morality or function" (*AR*, 17–18). But his conception of beauty here is narrower than Kant's and is more like the ancient Greeks' harmony and proportion. If he adopts this definition of beauty as an abstract and external principle (which he has already, incidentally, denied in the passage above edited out of *Power in Men*), he must then attribute as fundamental to art more than beauty and even deny beauty to some art. One of the things he proceeds to add to his definition is "direct knowledge of the world" (*AR*, 18). (Some aestheticians identify this with beauty on the assumption that to know anything directly *as itself* is to apprehend its internal harmony and thus its beauty. But Cary would argue that this is really a moral or religious value.) Later on in *Art and Reality* he seems to enlarge the term "beauty" from the Grecian toward the Keatsian equation of beauty and truth, but there is always—as perhaps there is in Keats—a lingering of the old idea. He cannot quite allow the beautiful to include the disagreeable, though he sees that Flaubert gets his effect in part because of the ugliness he presents. This effect he still calls moral and not aesthetic. At the same time, the moral is *not* seen as an external principle, and so it tends to blend with the idea of beauty in the post-Kantian sense. In *Power in Men* (p. 235), Cary clearly refers to the argument of Kant's *Critique of Judgment* when he says, "notions of beauty commonly attach to single objects, so that each is a separate idea and there is no general principle at all." This notion has an ethical parallel in Blake's attack against external "moral law," which Cary adopts, with some addenda, bringing together ethics with aesthetics under an argument originally aesthetical in Kant. Beauty resides then in the full unfolding of a particular and is thus identifiable with what Cary calls the symbol. Art, employing language, which tends to move toward generalization, struggles with itself as medium to maintain the freshness of particularity, which is the nearest it can come to expressing the artist's intuition.

In every intuitive act and expression there is an ordering that is "creative." It appears that Cary must give either to intuition or to expression-externalization or to both a power like that which Coleridge calls imagination. For Cary, this power must take into account and act against the pressure of brute fact, so that it is not exactly an epistemological power. It is more a cultural or social force—a contributor to what Northrop Frye calls a "myth of concern." Insofar as it succeeds it "creates ideas, of which a very large proportion are, or become, ideas for action" (*AR*, 21). Cary summarizes this as follows: In the artist's act there is "a kind of translation, not from one language into another, but from one state of existence into another, from the receptive into the creative, from the purely sensuous impression into the purely reflective and critical act" (*AR*, 27).

M. M. Mahood (pp. 85–86) writes: "In all his accounts of the creative process, Cary distinguishes three stages: intuition, approach, and form. By intuition, Cary means more than sympathy or insight. It is an imaginative leap into a character's situation at a moment of tragic or comic crisis." But, of course, such characters are created by Cary; they are not there to be communed with previous to their creation.

Cary sees intuition and education falling into conflict in experience. The conflict is inevitable and necessary. Cary's child is a Blakean or Wordsworthian innocent, capable of direct intuitions unmediated by any language of forms. There is a mystery here that Cary does not try to explain except by the word "feeling": "the act of imagination, by which the simplest forms are grasped in relation, is always accompanied by a feeling about the object. A child does not merely see the form and colour of a chair or try to grasp its solidity and use, he feels something about it—recognition, curiosity, like or dislike" (*PM*, 233).

One of Cary's most charming examples is the following:

A small girl of seven once asked me if I would like a drawing. I said yes. She asked, "What shall I draw?"

"Anything you like."

"Shall I draw you a swan?"

"Yes, a swan"; and the child sat down and drew for half an hour. I'd forgotten about the swan until she produced the most original swan I'd ever seen. It was a swimming swan, that is, a creature designed simply to swim. Its feet were enormous and very carefully finished, obviously from life. The whole structure of the feet was shown in heavy black lines. The child was used to seeing swans on a canal at the end of her garden and had taken particular notice of their feet. Below the water the swan was all power. But for body she gave it the faintest, lightest outline, neck and wings included in one round line shaped rather like a cloud—a perfect expression of the cloud-like movement of the swan on the surface.

I was admiring this swan when an older child in the room, aged thirteen, looked at the drawing and said contemptuously, "That's not a bit like a swan. I'll draw you a swan," and produced at once a Christmas-card swan, of the commonest type. (*AR*, 32–33)

The second child had proceeded much farther along the road of education, and education is conceptual and destructive of intuition. Why, then, must we abide it? The main reason is that it is inevitable, like Blake's fall into experience. If adults don't provide a good education, then children will provide a bad one for themselves and each other. Cary goes so far as to suggest that by a process of contrariety there may be definite value in a quite rigorous education, but the results are unpredictable. It may produce genius; it may stifle it. In any case, even the original swan of childish art is not sophisticated enough in technique to "give any large meaning to the world" (*AR*, 50). The artist's problem is to master his conceptual education and to put it to use in the expression of his intuition, which one hopes has not been entirely destroyed by the education itself. This is what Jimson means when he responds flippantly to Sir William Beeder's remark:

> "My wife has made a special study of watercolour technique," said Sir William. "A very difficult medium."
> "Terrible," I said. "But her ladyship has mastered it. She's only got to forget it." (*HM*, 152)

He goes on to say,

> "Why, your ladyship, a lot of my recent stuff is not much better, technically, than any young lady can do after six lessons at a good school. Heavy-handed, stupid-looking daubery. Only difference is that it's about something—it's an experience. . . ." (*HM*, 152–53)

Luck, the mysterious—or something we can't quite control by explanation—plays a role here in providing the context for discovery. An object being painted will become something else as the painter works, seeking to complete his intuition, but also now facing the objectivity of the work itself. This happens in a passage from *The Horse's Mouth*, where Jimson creates fishes in his painting "The Fall" out of shapes of an indeterminate nature:

Flowers. I began the flowers, but they felt wrong. And all at once I made a thing like a white Indian club. I like it, I said, but it's not a flower, is it? What the hell could it be? A fish. And I felt a kick inside as if I was having a foal. Fish. Fish. Silver-white, green-white. And shapes that you could stroke with your eyebrows. (*HM*, 43)

The point to be added is that one must have the education to make this sort of luck, which is, then, not entirely luck. It is based on what Jimson ironically insists must be consciously forgotten. Cary's slant on this is again different from Croce's, since his strong sense of the growing separate objectivity of the art object requires that the object itself exert a considerable degree of control. After a certain point in composition, the writer—unless he is regarded as simply copying out a complete intuition—finds he is compelled to a choice he had not imagined. Thus we could say that the original intuition is rather obliterated and the object becomes an intuitive object of its own, that is, to be intuited for its potentiality. There is a strong sense of the objectivity of the work in *Art and Reality*. But there Cary insists that the artist is still attempting to express an original intuition. Jimson, on the other hand, seems to be in the clutches of the object, so to speak, and intuits new possibilities as he works. These are not the original intuition. Indeed the foal's kick in the passage quoted comes midway in Jimson's work with "The Fall" and refers him into the work itself. On the other hand, Jimson also argues with Nosy Barbon that he likes only to *begin* pictures, which can mean that he is always tormented by the loss of the original intuition. I shall return to this important point.

In either case, for Cary the object achieves its separateness. Only by regarding it as an *other* can the artist bring his own critical powers to bear upon its completion. This is important because, after all, the artist is dealing with something and must have some freedom from that thing in order to do so. A whole theory of freedom in Cary is tied up with this.

Cary uses in a curious way other language having to do with what the artist expresses. He says that the artist "wants not only to express his unique idea of things, but to communicate it. He is, in fact, almost invariably a propagandist" (*AR*, 91). The terminology is loose. Cary does not have in mind a separable idea, a moral code, prescription, or proscription as such, but something more like what Kant called an "aesthetic idea." He uses the term "propagandist," therefore, in a special sense. It sounds at first as if the artist is to move people to action in any possible way. In another place, he remarks that all serious artists preach. And he goes on to argue, "They are perfectly convinced of the truth as they see it, and they write to communicate that truth" (*AR*, 109). But having embarked on his argument in this style, Cary must next separate truly artistic "propaganda" or "preaching" from the kind to which these words usually refer. This takes him back to the venerable distinction between allegory and symbolism. Ingvar Söderskog (pp. 15, 18) notices this and remarks that Cary's use of "allegory" seems to be a derogatory word derived from the symbolist tradition rather than a technical term: "It is unfortunate that, rather than describe allegory as the opposite and ruin of the symbol and the representation of 'character,' Cary did not try to level the distinction." Not to "level the distinction" raises many problems. A strong argument can be made that the truly "symbolic" is that which evades "translation" and this can only be the solid and realistic. This is, I think, what impels Michael Echeruo (p. 69) to write that Cary "always preferred to contain the symbolic meaning within the confines of realistic fiction." Allegory, always loosened from particularity, is for Cary purely conceptual: "Allegory gives a clear, a definite meaning; not to the soul, but to the conceptual judgment, and in a form of dry precept whose falsity is at once detected by the soul" (*AR*, 163). A cancelled passage says of the symbol, "We might say, therefore, that it is actually in the symbol that we attain the union between concept and intuition, the junction of mind and body, in a common reaction. For the symbol carries both conceptual meaning and the overcharge of emotion. It pays for this quality in vagueness and imprecision" (*OC*, Box 232). Up to the last sentence the passage celebrates the symbol in a way reminiscent of romanticism, but Cary gives nothing of romantic mystery, spirit, or transcendence to the symbol. It is not miraculous; it does not transport us to a super-reality. It is social and cultural, and as such it is quite fragile and can easily be destroyed. A compound of concept and intuition in its birth, it easily deteriorates into pure concept by repeated use. When this occurs, a new symbol must be generated.

The theory of the symbol is fictively Gulley Jimson's before it is Cary's, that is, it is developed by Jimson in *The Horse's Mouth* by means of his use of Blake's poem "The Mental Traveller" years before Cary expressed it in *Art and Reality*. "The Mental Traveller" presents a dialectical situation which expresses itself in fallen history as an endless cyclical recurrence: It involves a male and a female principle, the male representing roughly the active creative imagination and the female representing nature and the materials of experience to be shaped by the imagination. The female is by turns old woman, mother, virgin, and babe; and the male is infant, child, flaming youth, and old man. As the male grows older the female grows younger and vice versa, so that the cyclical relationships are old woman-babe, mother-child, virgin-youth, babe-old man, and so forth. In one of the earliest interpretations of Blake, W. B. Yeats wrote that "a perfect mystical symbol or fable can be read in any region of nature and thought—mineral, meteoric, religious, philosophical—it is all one. Things we have to give in *succession* in our explanatory prose are set forth *simultaneously* in Blake's verse" (*The Works of William Blake* [London: Quaritch, 1893], I: p. 287). This idea has some similarity to Cary's idea that the symbol is not subject to division, though Cary's symbols are secular rather than mystical. Söderskog (p. 20) identifies Cary's "symbol" with Blake's "allegory addressed to the intellectual powers while it is altogether hidden from the corporeal understanding." One ought to note, however, that elsewhere Blake uses allegory in a derogatory sense, much as Cary himself does. It is likely that Cary's derogatory use of the term stems in part from Blake.

According to Yeats, the conceptual power, working upon the symbol, forces it into succession. Thus interpreters, who are conceptualizers or allegorizers of symbolic utterances, must speak of "levels" of meaning and set these "levels" out in succession, while the symbol itself manages to say everything at once. In the terms in which we are speaking, the total poem, though composed of symbols, is itself a single symbol. Cary remarks:

> [T]he form of a book, page by page, is not the book, the work of art. All these separate pages and chapters, like the movements of a symphony, do not have a complete significance until the whole work is known. They are, so to speak, partly in suspension, until at the end of the last movement, the last chapter, they suddenly fall into their place. This is only to say that the separate forms do not possess their whole content until the work is complete. That's why I call the book a total symbol. It is both richer than its parts and actually different from them. (*AR*, 103)

This goes beyond Yeats's statement that the symbol contains in unity what explanatory prose lays out in succession. It indicates that the symbol contains more than the attempt to lay out its "levels" successively can ever express.

Cary is not discussing only those books that we now formally classify as artistic. He holds that the expression of a philosophical system should be regarded as a total symbol, and that an artist's total canon becomes a symbol, too.

> But symbols decay. Each one tends to sink into the empty object, the bare concept-label, the mechanical sign or gesture. The word becomes a word from a dictionary. The brush stroke, the style, of a painter becomes by repetition a term in his expression, analogous to a word. It is part of his language. He always makes that statement in that form. The new critics learn that language and teach it to the public. . . . The illumination has become common daylight. (*AR*, 71–72)

The symbol has been conceptualized. Cary has appropriated here his own experience of artistic fashion and Blake's cyclical vision of creativity—"prolific" and "devourer"—for a social theory of artistic change. In Blake the prolific are the creators, the prophets. The devourers are the "churches" and the rationalists. The prolific provide the food, the devourers digest it or use it. Blake said two important things about these two classes of men: first, that the "prolific would cease to be prolific unless the devourer as a sea received the excess of his delights"; second, that "these two classes of men are always upon earth, and they should be enemies; whoever tries to reconcile them seeks to destroy existence" (*The Marriage of Heaven and Hell*, plates 16–17). Cary goes along with this, pointing out in "Liberty or Freedom" that there is always something potentially dangerous about the free imagination, which is the Blakean prolific:

> I am not afraid for freedom, I am afraid for the world if it cannot manage freedom. For it is a most mysterious and terrible power, secret and eternal. It is born in every child and sets to work at once to create a world according to that child's desires. It uses every weapon to achieve its aims, and is infinitely cunning in the invention of new weapons. (*OC*, Box 242)

This aspect of freedom is clearly like Blake's Orc, and it requires discipline, control. Even Jimson in his ironic way argues this point to Nosy Barbon:

> All art is bad, but modern art is the worst. Just like the influenza. The newer it is, the more dangerous. And modern art is not only a public danger—it's insidious. You never know what may happen when it's got loose. Dickens and all the other noble and wise men

who backed him up, parsons and magistrates and judges, were quite right. So were the brave lads who fought against the Impressionists in 1870, and the Post-Impressionists in 1910, and that rat Jimson in 1920. They were all quite right. They knew what modern art can do. Creeping about everywhere, undermining the Church and the State and the Academy and the Law and marriage and the Government—smashing up civilisation, degenerating the Empire. (*HM,* 26)

Blake's "Mental Traveller," which I shall discuss only in part here because it comes up again in chapter 4, helps Jimson, who is one of its devourers, to fix down his sense of the history of modern art, particulars in the world around him, his own career, his relationship with Sara Monday, and the gap between intuition and expression. But Jimson is not the usual kind of devourer, i.e., interpretive critic, for he does not offer a sustained conceptualization or allegory of the poem. Instead he subtly reveals how as a fable it can be read in any region of nature. The poem moves in and out of his own story.

The art he finally comes to—the large symbolical works with biblical subjects, "Jacob and his Wives," "The Holy Innocents," "The Living God," "The Fall," "The Raising of Lazarus," "The Creation"—is not publicly understood, though the work of his earlier period is now appreciated and even represented in the Tate Gallery. Are Jimson's biblical works fated to die, as all symbols apparently must? Certainly Cary's making them suffer destruction at the hands of vandals, bishops, or councilmen is telling us something about what can happen to symbols. But the answer is more complex. Most of Jimson's works are destroyed; but symbols can be reborn—if they survive. Two anecdotes in *Art and Reality* treat the irony of this. The first tells of Cary as a young boy of sixteen meeting an old painter, formerly popular, now annually rejected by the Academy. He belonged to a dead fashion or system of symbols and could not understand what had happened. Cary turned this destitute old man into Jimson's father for *The Horse's Mouth,* and one suspects that some of Jimson's drive to achieve always new forms of expression is meant by Cary to express a fear of his father's fate. Ironically, Jimson's own fate is to be apart from the fashion and to suffer for it.

The second anecdote tells of a Victorian painting that Cary inherited, having seen and disliked it forty years before, only now to realize its definite merits. In some curious way it had been reborn:

From a contemporary portrait, or rather a portrait only a few years out-of-date, of two ladies and a child, the ladies in fashions which had just become ridiculous, in a room whose furniture had lately become demoded, the picture was changed into a period piece. Added to its effect was all that had been felt and written about the Victorian age by historians, by novelists, in those forty years. Thus the whole mass of associations belonging to that picture and to the late Victorian style in which it was painted had become, not only enormously enlarged, but formalised within the idea of a period. This idea, the idea of a period and its character is, of course, also the creation of art. And as soon as it acquires a form and a meaning, it has a very powerful supercharge of value, not only aesthetic but general. (*AR*, 80–81)

At the same time it is conveniently removed from the realm of contemporary controversy and is no longer subject to imitation or revolt, though, one might observe, it is permitted to be used as "influence."

This view of the art of the past is one of Cary's most interesting contributions. His approach to symbols is unusual in acknowledging flux and movement. He is not content with building an abstract, Platonizing conception of the symbol. Dead systems can be reborn into a new but different kind of life. The argument depends on his other view that there is also something enduring, though in this case constant, about human nature. The constancy is twofold. First, there is the fact of human creativity and its demand to express its unique intuitions, and second, there is the reality of brute fact and the accompanying changeless moral issues that are generated by the clash of creativity with fact. Every human age builds its own symbolic systems and its own creative response to the reality of brute fact. A symbolic system that is no longer the battleground of fashion becomes, as it recedes into the past, the image of a free human response to the basic reality or chaos with which all men must cope. Its actual advantage as an object of apprehension is its distance. Because it is anchored in the past and is so fully delineated in the way Cary describes it in the previous quotation, it is more complete than the art of the present is ever likely to appear to us. This argument seems to me as good as I have seen for a traditional liberal education in the arts and why it should not concentrate exclusively on the present. In a creation from the past the fundamental human issue of trying to construct meaning is fully played out. We observe this. We do not, I think, merely evaluate it, but only come to *understand* it, all passion spent. As we do this we come to know better the conditions of our situation. Without this distance, without these completed and then reborn systems of the past, we remain locked within the not fully understood and incomplete systems of our own making: "A period can never know itself. It always appears to itself to have no special craze, no special bias, to be remarkably well balanced and objective in judgment" (*OC*, Box 241). Thus it requires the presence of other ages to joggle its own complacency.

The fact of change is paramount. A society receives and accepts the symbols that are ordered by a just previous generation of artists. Our contemporary existentialists are living what the artists of a previous generation intuited, expressed, and thus invented. We are the devourers of those intuitions. Meanwhile contemporary artists are intuiting the reality to be devoured in time by a later generation. Thus the artist appears to be ahead of his time, though he is expressing his intuitions of a world present to him. Society, devouring the recent past, never achieves a completed picture of itself. The reason is that art holds to the particular; the devourer abstracts.

I have quoted a remark by Cary arguing that a book is a *total symbol*, the parts in suspension until the whole is grasped. So, too, for Cary, with the total symbolic system that is an age, to which the separate, smaller total symbols contribute. We come to know it whole only in retrospect as we view the sum total of the work of an age. Our response to it is free: "It is no longer subject to imitation and therefore it has acquired all the virtue of a unique and original attitude towards the world, a virtue it lacked in its own time. It is no longer a specimen of popular exploitation" (*AR*, 82).

Cary's cyclical idea is without question derived from his close study of Blake, where the matter is treated not only in "The Mental Traveller" but also in Blake's development of the figure of the revolutionary Orc and the conservative Urizen. In Blake the young Orc becomes the Urizen of the next cycle. Cary recognizes why this is so:

> The reason why the young revolutionary becomes the old conservative is not some disease of age, but simply the fact that he has created in imagination that world, a free revolutionary world, which is being torn from him. We live in the creation and it presents us with two kinds of tragedy: that of the young genius who desires to create his own new world, in politics or in art, and is defeated by the academicism of those whose art and reputations are threatened by his

innovation; and that of the conservative whose world is being destroyed. (*AR*, 74)

In his earlier work this Orcan fate was not so apparent to Blake, but
soon he saw the necessity of separating the fundamental spirit of
creative activity from Orc and giving it a name of its own. Thus he
appropriated Los to stand for this spirit. Los is the father of Orc,
that is, Los's creativity can express itself historically as this revolutionary force, which dies into the "old Church," as Jimson calls it,
after Blake. Fundamentally, however, Los is the enduring power of
creativity in which Cary also believes. This is the power, among
other things, of getting outside the prevailing systems and gaining
the freedom to see the thing itself. But to express this new intuition
is to begin the building of a new symbolic system, with all the difficulties that involves. Cary no doubt appreciated Los's statement:

> I must create a system or be enslaved by another Man's.
> I will not Reason and Compare; my business is to create,
>
> (*Jerusalem*, 10)

reason and comparison being the characteristics of the prevailing
system as Blake saw it in his own time. In "What Does Art Create?"
Cary developed his dialectical view of art:

> [A] man, as he grows older, moves in a world entirely created by art.
> He sees nothing but concepts. . . . Dead concepts convey no excite-
> ment, no thrill of feeling. [Here Cary describes J. S. Mill's account of
> being brought alive to feeling again by Wordsworth's poetry.] The
> penalty of freedom is creation, and without a ceaseless creative
> effort all things die. We say often that the very fabric of the world, of
> this room, is maintained by nothing else than a continual act of the
> imagination.
>
> Therefore we say that, in the final resort, what art creates and re-
> creates in every generation is life; I mean life as a joyful and signifi-
> cant experience. Without the arts, the continuous effort of artists,
> recreating and revealing, men and nations would very quickly die
> from mere disgust. . . . On the other hand it is precisely this contin-
> uous effort of new creation, of new ideas, which keeps the world in
> a turmoil and threatens always to shake civilisation to pieces. (*OC*,
> Box 249)

In *The Horse's Mouth* there is an interesting passage that deals
directly with the matter of how we tend to live *in* our symbolic systems and how intuition must break through them to the expression

and eventual establishment of a new system, which in turn must be broken through. Jimson has been brought by Coker to Hickson with the intention of gaining what she regards as a fair price for Jimson's paintings. Jimson attempts to separate himself from the discussion and begins to generate an idea for a painting in the process of thinking about his friend Plant's Spinozaism. Plant is a contemplative, a gentle abstractionist. Jimson says, "Contemplation is not the doings. It doesn't get *there*, in fact." And he continues:

> Contemplation, in fact, is ON THE OUTSIDE. It's not on the spot. And the truth is that Spinoza was always on the outside. He didn't understand freedom, and so he didn't understand anything. . . . Freedom, to be plain, is nothing but THE INSIDE OF THE OUTSIDE. And even a philosopher like old Ben can't judge the xxx by eating pint pots.

He proceeds to compliment Blake, who, he concludes, had it right:

> Whereas old Bill, that damned Englishman, didn't understand anything else but freedom, and so all his nonsense is full of truth; and even though he may be a bit of an outsider, HIS OUTSIDE IS ON THE INSIDE. (*HM*, 103)

This passage seems to be related to Blake's treatment of his own symbols of circumference and center, expansion and contraction. In Blake the whole effort of imagination is to expand the "selfish center" of one's consciousness so that it is the circumference of one's experience, orders that experience by containing it formally. The consciousness as a selfish center makes everything around it, including its self, into a Lockean world of primary existence available for analysis. The expanded consciousness at the circumference has shaped its experience into what Cary would call "meaning," containing it in the forms of one's art, in an act like that of Los walking around the walls of Golgonooza. Jimson elsewhere calls this act throwing a "loop of creation" around experience with the "eye of imagination" (*HM*, 222).

Playing the terms "outside" and "inside," Jimson argues that one can be outside something in three different ways. In one sense, to be outside is to be an outsider, to be cut off from things, as contemplation and abstract thought would do. This outsideness Blake would actually call being at the center. This is why Blake says the "selfish center" is outside. In another sense, to be outside is to have thrown a loop of creation around experience and thus to have made of that experience an inside, given it a total form or symbolic status. This is the ordering and creation of the artist that Cary talks about in *Art and Reality*. It is to "catch the old mole where he digs," which is a Jimsonian proverb of Hell (*HM*, 103). In a third sense, to be outside is to be outside the prevailing fashion, going one's own way, as both Blake and Spinoza were. Jimson is well aware of this third condition, being this kind of outsider himself.

Art and Reality talks about the birth and death of symbols, about originality, and about the need finally for a conceptual education. Jimson's and Cary's own relation to Blake must be observed here in the light of some of these ideas. Cary refers in *Art and Reality* to the new cathedral at Coventry and mentions the strife over its design, some wishing to see a Gothic building of the old style and some demanding a complete break with the past. Then he remarks, "What was really wanted at Coventry was what the church has had so often before, a new style, which refers to and recalls the old" (*AR*, 60). I have already remarked that in Cary's view of tradition there is no idea that a later writer misinterprets his illustrious predecessor in order to evade domination while still attaching himself to tradition, as in the theory of Harold Bloom; nor does Cary quite limit his view of tradition and influence to the idea that the poet is passing onward an archetypal vision, as Blake, according to Northrop Frye, imagined Milton to be doing with the Bible. Instead, Cary imagines Jimson, and himself, confronting Blake, and recognizing that he can use Blake to reveal something about *his* experience, which is temporally different from Blake's, yet similar, too. In this sense Jimson is expanding Blake into a new age, perhaps ransacking Blake for those potential and latent elements of Blake's vision that Blake himself did not emphasize or develop or left implied or simply didn't notice as possibilities. This is, in one sense, a passing on, such as Frye has observed, but it is more than that. It is a proliferation after a devouring; or it can be described as a bringing to life of latent possibilities implicit in or suggested by a predecessor. This is one of the reasons that Jimson portrays himself as a rogue who will steal anything not nailed down.

The *First Trilogy* might possibly be observable as a symbol from which the preceding concepts were generated. This would make *Art and Reality* a devouring commentary on the trilogy. Obviously Jimson is Cary's most complete delineation of the artist or creator of symbols, and it is not surprising to discover that much of Jimson's behavior can be explained by reflection on the gap Cary finds between intuition and expression. I shall return to this, but first we should consider Cary's art, not Jimson's.

Let us assume from the preceding discussion that among Cary's views are the following: Everyone is alone in mind and must make meaning out of his experience; there are few questions which can be answered with a simple true or false; instead the problem of most statements is their degree of imaginative adequacy; adequacy is a matter of not only whether a view is in accord with brute reality but also whether it offers enough of value to the social world in which man moves; each person expresses only part of his original intuition.

These principles center on the perceiving, thinking, acting consciousness. If Cary were compelled to order in priority the Aristotelian elements of the literary work—plot, character, diction, etc.—character would have to come first. However, Cary's attention to the outer world of fact prevents him from adoption of a purely autobiographical expressiveness. He does not indulge himself in egotistical sublimity, though he creates characters who do. These characters are distanced by the author's adoption of different narrators for each of the novels of the trilogy, so that the narrator of one is observed by the narrator of the others. At the same time, this triple focus is an attempt to enlarge the circumference of the whole. The world of meaning is something built by our experiencing and evaluating the blending and clash of the meanings each character creates. There are not simply true or false views so much as meanings of various adequacy, sophistication, or fullness. We can learn from the expression even of a limited view because after all it *is* someone's view and symbolizes the world of that person, and it impinges on ours; it becomes part of the brute fact that *we* must take it into account.

Writers on Cary have argued for various structures informing the *First Trilogy*. Golden Larsen finds in it "the archetypal pattern of the *Fall and Redemption*" (p. 99). Wright emphasizes the mediations of the female figure between the figure of creator and figure of preserver (p. 24). Stockholder finds various threefold structures (pp. 232–33). Echeruo finds that each novel of the trilogy provides a different "center": *Herself Surprised*, the "emotional center"; *To Be a Pilgrim*, the "intellectual center"; *The Horse's Mouth*, the "existential core" (p. 70). These abstracted structures are of variable value as help to a reader. My approach begins by observing that as the three speakers of the *First Trilogy*—Sara Monday, Thomas Wilcher, and Gulley Jimson—not only view each other but also build up a total symbolic structure of interrelated parts that is Cary's expression, they reveal a hierarchy of consciousness. It may be useful at the distance at which I am operating to see these levels in Blakean terms; the most sophisticated consciousness of the three, Jimson, uses them to some extent himself. I reduce them to a brief chart. It can provide a reasonably satisfactory explanation of the "abstract real" structure of the trilogy.

Jimson	Prolific	Los	Reprobate	Male	Circumference
Wilcher	Devourer	Spectre	Redeemed	Hermaphrodite	In-between
Sara	Nature	Emanation	Elect	Female	Center

In Blake's terms, Jimson is the "prolific" creator of expressions, while Sara is, in some aspects at least, the nature that has been captured in artistic form. She is Jimson's "spiritual fodder" (*HM*, 52) and gyres back and forth in his eyes between the distant elusive nature and the captured form described in Blake's "Mental Traveller." Of course, that is Jimson's view. In the trilogy as a whole, at the most abstract level, Sara plays the part most representative of instinctual, unthinking survival. One is tempted to call her the emanation, which is the female principle of Blake's poems and, to the subjective imagination, the objective world. She is treated by Jimson, when he is in his creative, that is, fiction-making frame of mind, as the eternal female. As all of these things she occupies the center of the trilogy and forms the principal link among the books. She seems also, of the three consciousnesses, most at the Blakean "center." Gulley says that she can mother a man; in Blake's terms this says that she envelops him. And that means her men are external to her. But this is a bold Blakean application, and it doesn't quite work, for Sara possesses her own mode of artistry that takes her, in its limited terms, to a sort of circumference. Her artistry is her power to fashion recalcitrant materials into a home or nest. This power, which reveals itself in her shrewdness, deceptiveness, and improvisation, is virtually instinctive with her. (Jimson is exceedingly sensitive to it and, after Blake, he calls her religion "female religion." Wilcher is aware of it, though he has not successfully named it.) This power doesn't really throw a loop of creation around anything in the sense in which Jimson uses that expression, but it is fundamental because it organizes things for survival and pleasure. It is a power that Cary, unlike many writers, never overlooks or fails to respect.

Jimson stands opposite to Sara as the artist figure, or, in his own mind, a son of Blake's Los. He is male to her female, circumference to her center. He is more than a Sara-watcher, he is a Sara-knower; he tries to give her a meaning and contain her in his vision, though he recognizes that his vision contains only "some of her." And he is right about this. Nor is he always at the circumference: Like Los he allows "his fires to decay," as, for example, when he assaults her. But he is fundamentally a Blakean "prolific," maker of symbols that others can devour and thus conceptualize, if they do not destroy them, just as they have begun to accept and understand and thus devour his earlier paintings of Sara. Indeed, his painting of Sara in the Tate Gallery is already being copied by students.

It is also to be noted, however, that Jimson, though a son of Los, is under greater pressure from the culture than even Blake imagined or at least set forth in his treatment of Los, tense as Blake's treatment may be. This is shown in many places and particularly in Jimson's being reduced to copying himself at the Tate in order to raise funds. This is the artist's life pathetically copying itself, Jimson's career corrupting itself, Jimson imitating his imitators—and sadly in the cause of continuing to paint.

It is easy enough, as Jimson does, to cast Wilcher in the role of the Blakean "spectre," which has lost the proper circumferential relation to its emanation and wanders through the world searching for it. This is reflected in his perverse exhibitionism and his behavior with Sara, who reports:

> Mr. W. would never allow me to shew him any kindness, or rather, I saw that it upset him. I must never allow a dear to slip out, and if I had to touch him for any reason, I must do it as a young nervous creature, with a quiet movement and a steady still hand. For if I seemed to pet him, he would jerk away and say something cool and businesslike. "Come now, it's late," or bring in some conversation about the house. At first I thought he kept me at a distance for fear that I would grow conceited and make myself a nuisance to him, as I daresay other women had done. Afterwards I saw that he was nervous of kindness; and perhaps he was afraid of women. He had learned one way to deal with them and so he could not risk any other. (*HS*, 175)

As we see him in *To Be a Pilgrim*, he has lost even the relationship he had with Sara and tries for a time vainly to recapture her in a fantasy of the future. At the same time, too, like Blake's universal man Albion, he claims that for a time he had lost touch with England itself, which in Blake is one form of Albion's emanation. As a lawyer, Wilcher is also connected to the spectre, external law in Blake's cosmos having been created by Urizen when he fell into the spectral state. Urizen's intention was to control and order nature not by means of a loop of creation but by the chains of moral law. Wilcher, himself, until the very end, when he decides to leave no will, would frantically control the future by legal maneuver. He has rewritten his will thirty-one times.

If Jimson and Sara can be identified with the male and female of Blake's "Mental Traveller," Wilcher seems like the "hermaphrodite" of *Milton* and *Jerusalem*. In Blake, the hermaphrodite represents not an androgynous union of the sexes but the split and warfare between them in the body social. The true relation would be one of contrariety, which can become prolific—the seed in nature; the hermaphroditic relationship is negative and perverse. In sum, Wilcher suffers division and irresolution and is Blake's lost traveller. He is endlessly analytical and must turn everything into abstraction. He is what Blake would call an allegorist. Jimson recognizes all of this in him, but not his hidden humanity:

> [M]en like Wilcher . . . don't look upon you as human. You're a Lost Soul, or a Bad Husband, or a Modern Artist, or a Good Citizen, or a Suspicious Character, or an Income Tax Payer. They don't live in the world we know, composed of individual creatures, fields and moons and trees and stars and cats and flowers and women and saucepans and bicycles and men; they're phantoms, spectres. And they wander screaming and gnashing their teeth, that is, murmuring to themselves and uttering faint sighs, in a spectrous world of abstractions, gibbering and melting into each other like a lot of political systems and religious creeds. (*HM*, 186)

There is a great deal of pathos in Cary's treatment of Wilcher but not in Jimson's. Wilcher, like Urizen, is disturbed over the condition of things and doesn't really want to have been or to be what he has been. He would like to achieve a circumference, but he must discover how. He has no capacity to deal with present or future except through memory, which Blake, seeing memory defined in eighteenth-century terms as merely the product of the association of existent ideas into new combinations, opposes to inspiration. He is a devourer, but he is also what Blake would call a "redeemed."

[T]he Elect is one Class: You
Shall bind them separate; they cannot believe in Eternal Life
Except by Miracle and a New Birth. The other two Classes,
The Reprobate, who never cease to Believe, and the Redeemed,
Who live in doubts and fears perpetually tormented by the Elect.

(Milton, 25)

The redeemed can be saved for the imagination, and Wilcher, because tormented and searching, is redeemable. Caught in the allegorical world where Jimson perceives him, he is struggling to escape. There we see him asserting, for example: "A real discovery is not a thought; it is an experience, which is easily interrupted and lost" (*TBP*, 16). There is, however, another focus which we must remember with respect to Wilcher. We should not stretch Wilcher on a Blakean bed in the way Jimson does, no matter how full of insight that act is. For Wilcher is perceivable in terms of a symbol offered by John Bunyan—the pilgrim. To take him seriously in Bunyan's terms is to acknowledge an idea inescapable to a close reading of Cary—that the intellectual vision of Blake may be more sophisticated, but redemption is possible at other levels, which ought never to be looked down upon.

In the Blakean arrangement, which makes Wilcher the redeemed, Jimson is the reprobate outcast figure, though he is *not* Wilcher's redeemer. Sara is a Blakean Elect only in that her nature is fixed. Strictly speaking, she is not one of this Blakean triad, which is all male.

	Profession	Self-description	Intent	Normal Genre	Tone of Voice
Jimson	Artist	Son of Los	Art Object	Memoir	conscious ironic statement
Wilcher	Lawyer	Mr. Facing-both-ways	Private Statement	Journal	consciousness of irony in the world
Sara	Homemaker	Criminal	Public Statement	Confession	unconscious irony

The Blakean roles of the three narrators affect the kind of statement each makes, as summarized in the chart. Sara is described by Cary in his introduction as having a "secret instinctive and everlasting design to build herself a nest somewhere" (*HS*, 8). The so-called archetypical nature of Sara as "essential woman, the wife, the mother, the homemaker, an eternal figure, who keeps the world going" (Malcolm Foster, p. 381), has been mentioned by virtually all the commentators on the novel, including Cary himself. Foster even connects her physical being to the "statues of the ancient goddesses, who embodied the essence of woman" (p. 381). But Sara's uniqueness has been less mentioned. By the time we see her writing she is no longer a wife but a widow, estranged from her children apparently, and, though a homemaker, unable to make the home she would really like with Jimson. As a writer she is also instinctive in her use of homely figures of speech from the range of her experience. These figures suggest that the range is narrow, but she makes full use of what is available to her, and she achieves truly moving passages when she speaks of kitchen and garden. She colors the facts, moralizes conveniently, verbalizes sentimentally and in hackneyed fashion, yet her language is effective. She *uses* language as one uses an arm. She does not control the irony that the novel itself contains. The irony is outside her, and she is unaware of it. Her artistry is thus limited, and she remains more a character in a novel than a writer of a book. This is not to say that Sara has no prose style. Andrew Wright (p. 118) has remarked that one of the excellences of *Herself Surprised* is its "plain" style. Golden Larsen (p. 124) has rightly remarked that her signature is "stamped on every page and reflected in every sentence." The novel is without question a *tour de force* in this respect. Her memoirs are written for the pulp trade and for money, which means that they must have some lurid interest while at the same time they are enveloped in a form of conventional morality. Her "confession" appears to us to have too much external purpose. She calls herself a criminal, but she hardly believes that she really is one because she does not live a moral code. She can't, therefore, really *imagine* herself as what the law has told her she is. She accepts the judge's verdict and his chastisement, nevertheless, but she doesn't *feel* their meaning, and her story as she tells it does not include her guilt or anyone's guilt in the way it presents the world to us.

Instead, her world is an instinctual world. She may be thought of as an artist as we think of the spider's web-making as artistry. It is not children's art—the art of innocence—but it has affinities to it. The surface of her language is opaque by a design that operates in her instinctively, created by a combination of intellectual limitations and her craftiness. Only we as readers are in a position to know that she reveals more about herself than she can imagine about herself. Neither introspective nor rational, she simply endures. She is strongly intuitive without nearly as much conceptual power, so that her intuition is not given conscious shape and remains pragmatically directed. Yet we must not assume that she does not have Cary's respect. Her power is fundamentally human and capable of good, for she has enormous capacity for sympathy, and her opaque language somehow conveys this in spite of everything one can say against it.

Wilcher reveals a higher, though not necessarily more interesting, level of consciousness. Sara accepts for herself the word "criminal," but she neither believes nor disbelieves it. Wilcher calls himself "Mr. Facing-both-ways" and believes it. For two reasons: he believes in the "reality" of such "allegoric" abstract terms, and he does not have any conscious reason to lie, because his journal is relatively private and addressed principally to himself for purposes of learning the truth. He may not always succeed in escaping self-delusion or his own unconscious motives, but his effort is sincere. Very sincere, to the extent that it is rarely ironic in statement, though appreciative of the ironies in many situations that he observes. The privacy of the statement is consistent with Wilcher's spectral state. He is the artist of introverted self-analysis. It is an incomplete art because rather than making a circumference of the self it anatomizes the self and thus externalizes it, just as psychoanalytical writing is incomplete as art. Wilcher simply does not have the tools to reach a circumference. Yet he does manage, as his journal proceeds, to expand his center somewhat. He is torn between his possession of things and his sense of the spiritual encumbrance of these things. The journal is the *scene* of struggle.

Jimson's memoir is the *expression* of a struggle that is imaginatively ordered and given meaning by the narrator himself, while *we* watch Wilcher's struggle to give his life meaning, and *we* give meaning to Sara's existence. While Sara is inside her country maxims and Wilcher tries to find life in dead langauge, Jimson invents new possibilities by using the art of the past in combinations with new intuitions. Jimson's difference with Mr. Plant illustrates also his difference from Wilcher. Plant has tried to find some "meaning" in the loss of his hand. Jimson argues that he is simply wrong "about the meaning of the world. The world doesn't mean anything to anybody except what the thrush said to the snail before she knocked it on the brick. GET ON OR GET OUT. LAZY BONES" (*HM,*

44

208). This does not mean that Jimson believes the world isn't there, only that one has to put meaning into the world, not take it out. Jimson writes a self-conscious, radically artistic work. It has its own egotistical and thus central defensiveness, but Jimson protects the work by infusing it with a considerable irony of statement. As a "defense" of the artist it is formally self-confident, contrived, and exuberant. Jimson's own reported actions are often outrageous, but they are given a context in which they accumulate meaning. That context is the total symbol of the artist's social and cultural plight. In chapter 26 there is a sort of microcosm of that symbol where it has been discovered that Mrs. Coker has used "The Fall" to patch the roof:

> "A wonderful picture like that," said Nosy. "P-put on the r-roof."
> "A serious thing for me," I said. But I almost burst out laughing at Nosy's indignation. And I decided to give way to my gaiety. It's not an easy thing to do when you have a real grievance, and if I had been fifty years younger I shouldn't have done it. But for some time now I had been noticing that on the whole, a man is wise to give way to gaiety, even at the expense of a grievance. A good grievance is highly enjoyable, but like a lot of other pleasures, it is bad for the liver. It affects the digestion and injures the sweetbread. So I gave way and laughed.
> "W-what is it?" said Nosy, quite terrified. He thought I was going mad with grief.
> "I was laughing," I said.
> "You are too g-good, Mr. Jimson, too n-noble. You oughtn't to f-forgive a crime like that—a crime against s-s-civilisation. I'd like to cut that old woman's throat. I'd like to cut the whole B-British throat. The d-dirty fff-philistines."
> "Not exactly noble, Nosy," I said. For it's dangerous to be thought noble, when you're only being sensible. It causes fatty degeneration of the judgment. "The fact is, I was sick of that god-damned picture."
> "It was the f-finest picture I every saw," said Nosy, getting angry with me. "You m-mustn't s-say such things."
> "I never knew how I hated it," I said, "till now. I've disliked all my pictures, but I never hated one so much as the Fall. . . ."
> "But what I do like," I said, "is starting new ones." (*HM*, 169)

The balance and pathos of this chapter is the balance and pathos of the whole book observed as Jimson's utterance. Jimson treats the situation ironically, for that is a mode of managing imaginatively all the brute reality that he cannot control. It is a way of objectifying, of giving meaning to as much experience as he can throw a loop around. But no art is perfect, and Jimson's suffers from a sort of desperation that gives it pathos.

The usual cliché is to argue that one should not give way to morbidity or discouragement. Jimson desperately turns this upside down and insists in a supreme irony that he ought to give way to gaiety, though this is clearly a discipline he has taught himself, and one that sometimes fails him. His implication is that his view, if nothing else, is the practical one. And this becomes in turn an ironic comment on the usual attribution of impracticality to artists. Jimson's practicality is at a very cerebral level. Cary remarks in his introduction to the novel: "[Jimson] makes a joke of life because he dare not take it seriously. He is afraid that if he does not laugh he will lose either his nerves or his temper" (*HM*, 7). This is certainly an accurate remark.

Jimson's argument that he has come to hate his picture and that what he really likes is starting new ones is also a form of self-protection. There is more involved, of course—a certain perverse delight in initiating Nosy into the hardships of experience, an acknowledgment that painting is really hard work.

This matter of starting new pictures takes us back to our initial concern with the gap Cary perceives between intuition and expression in *Art and Reality*. Yet Jimson's attitude and the treatment Cary gives to Jimson in the novel seem to me more sophisticated than the theory of *Art and Reality*. Though Jimson prefers beginnings, hates the "hell" of subsequent composition, and loves the meaninglessness of the pure materials of his art, he does not really argue that the process of composition is a torment *because* of the loss of the intuition. Instead, his emphasis is on the otherness and domination, past a certain point in the process, of the object itself. He recognizes that once the human hand introduces meaning into the material, that material must be dealt with. At the same time, he acknowledges at least tacitly that the original intuition is not necessarily any longer the issue. The problem has become the working out of the possibilities inherent in a situation that changes as the object takes on its own existence. This is sometimes depressing, sometimes not—not because of the artist's implicit comparison of an original intuition to the object but because of the widening or narrowing of his choices. When Jimson returns from jail to view "The Fall," he sees it anew:

Why, I thought, it's not bad in places. It might be a good thing. The serpent wants to be a bit thicker, and I could bring his tail round to make a nice curl over the tree. Adam is a bit too blue, and Eve could be redder—to bring up the blues. Yes, yes, I thought, getting a bit excited, as I always do when I come back to work after a holiday. I've got something there. Adam's right leg is a gift, whatever you may say. Nobody has done that before with a leg. What a shape. I must have been tight or walking in my sleep when I knocked that off. (*HM*, 15)

Which suggests that the intuition that originally set Jimson going is lost and that it does not really matter. The same is true when Jimson, working with the object, changes some flowers into a "thing like a white Indian club" and finally into a fish (*HM*, 43). We have here a series of intuitions, if you will, but intuitions *into* the materials, not previous to their existence. Most artists will acknowledge a certain pleasure in these events.

Finally, Jimson's arguing in behalf of beginnings is put into the context of his social situation and is thus given a non-theoretical basis that, though impure, is true to experience. Therefore, I suggest that Cary is more sophisticated when he moves toward the particularity of art than when he attempts to generalize and lift the artistic process out of the fabric of life. His art betters his theory and places emphasis on the whole building process and the successes and failures all along the way. On this matter Cary of *The Horse's Mouth* is closer to Blake than to Cary of *Art and Reality*, for in the former the Blakean emphasis on process is paramount. Jimson's power to endure, to begin again and again, always to renew his exuberance for his craft makes him a son of Los and makes it possible for his own particularity to rise to the representation not just of the predicament of the artist but of the endurance of art itself as a human symbolic form of activity. The Jimsonian conception of the symbol is of a thing made, and ultimately—though it may not have much of the original intuition in it, whatever that may have been—it does have *something* to it. In a draft for *Art and Reality*, Cary calls this quality, as apprehended by the observer, "realization," though in *Art and Reality* he finally calls it the "intuition" as the reader receives it. To call it "intuition" is to imply that there has been conveyed to the observer the artist's original "intuition." But Cary has already argued in *Art and Reality* that this is virtually impossible and has rendered it possibly irrelevant in *The Horse's Mouth*.

The "intuition" or "realization" or whatever it is that Cary's novel conveys to us is more true—that is, adequate—than his theory, for in *The Horse's Mouth* the artist is presented to us as involved in the whole process of creation. The conceptualizing of that realization, which is being partially accomplished in this chapter, is part of the *use* to which we put the symbol, part of the devouring of it that is a phase in the inevitable round described by Blake and by Cary himself. In a typescript Cary wrote:

> [W]e live in a world dominated not only by the symbolic forms created by and for art but by the ideas, the acts of the imagination, by which philosophers, poets, writers generally, artists of the mind, have imposed upon the chaos of events, the everlasting conflict of wills, a formal unity, necessary to them as artists, to build a work of art, and so communicate not only feeling and fact, but a meaning, that is to say, a possible true picture of the whole. (*OC*, Box 232)

The shape that Cary gives to his trilogy as a whole is that of the gradual sophistication of the power of creative ordering—from the more rudimentary artistic ordering of Sara to the symbolic form of Jimson, shown in the chart.

	Influence	Quality of Prose	Ultimate Language	Philosophy
Jimson	Blake	particularity	symbol	symbolic form
Wilcher	Bunyan	generality	allegory	"Platonism"
Sara	Yonge	opacity	maxim	pragmatism

Sara's reading of Charlotte M. Yonge has affected her somewhat unconscious tendency to regard language as expressing truth best in the form of what Wilcher calls her "country maxims" (*TBP*, 320). These maxims vary in imaginative intensity; it is interesting to see that those Jimson remembers are generally more interesting than the ones Wilcher recalls. For the most part their originality can be drained by prolonged use, and they are a sort of opaque screen behind which Sara's hiddenness is paradoxically made revealing. Their aim *seems* to be to reduce the meaning of any action to precept.

This is by no means to say that the novel is a failure because of Sara's language. It is a book written by Cary, not Sara; and it is designed to reveal the true relation between Sara and her precepts. Further, she has her own sort of artistry that is constantly breaking forth to surprise us (and no doubt her) and to please us as well.

Yet, her artistry seems unconscious. (The psychology of this would have to be explored; I use the term "unconscious" not in the psychological sense but only to describe an absence, though obviously in some systems of psychology more is involved.) The irony, at any rate, is *outside* Sara, for her desire to make a moralistic "confession" is convention more than it is conscious irony. As a result we can characterize her sense of the ultimate aim of language to be the maxim, which makes language a container of *illustrations* of the way people ought to behave in order to survive. If one were to pin a philosophy to that it would be pragmatism, which must consider language itself as a tool or an object for use. Reality is not located *in* the maxims; they remain a commentary generalizing from events.

As we move up the scale of consciousness, with Wilcher language begins to harbor a greater degree of reality in the form of what the romantics called allegory. Wilcher's author is Bunyan, and his own greatest desire is to become a true pilgrim, to be gathered into the traditional allegory of spiritual quest, to lose his individuality in the "Platonic" symbol, to be—as he comes to learn and accept—what he really is not. I borrow the term "Platonic" here in the special sense employed by John Crowe Ransom in his well-known essay "Poetry: A Note in Ontology": "Platonic poetry is allegory, a discourse in things, but on the understanding that they are translatable at every point into ideas. . . . Now the fine Platonic world of ideas fails to coincide with the original world of perception, which is the world populated by the stubborn and contingent objects." Reality inheres for Wilcher in the "Platonic" abstraction, the general that not merely stands for real particulars but is actually the truth that these particulars strive to become. But Wilcher cannot escape his uniqueness and is facing both ways between the unique individuality that he wishes to consider merely the example and the archetype, Platonic form, or precept. Jimson, of course, knows this about Wilcher and describes him as seeing people always in general terms.

By contrast, Jimson makes Blake's argument that only individuals exist, though as we shall later see with an un-Blakean bitter twist. The ultimate language for him must be that of the symbol, where the unique is treated in a created context. Sara's maxims are metaphorical in form, but they are similes in substance and are always pragmatic and illustrative. Wilcher is tormented by his tendency to take his metaphors literally, which is like affronting gravity. He must turn his sister, brother, and others into types before he

Cary's voice self-consciously and directly uttering a statement. Rather, his authority, or the trilogy's authority, if you wish, is constituted by more than the totality of the fictive voices he has created and their interrelations. It is a "whole of meaning" or "total symbol." Further, Cary differs from Blake in embracing the whole process. His Sara is not the terrifying Rahab or Tirzah of Blake's prophecies, but a creature exuding sympathy; his spectral Wilcher is redeemed as a pilgrim; and his son of Los, Jimson, if not a murderer, has at least committed manslaughter. Obviously, there are some particulars for us yet to consider.

3
Freedom and Point of View
First and Second Trilogies

We have noticed that according to Cary the artist is faced at some point in the creative process with materials that have taken on an independent existence, presenting unforeseen problems and possibilities. A parallel situation confronts the politician, and it requires imagination and flexibility—the freedom to improvise—in at least as great measure as it does for the artist. Indeed, the politician's situation may contain more "chaos," for history is a flux and its materials explosive. Fundamental here is Cary's notion of freedom. It contains its own paradox, which is that man is condemned to exercise freedom, that is, be freedom's prisoner. This paradox is important to an abstracted or distanced notion of the second trilogy, and Cary presents it at length in *Power in Men* and applies it in *The Case for African Freedom* and *Britain and West Africa*.

Michael Echeruo (p. 10) is quite correct to remark that Cary's real interest is not in "politics as such, nor in government . . . but in the management of metaphysical and human order," and Jack Wolkenfeld (p. 157) is not wrong to declare, "[Cary] has only one major concern—the actual position of individuals in the many-sided reality in which he lives." But both remarks do tend to ignore the fact that Cary's notion of politics, like his notion of art, is extremely broad. Often he makes the word expand to cover all human relations and forms of human order. On the other hand, he sometimes contracts the term to make a specific point. For example, in *Power in Men*, he remarks, "Man is not a political or economic animal. He is moved by sympathies, tastes, faiths which have nothing to do with politics" (*PM*, 35). The reason for this particular contraction is that here Cary is strongly opposing any purely behavioristic or mechanistic theory of man that deprives him of his freedom, reducing him to an entity in an abstract notion of social order:

The word 'economy' must not hide the reality of a social order which is not fundamentally economic. Men and women are not units in an economic structure, they are living souls who are ready often to ignore even the primary needs of their bodies for some ideal satisfaction. (*CAF*, 132)

But whether Cary expands the notion of politics (as he must if he is to employ it to describe the *Second Trilogy*) or contracts it to mean something like "professional affairs of state," he makes it clear that the distinction between political and other kinds of power is not real (*PM*, 10).

This takes us back to Cary's major political treatise *Power in Men* and the words "power," "freedom," and "liberty," which are central to it. Never actually a member of the Liberal Party or even of the Liberal Book Club, for which he wrote the book, Cary thought of his own sentiments as liberal. The publisher's change of the book's title, resisted unsuccessfully by Cary, from *Liberty and Freedom* was, I think, a good idea after all. The reason is that Cary does not consistently distinguish between liberty and freedom; both become subsumed under the term "power." This does not hurt the argument, but it has impelled some of his critics to try to clean up the presentation by making a distinction between the two words that would be sensible were Cary actually to have adopted it consistently. Wolkenfeld (p. 161) describes Cary's liberty as what gives men power to control their lives and his freedom as the ability to make decisions. Echeruo (p. 13) calls freedom the creative power of man as a "virtually self-determined actor" and liberty "the availability of those conditions which give this innate power an unrestricted scope for full realization." Neither of these definitions is quite accurate, because idealized and neater than Cary's actual use of the words turns out to be. I shall not attempt to distinguish rigorously Cary's two terms from each other, let alone break down "freedom," as Wolkenfeld does, first into moral freedom and freedom of the mind, and then into external and internal freedom. Rather, I shall only say that "freedom" seems, most of the time, the more fundamental term; "liberty," some of the time, more closely associated with politics and social situations.

A passage from an early draft of *Power in Men* makes this distinction. Cary is speaking about the problem of government in an autocracy:

It can push its people about, it can shout at them, but it cannot tell them what is going on in their minds, and especially their imagination. Because the imagination is free by nature. It is of course the source of all creative power, of every plot and revolution.

When you read in the papers that freedom is in danger, ask yourself whether the writer means this real freedom, or liberty. Liberty is an idea, a conception, a set of rights secured by man-made laws, by democratic constitution. These liberties are always in danger, but freedom, the free mind, is real and indestructible. It can be limited by a bad education, but it cannot be destroyed. (*OC*, Box 242)

Another deleted passage says:

> Freedom and liberty have two aspects from outside and inside the man. From without freedom is absence of prejudice; liberty is absence of restraint; from within they are power to seek truth and power to seek action. (*OC*, Box 267)

Cary probably deleted this passage because his book turns out to be an attack on liberty as absence of restraint; he never completely straightened out his use of the term.

It is best, in any case, to begin with Cary's notion of power. This power is not a derived power. It is in human nature as a given, and for that reason it is a mystery. Further, as a word, it is "abstract," because like the Kantian form of beauty, power is unique, that is, it is entirely individual to each human being, thus undefinable. This power—expressing itself in freedom and liberty—

> is real in the strictest and profoundest sense. It belongs to ultimate reality. It is present in all purposive action, from the slightest muscular movement of any living creature to the grandest ideal construction of the poet or the artist. (*PM*, 7)

It is more fundamental than reason and intellect, and both depend on it. Again a passage from an early draft is most explicit:

> Man is born the most dependent of creatures, and he began as a race in extreme weakness and dependence. But everywhere he is growing more and more into freedom, for freedom is power. It is the power in the soul to think for oneself and to think secretly; to choose a course of action and wait years to achieve it; to satisfy ambition and indulge a passion. It is not only a secret power, it is a final power in the world, everlasting and unconquerable. (*OC*, Box 236)

The paradox that man is condemned to exercise the power of freedom and is therefore its prisoner exists because of the great variety of possibility this power offers. Men must construct their ideas of things. Even an apparently passive response to the real will eventuate in some sort of world-view having been created. Men are born "almost without instinct and are compelled therefore to form their own idea of the world, their working map" (*SE*, 157). They are alone in mind, though not in sympathy, and as a result they must make the map by themselves.

But there is something odd here; one wonders to what extent this power to make freedom is not, after all, determined and therefore not free after all. One notices that it is not really an intellectual power. It is more like an instinct. It is clearly tied up with intuition, a return to a clear apprehension of the real. Cary reverses the notion that we are determined in emotions and free in reason by the trick of enlarging the idea of "emotion" to include "feeling" and "sympathy"; these terms incorporate the act of going forth rather than of simply responding to a stimulus. Still, one senses in Cary that this power is a fallen power ("The fall into freedom," Jimson exclaims), and it is the source of both torment and satisfaction. The power must be exercised. So freedom can go wrong, and often we see it go wrong especially in the action of the *Second Trilogy*, where too often in situations of exhaustion, frustration, despair, and loss of original inspiration the compulsive dark side takes over. This relation of freedom, as Cary uses the term, to compulsion is never quite faced in Cary's speculative writing, but it comes up as an issue with several characters in the trilogies. Jimson even recognizes it in himself. This makes us conclude again, as we did in the previous chapter with respect to artistic activity, that it is in the novels that Cary articulates the particular real, from which his notions of the "real" and "freedom" are abstracted.

Cary never tires of saying that freedom is not the undiluted absence of restraint. That would be ideal, and real only as an ideal. *Power in Men* is an attack on the idea of liberty as, in reality, the absence of restraint. For Cary, governmental power is derived from the innate real power of individuals. All government arises from the exercise of individual power or the abdication of it, for better or worse. This power, Cary asserts, acts "without regard to theory" (*PM*, 245). Cary wants to show that over the long haul it is an ineradicably positive force which, if frustrated, will express itself in some way or another. To define it as an absence would be to disregard its presence in its many manifestations. But to define it as Cary does is to imply that it is irrational and rather like the inspiration that possesses the hapless rhapsode of Plato's *Ion* or the dangerous poet of the *Republic*.

Cary sees that all government, through its derived power, imposes restraint and must do so for the support of general liberty: "Because of freedom there must be government" (*OC*, Box 242). He has utterly no patience with the cult of the noble savage, and he speaks harshly of "the abuse of civilisation . . . begun by Rousseau and continued by reformers, by neurotics, and of course by those who, wishing to be unconventional, succeed only in being commonplace" (*CAF*, 111). Cary is well aware of the contradiction among the early British liberals, who defined liberty as absence of restraint, but went about drawing up acts of restraint in order to further individual liberty. This is the sort of contradiction Cary likes to contemplate, because it demonstrates that it is right to acknowledge that the practice of freedom takes precedence over theory. The government to which Cary attaches Chester Nimmo, the Liberal government

> of 1902–1914 [the Liberals did not actually come to power until early in 1906] is justly thought one of the greatest in British history. But its achievements were all in the teeth of the old theory that state regulation was the enemy of private liberty. . . . But the fundamental creed of liberals was still the same: that liberty was absence of restraint, and that state action was therefore an evil. Thus liberals were in the position of fighting state socialists, for proposing exactly the same kind of legislation which their own government had started. (*PM*, 30–31)

But there comes a time when an inner division like this takes a heavy toll. This was one of the reasons the Liberals fell. That fall has been the subject of many books, often in violent disagreement. One thing, however, seems incontrovertible: The old slogans had worn out and had become remote from actual political practice, just as Cary indicates. Absence of restraint, if it was not always so, became an empty abstraction that actually frustrated human freedom. It could not bottle up human power forever.

There are, of course, some restraints that should never be present. General censorship, Cary agrees, is one of these, though even here he approves of censorship in individual situations where actual injury is feared and in certain other quite specific cases. Generally, however, he thinks the history of censorship has been one of "imbecility" (*PM*, 204). Restraint is even necessary in education, or at least compulsion is. Education is the key to liberty. Children ought to be compelled to go to school in order to increase their true liberty, to become less "parochial in outlook and childish in imagination" (*CAF*, 112). A teacher is not removing restraint in this act of liberation. He does not "draw out anything hidden in the child. . . . He gives instruction" (*PM*, 213), or at least he ought to. Good ideas—that of tolerance, for example—can be taught, and they contribute to the general liberty. In *The Case For African Freedom*, Cary asserts that human power is always pressing for more freedom. But:

> You cannot give liberty to people by a wave of the hand, as you throw open a cage. If you attempted it you would find your victims, like cage birds turned loose, would only injure or poison themselves. (*CAF*, 26)

They must be ready by education and industrial development for democracy, or the experiment will result in a turning toward chaos and tyranny in exactly the same way that Blake's Orc overthrows Urizen only to become a new Urizen. In other words, liberty comes at the end of a political process, not at its beginning.

There is no doubt that Cary was strongly influenced by Kant in formulating his idea of freedom and the political ideas that flow from it. Kant, in Cary's view, recognized that any time a man says "I ought" he assumes that he has a free power, otherwise the statement would be nonsense. Freedom involves moral choice; in other words, it is the ground of values, and without it there could be no moral issues.

In *Power in Men* Cary does not anticipate many recent political problems: the population explosion, for example. Also, he tends to separate work from satisfaction and distinguishes it too simply from leisure. But the book remains a testament to beliefs from which he never swerved in the rest of his career.* Yet it is in the

---

*Both Wright and Foster speak of *Power in Men* having been heavily cut by an editor. The three typed drafts in the Osborn Collection reveal an early version on thin paper of 154 pages, divided into chapters as follows: "Real Freedom," pp. 1–25; "Real Freedom," pp. 26–55; "Freedom and Authority," pp. 56–62; "Ideas of Liberty," pp. 63–71; "Anarchist Theory," pp. 72–102; "Ideas of Liberty: Legal," pp. 103–54. It was heavily revised to become a second typescript. This typescript was in

more practical political writings on Africa, where he focuses on a specific situation of a real people whom he had himself observed, that he is most eloquent:

> The final question, in short, is, do we believe in freedom, or not? Freedom runs great risks, and suffers great misfortunes. It is not the key to a golden age, which will never exist on earth or anywhere else. It is not a formula for perpetual peace of mind or body; it is not the sesame of an escapist. It is only, in the strictest sense of the word, the life of the spirit; eternal life; the power of the individual soul. A free man has mastery, so far as possible, of his own life. . . . he needs for that mastery as much wisdom as he can get. In so far as he refuses, consciously or unconsciously, to seek the truth, or to take responsibility, he is abdicating from freedom; he is making himself a slave of prejudice and fear. (*CAF*, 111)

Here Cary was deeply motivated by personal experience. It is a motivation consistent with his sense of the real as particular. But his novels contain more of the paradoxical nature of the power of freedom and more of its tragedy and comedy than do his political writings, speculative or practical.

Cary is a political novelist in the *Second Trilogy* in the narrowest sense because he writes about a politician, but he is also one in the largest sense because he is supremely interested in the individual's relation to a social real. In *The Horse's Mouth*, the incident of the sculptor Abel's struggles with his stone is a treatment not so much of a social as a material real, a natural *other* to be shaped. Dealing with a social real comes to prominence, though it is of course present in all of Cary's novels, in the *Second Trilogy*. The *Second Trilogy* is about a social real which is *there*, not like a stone but as a capricious, chaotic shape-changer, a "tumult of accident" (*OC*, Box 200). Like all of Cary's work, the trilogy is concerned with the individual's power to deal with this difficult *other*. Inside a social situation, there is both liberty and captivity, and the power that makes for liberty in one situation may result in captivity in another or even

---

turn heavily revised in style in red ink by some editor, much to Cary's irritation. On it he makes his own changes, including reductions, but tells his typist to ignore entirely the editor's changes. The alien changes in red ink must be what Wright refers to, but they had no effect on the final version. The third typescript, on heavy paper, is the one prepared for the printer by Cary. There also were probably cuts made on some other typescript before preparation of the third typescript. In my opinion, the deletions Cary did make are in no way harmful to the final text.

captivity in the same situation if it persists. This happens over and over in the *Second Trilogy*. Hardly a character on its stage for any length of time is not involved personally in it. It is not a theme; it is the real.

Perhaps there is something about a novel deeply concerned with art that contributes to the possibility that characters' roles may seem to be fixed, from a distance at least. A charting of the speakers of the *Second Trilogy* is much more difficult. Indeed, one quickly concludes that they may have been constituted to evade charting along the lines I employed for the *First Trilogy* in the previous chapter. Andrew Wright remarked in the first book written on Cary:

> Cary portrays again and again the same three people because for him it is the commonness of the human dilemma which is compelling. The man who must create, the man who would preserve, and the woman who as female resembles both one and the other but also differs from either—these are the types to which Cary mainly confines himself because, for all their singularities, they constitute in Cary's world the defining limits of human possibility. (p. 72)

This is to stand quite far back to get the broad view, and Professor Wright, who is writing an introduction, knows that well enough. We might call it a sort of Wilcherian approach; in the practice of Cary criticism, it was a necessary first step, and I am thankful it was so well done. Unfortunately, the criticism of Cary has not often managed to approach much closer to the characters of the *Second Trilogy*. It has suffered confusion and annoyance, perhaps because things do not work out quite according to the grand plan of types that Wright laid out so early and Cary insidiously supported in so many of his didactic remarks to his readers. Wolkenfeld remarks (p. 114) that Cary thought in types of characters, though his characters are also specific. He regards the *Second Trilogy* as "more confusing than the *First* because its categories are less clearly visible" (p. 90). However, the basic types are, in his view, still there. Observing Nina Latter, he remarks that she belongs to more categories than Sara Monday, who is simpler. He notes (p. 94) a greater irony in the *Second Trilogy* than in the *First*. I suspect that these remarks are somewhat overburdened by the theory of types. I believe that Malcolm Foster's anxiety about the *Second Trilogy*, shared by many critics, has to do with Cary's breakdown of the types, making them far less useful for interpretation. Foster believes that the *Second Trilogy* is not as unified as the first, its theme far less

59

clear, and its chronology "too vast." Further, he says, Cary has a severe problem making Chester Nimmo and Jim Latter characters with whom we are sympathetic. I believe Wolkenfeld's observation that there is more irony in the *Second Trilogy* has to do with these matters. The so-called diffuseness and vastness and the problem of sympathy are all deliberate on Cary's part. They are the result of his effort to do justice to his political theme. If we follow these matters out a bit by giving attention to the characters, we shall find that they and their situation are quite different from those of the *First Trilogy*. Comparison to it needs to be made with respect to these differences more than with respect to the matter of types.

The chronological spread of the *Second Trilogy* is broader in two ways. First, two narrators pay attention to their youth, while only Wilcher pays a lot of attention to his youth in the *First Trilogy*. Second, the presence of English political and social history pervades the *Second Trilogy* in a distinct way, Nimmo's rise and fall being a microcosm of English liberal politics during his career. True, the *First Trilogy* makes a similar effort with Gulley Jimson and his artistic career as a compressed version of the history of modern English art, and Wilcher chronicles broad social changes. But Jimson's effort is relatively restricted to chapter 13, which doesn't fit very neatly into the movement of Jimson's narrative. It is, in fact, a late interpolation. As a miniature history of modern English art, it is closer to what Helen Gardner complains about with respect to the *Second Trilogy*: "For all its skill and interest, Cary's second trilogy suffers from being so much based on what he called 'research,' so little on memory" (*SE*, viii). I respectfully disagree with this assessment. It is chapter 13 of *The Horse's Mouth* that has the appearance of "history," of appendage, and of a cuteness that goes on too long. *To Be a Pilgrim* treats of broad trends that have familiar names: Victorianism, the Decadence, the First World War, and so forth. Actual political history in the *Second Trilogy* is far more closely interwoven with the characters' lives. Jimson is an individual artist, ahead, behind, or outside his time. Wilcher is a spiritual outsider. Sara lives in a world much more fundamental than that of political history. Chester Nimmo, on the other hand, represents his party and participates in the events of the time, even down to the Contract Case, a parallel that Cary contrives for the infamous Marconi Case of 1912–13 that implicated Lloyd George, Rufus Isaacs, and Herbert Samuel—all Cabinet members. It is important to note, however, that the fictive parallel is carefully distinguished from the historical Marconi Case. Nimmo remains fictive and particular.

Cary did not intend Nimmo allegorically to "be" Lloyd George any more than he intended the Contract Case to "be" the Marconi Case. In a note he wrote: "Not Lloyd George. I don't like novels which pretend to give the history of real people. I'd rather read real history" (*OC*, Box 288). Cary brings together in his three narrators various aspects of the political scene, for example, Nimmo's evangelicalism, Nina's class attitudes, and Jim Latter's colonial experience. George Garrett (pp. 245–56) has detected in the *Second Trilogy* an "impatience with the guise of *fiction*." I am not sure what he means by this. The presence of historical detail cannot be to what he refers. Rather, it must be a certain harsher tone or attitude, which we have tended to associate loosely with the word "realistic." There *is* a difference of tone, and Garrett perceives it as "perhaps, a streak, a shadow of ineradicable pessimism" (p. 252). But this seems not quite right as a way of describing the difference when we look back at the *First Trilogy* and observe Sara killed by the man she most loved, Wilcher bereft of nearly everything but his memories, Jimson's most ambitious works destroyed, Plant's hand amputated, and Rozzie dying after losing her leg. It is something in the handling of the situation that leads Garrett to his observation, not merely the fates of the characters.

Perhaps it is that there is greater surface ambiguity in the *Second Trilogy*, reflecting the deeper ambiguities of situation in political life. This is saying a great deal, for there is quite a lot in the *First Trilogy*, but there it lies for the most part in the elusiveness of Sara's "nature" and the irony of Jimson's expression. In the *Second Trilogy*, it usually comes to invade the events—the "facts" themselves. This ambiguity is one theme of Nina Latter's discourse in *Prisoner of Grace*, and though Jim Latter sees no ambiguity in the facts or their interpretation, we are less convinced. Of the three narrators, it is interesting that Chester Nimmo has the firmest hold on events, though the whole trilogy turns on the ambiguity of his character.

There is a more complicated set of relationships among the characters of the *Second Trilogy*. In the *First Trilogy* Sara's narrative involves both Wilcher and Jimson, but except for their one meeting, they are treated separately according to chronology. Wilcher has virtually nothing to say about Jimson, and Jimson treats Wilcher briefly as the Blakean spectre. By contrast Nina Latter's discourse intimately involves both Jim Latter and Chester Nimmo, and without strict chronological separation. Jim Latter's narrative involves Nina and Nimmo in the same way, and is constructed around scenes involving the three of them. There is no mention of Latter in

Nimmo's memoir, and only brief mention of Nina, but when we read it we suddenly realize about two-thirds of the way through that Nimmo has been writing, indeed dictating the whole of it, to her, and that it is both a lovemaking to and chastisement of his re-married former wife. This sly trick, which is of course also Cary's trick, requires us quite suddenly, two-thirds of the way through the novel, to see the whole all over again.

Cary has a habit of doing this to us. Jimson himself is a master of it, as he shows in several conversations with Nosy Barbon, who is made thereby to see things suddenly from a new perspective. Chester Nimmo's political acts frequently have this surprising quality. Nina is often made to see differently by having to reconstitute her world to include them. Cary's whole trilogistic approach does this sort of thing on the larger scale.

In making it far more difficult to label his narrators, Cary now forces us to make qualifications and recognize reversals. One might think, given previous critical treatment of the women in Cary as nature and the eternal female, and the clear connection of Jimson and Wilcher (though we must remember that this is in Jimson's mind) with Blake's Los and Spectre, that we could say: Nina = Nature and Enitharmon, Nimmo = Los and the prolific, Latter = Spectre and the devourer. But as we proceed we grasp that Nina is quite another nature, that Nimmo, who is clearly a prolific political actor, also plays a spectral role (he has no natural children, for example, and he pretends to be the father of Jim Latter's). Likewise, Latter is at least naturally prolific enough to be a father, though he is a devouring drain on the resources—monetary and emotional— of the family he does acknowledge. This is not merely a reversal of the *First Trilogy*; it is a scrambling of the types and makes us begin again in our responses to Cary's characters. This requirement that we begin again is characteristic of Cary's method inside each novel as well as from novel to novel and even trilogy to trilogy.

With respect to Blake's reprobate, redeemed, and elect, which fitted the *First Trilogy* to some extent, there is an ironic reversal back to the Calvinistic meanings Blake originally ironically reversed. Nina Latter is reprobate in Calvin's sense from Latter's point of view, though Nimmo treats her as his redeemer. Nimmo treats himself as redeemed in Calvin's sense in *Except the Lord*, though he is reprobate in that very same sense to Latter. Latter is elect in Calvin's sense in his own story, but elect in the Blakean sense to Nimmo, who regards him as a rigid, childish fool. (Nimmo, of course, believes that one must manage such fools.) Nina sees herself in neither the Blakean nor the Calvinistic senses of these terms. For her, both sets would be too fixed and on either side of a truth both complex and shifting. Nimmo believes the view he achieves (or is it recaptures?) is a liberation. Latter is captured by his. Nina imagines herself a prisoner, and the important scene at the train station with Nimmo plays out her sense of this; but we read the scene somewhat differently. If she sees herself imprisoned by Nimmo and grace, we see her also as captor of both Nimmo and Latter. And we see her having made a free choice. Nimmo's narrative presents him as a pilgrim into his past, but we see him less a journeyer than a maker—a mover and shaker in the current jargon—in politics, though it is easy to let that notion of him be replaced by "wangler," one of the set of derogatory terms Latter uses to describe him. Both are true, perhaps necessarily true, as Nina seems to realize. Jim Latter presents himself in his narrative, and in his physical bearing, as a soldier. But his military career was not a success. He has been most of the time a remittance man sent to the colonial service in order to keep him out of trouble with debts at home. (Also to keep him away from Nina.) None of the three, then, is entirely what he or she purports to be. But none is *not* entirely what he or she purports to be either.

One might expect this ambiguity to go deeper, and it does. Nina's discourse purports to be a defense of Chester Nimmo's career, but it is self-centered and ends up an expression of herself more revealing than her ingratiating tone—which has usually gotten her what she wanted—would normally lead us to expect. She has a quality of self-indulgence that she confesses to, and her book is a self-indulgence. Her apparent boldness in revealing self-indulgence comes out of a security born of her class; though, for reasons we shall consider, Cary makes her an orphan. Her style is exceedingly literate—as befits her class and her great pleasure in reading. It is self-confident in a way that is occasionally insufferable to Nimmo, who is of a different class and whose own style is so antithetical to hers. Her style includes many parenthetical utterances. Cary said he wanted her to have a "brackety mind," and these utterances express, among other things, her capacity to see complexity, though in some respects she appreciates the simple. The simple things she does like—usually having to do with her own pleasure—are made possible by a complex social and class structure, in which she is in a favored position.

Unlike Nina's literary background, Latter's and Nimmo's are clearly limited, Nimmo's being more capable of expansion, perhaps. What does affect their narratives is deeply ingrained in them. Nimmo's reference to Psalm 127 expresses, of course, his religious background. His memoir takes the form of a didactic morality of the prodigal son or brother who has left the fold, journeyed afar, only to return to the source of inspiration. It means to have an effect—an inspirational religious effect on its reader, and a political effect, both on Nina and others. It is also a kind of confession. But the confession is part of a campaign. It is meant to kill more than one bird and expresses one of Nimmo's main qualities, the multiplicity of his own motives in any one of his acts. Running in the design is a particular device that is not mentioned by its Wordsworthian name: the spot of time. It is a form perhaps so deeply ingrained in the literate English consciousness that identification with Wordsworth is probably an overspecification of the text. Still, it was Wordsworth who could be said to have made from a Methodist method a literary form. This would be appropriate for Nimmo's own evangelical background. Indeed, Nimmo tends to return it to its religious sources. The spots of time he employs are different in important ways from Wordsworth's in their more directly didactic or illustrative character and their design on the reader. As such they are perfectly natural to Nimmo, who thinks any statement ought to get something done. Wordsworth's *Prelude*, which is much more internal, does not use spots of time with a direct design upon the reader; the whole poem demonstrates how spots of time work, but the spots don't often carry individual moral messages in the explicit ways that Nimmo's often do.

Jim Latter's narrative is dictated in the anti-literary style of a military report, though there are constant lapses into bitter humor and sentimentality. He calls it a "statement," but it is formally a confession. Latter's style puts immense emphasis on fact, but the result is our questioning almost all his facts except the simplest ones of date, place, and time. His discourse is only formally a confession because in the end it is really an accusation, bill of particulars, and judgment on his wife, on Nimmo and, finally, on the world.

Latter's favorite poem, in what one imagines is a rather narrow range of literary experience and appreciation, is Richard Lovelace's "To Lucasta, Going to the Wars," the theme of which, of course, is honor. One does not imagine that Lovelace's poem influenced Latter so much as to appeal to some inclination already present in him, while one imagines the psalm to have actually influenced Nimmo's development. In the light of the denouement in the *Second Trilogy*, both poem and psalm play ironic roles, though by no means for their narrators.

Latter's emphasis on honor is, among the three narrators, the strongest commitment to abstraction, and the most dangerous commitment. It ends in the most appalling dishonor. There is a parallel irony in Nimmo's emphasis on family, for he has no children, and Psalm 127 speaks of the importance of children above all things. Nimmo, who has considerable imagination and creative powers, tries to create fatherhood by means of a fiction that can't be sustained. Latter's "honor," after his initial dishonorable failure to marry Nina when she becomes pregnant, requires that he refuse to acknowledge his children, which he honorably persists in doing, after an early confrontation with Nimmo and Nina, to the end. In a moving moment of exhaustion and despair that takes Nina by surprise, Nimmo, who has attempted the fiction of fatherhood, acknowledges that he has no children. A false father, Nimmo tries to be a true one. A true father, Latter is a false one. There is also a complication in Nina's motherhood, which is but a hint in comparison to the clearly ironic fatherhoods of Latter and Nimmo. She tends to flirt with her son Tom, or rather, allows her son Tom to flirt with her, and for a time treats him as her escort, almost her lover.

These complexities are designed to put a greater stress on our sympathies, while yet requiring us to acknowledge *in such a situation* a certain justice or insight or even attractiveness and rightness in certain actions. In the *First Trilogy* we are inclined to sympathize with some of our characters' compulsions and freedoms. They are made sympathetic through their styles. They tend to reveal deeper sides that are attractive. Sara reveals a homely sensibility that grows on us, and in fact pleasantly surprises us. Wilcher reveals a certain wit and sympathetic earnestness that makes us revise our opinion, formed by *Herself Surprised*. Jimson's cleverness, his genius, his capacity to laugh, his self-discipline (even though it fails him) impress us. We are in danger (and the danger is deliberately created), as some critics have been in danger, of forgetting (but in the end we do not) that Sara is a thief and sly conniver, Wilcher sexually unstable and an ornery miser, and Jimson a violent man guilty of theft, vandalism, and, at least, manslaughter.

In the *Second Trilogy*, the good qualities of the characters are not in the forefront. These qualities are so consistently undermined that we suspect Cary has deliberately reversed the pattern of expectation built up through the *First Trilogy* in order to make us think again. With Jimson, for example, we reluctantly admit his attack on Sara. With Nimmo we reluctantly admit his one-time political genius. But it is not a matter of simple reversal. Nina's sense of honor and fairness, which is the initial impulse for her book, comes out of the sort of training typical of her social class. It is unfortunately infected by her special brand of flaccidity. Sara says at one point that she was so surprised at herself that she wondered if there was anything she wouldn't do. Nina comes to impress us as someone whose code would not let her do certain things, but we suspect that she might excuse almost anything in someone else. At the same time, we recognize that she is very perceptive. In Nimmo we are faced with the problem of admiring his faith and hating his wangling. And the two are not separate, since the prose style seems to include both. Cary will not let us out of this uncomfortable state. We are forced, virtually against our will, to weigh up the issues, only to weigh them again in the light of new events. A lot of this involves Cary's desire that we come to grasp his notion of the politician.

Jim Latter's sense of injustice is for some readers, perhaps, his most insidious trait—a trap. He offers many attractive passages of wry wit, but all filtered through an exceedingly rigid mind. Cary himself even went so far as to describe Latter as a paranoid—one of those statements by authors better not uttered. Behind these speakers one discovers a harsher authorial voice than in the *First Trilogy*. The "real" is, however, the same real. Indeed, it covers much of the same historical time, and some of the events of both trilogies take place in Devon, though Cary never connects the two trilogies through event or character. The "real" is a real that is never very pretty. It is a real of injustice, sickness, pain, and bad luck. The characters embody the paradox that their free power is also their captivity, and their freedom can *turn into* compulsive behavior: Nina's flaccidity, Nimmo's wangling; Latter's avenging rigidity. In the *First Trilogy* what we see as compulsive behavior— Jimson's irony, Sara's nest-making, Wilcher's strange ambivalence— seem at least sometimes saving graces. Not in the *Second Trilogy* where they appear deeply involved in the tragic consequences. Freedom itself has become a dangerous thing.

That brings us to the problem of Cary's authorial presence. His

voice never speaks directly for itself, but always through a character. The question of authorial voice or what appears to be lack of
the same has dominated the academic criticism of Cary from its beginning and has led to quarrels about his own willingness to take a
position toward the behavior of his characters. Wright (p. 13) called
his multiplicity of viewpoints new to the novel; although he also
saw it as a reordering of the conventions of first-person narration.
Except in quite rare instances, the device is not, however, used to
reflect from different points of view on the same incident. When
this does happen, it is always a telling occurrence, as in Nina's and
Jim's interpretations of who came to whose bed when they were
children. But even in this sort of case—Jimson's meeting with
Wilcher as reported by both Sara and Jimson—there is often a difference: Sara reports what Wilcher told her about the meeting; Jimson reports the meeting principally to describe Wilcher.

Sara's narrative is written in jail in 1936–37. Wilcher begins to
keep his journal in 1936, and it ends in the autumn of 1938. Jimson
dictates his memoir in hospital in 1939. Nina writes *Prisoner of Grace*
and Nimmo *Except the Lord* in 1924. Jim Latter makes his statement
after July, 1926. However, as close together as their writings are
chronologically, the spaces of time that constitute their principal
subject matters are more discrete. Sara's narrative takes her up to
her imprisonment. Jimson's memoir is confined (except for a few
scattered recollections) to the years 1938 and 1939. The "current"
events that constitute the outer frame of Wilcher's journal occur between the end of Sara's act of writing and the beginning of Jimson's. These are mixed with recollections of the major events of his
lifetime. (He was born in 1867.)

The *Second Trilogy* is quite different in part because of the extended involvement of the three narrators with each other. Nina
and Nimmo write at the same time but about entirely different
events. Nimmo's narrative breaks off before his marriage to Nina,
and Nina's narrative, though beginning with her youthful relationship with Jim Latter, concentrates on Nimmo's career and her relationship with the two men. Latter's "statement" is concerned with
events occurring after Nina's narrative has broken off, and they all
occur within a few days. There is no way to line up the novels of
the *First Trilogy* with those of the *Second* with respect to this matter.
True, in each trilogy there is a novel which offers a panoramic
spread, but they have little in common otherwise. Jimson and Latter seem to sum up, and both are involved in denouements in

which they kill women, but Cary is using the parallels, if anything, for the sake of contrast.

These are matters that will come up again in the next two chapters. I want here only to emphasize the technical variety of the narratives and to note that each concentrates on different events. The binding together, as Wolkenfeld (p. 21) has remarked, lies in a "situation." This situation is the relationship of the three narrators. It is, in fact, two quite different versions of the old love triangle. Nimmo and Latter pay a lot of attention to each other. Wilcher and Jimson pay hardly any, and neither is aware of the extent and nature of Sara's involvement with the other, in the way that Nimmo and Latter have lived with each other's involvement with Nina.

Critics have characterized the intents and effects of these structures in a number of ways. Certainly the intent is not to raise the question of how one can ever find out what really happened. True, Jim Latter's story tantalizes us with this question, but even there it is a byproduct of a deeper purpose. It is, perhaps purposely, designed as an irritant to impel the reader to think *through* that question to what really counts. What really counts for Cary is what is inside people, and he takes some enormous and interesting chances here. Cary himself never indicates that an author ought to be objective, impartial, impersonal, neutral, or whatever; nor does he ever speak the modernist cliché that one should disregard the reader. With him it is all the opposite. A novelist must have a "consistent point of view" (*SE*, 150), and the reader "must not be confused, must not be jolted" (*SE*, 120). He wishes to be "clear, to avoid, especially, provoking in the reader ideas which have nothing to do with the theme" (*SE*, 120). But to avoid the reader's confusion ought not to be confused with requiring the reader on occasion to see things suddenly in a new light.

He goes on to remark that an author should keep out of sight: "An author has no more business in a book than the microphone on the screen. It is hard enough for him to give a clear coherent impression without unnecessary distractions" (*SE*, 120). The metaphor is somewhat misleading, but the second sentence helps to correct the impression. This is not an argument for impartiality; it is one for relevance and unity.

The events in Cary's novels are important, and the historical thread is carefully woven through the whole. In fact, Cary offers a fairly clear picture of the times—as clear as he needs to make it; and the actual structure of events (except for an unfortunate confusion in *Not Honour More*) is quite clear. But it is to be regarded principally as a means of expressing character in a social situation. Character is expressed in the act of construing the real; it is only natural that one think of these novels in terms of character before speaking of plot. Character takes us back to the matter of focus of narration, since it is the narrators' characters that interest us.

The quality in Cary that Wright, taking a page from Keats, calls both "disinterestedness" and his "broad sympathies" has been troublesome for some critics because they have been unable to locate Cary's *values* in the trilogies and suspect that those who do have actually transported them in from his speculative writings. Wright (p. 74) claims that Cary sides with the "creative man" and this is why "Gulley's defeat is a triumph and Wilcher's pathetic." But Cary's judgment goes beyond choosing the creative man, and as good an example as any is Wilcher, who (in terms that are meaningless when applied to Jimson) is "redeemed."

There are at least four critical attitudes toward this matter of values. First, one can assume that a novel really is Stendhal's "mirror in the roadway" and can be written in an entirely objective way, and that this is all right. Second, one can claim that it is not all right, an abandonment of moral responsibility. Third, one can argue that objectivity of this sort is really impossible, that the values come through unconsciously. Fourth, one can claim that the attempt at objectivity is "valueless" and therefore indecent. None of these will do for Cary. Cary's voice is present in certain ways, expressing moral judgments that at any given time may or may not be that of his narrator. Obviously this position requires a distinction between authorial stance, or what I shall call authority, and focus of narration.

The specific concern of those who worry about what they regard as Cary's moral flaccidity continues to be that he leaves everything up to the individual and thus falls into relativism. The most extreme proponent of this view is Robert Bloom, who in his book on Cary, as far back as 1962, expresses his opposition to the whole movement in modern fiction, which he claims effaces the author, satisfying itself with "analyses of consciousness for its own aimless, experiential sake" (p. x). Various critics take Bloom to task for pinning this label on Cary. Giles Mitchell (p. 118) has accused Bloom of "persistence in mistaking complexity for indeterminateness," but has not, I think, made a case that Bloom could accept. Both Wolkenfeld and Echeruo have entered the argument on the side of

Cary as moralist, Echeruo arguing that Bloom's demands on Cary are too stiff in moral tone. The argument takes us back to questions about the nature of fiction, as Mitchell sees (p. 116) when he says that Bloom's general principle is "perhaps not an altogether tenable view of the nature of art."

There is nothing wrong with bringing in Cary's nonfictional statements if they do, in fact, clarify what he is doing. Of course, they can never be substitutes for something absent in the work, but they can certainly make us alert to possibilities. Cary makes some important references, relevant here, to his debt to Kant:

> I read some philosophy at Oxford. . . . the only positive philosophical discoveries of any importance that I made were in Kant. I realized what he meant by the autocracy of the moral will, implied in the word "ought." (*SE*, 68)

Even earlier, he had written in a Kantian way about moral imperatives: "A man has no right to conceive of himself as a machine tool of a principle; he cannot get rid of the responsibility of moral freedom" (*PM*, 69). This does not sound like someone who is likely to avoid commitment. At the same time, it clearly sounds like someone who puts tremendous emphasis on individual moral responsibility. But allegiance to a given law is only obedience. The moral man knows his duty by reference to a "moral standard" that is known from an "idea of what the world ought to be." Fundamental moral standards are "the same everywhere." "All people admire courage, generosity, unselfish devotion" (*PM*, 69). "[L]ies are always lies, evil is always evil, public and private morals are governed precisely by the same law" (*SE*, 229). This may sound like passive allegiance to an external code, but Cary believes that the good can be apprehended directly without the mediation of reason. Cary expresses definite views about the existence of God "as a person," a "fact of experience" (*SE*, 7). Finally, he remarks that "all good novels, and especially popular novels, are about morals" (*SE*, 146).

Now, perhaps Cary was incompetent to express his views in a novel. Yet a number of critics have argued for his deeply moral concern at virtually all levels. Golden Larsen has seen his work as predicated on the idea of the regeneration of the spirit, though Larsen (p. 99) treats it on the abstract level of mythical pattern. Wolkenfeld (p. 187) calls the *Second Trilogy* a "positive work" that affirms "important fundamental values." Still, some have lingering doubts. A closer look is probably necessary before Bloom's attack on Cary's allegedly "mystifying liberality" and lack of conviction (pp. 39, 44) is laid to rest or, at the least, translated from these harsh accusatory terms into something that recognizes that there may be indirect ways to express moral vision in art.

The classic modern work on this subject remains Wayne Booth's *The Rhetoric of Fiction* (Chicago: University of Chicago Press, 1961), written in the tradition of the Chicago Aristotelians, Ronald S. Crane and Richard McKeon, and their school, and adumbrated in Booth's later influential work. He, too, has protested against the idea of the objective author and the unreliable narrator, and he praises Cary (p. 196) for abandoning that focus of narration in his posthumous novel, *The Captive and the Free*, where he thinks it could not have worked successfully. (The reason, however, that Cary did not use the trilogy form is that he knew he was dying and had time to write only one novel.) Like his well-known predecessor in the field, Percy Lubbock, Booth finds Henry James most interesting in his remarks on techniques of narration, and he notes at once two things pertinent to Cary's work: James thought the most interesting themes reflect the moral ambiguities of life, and his interest in realism did not lead him to believe that signs of the author's presence in a work were inartistic (pp. 49–50). Booth's view is that in any case the author cannot erase what I call his "authority." This "authority" for Booth is an ideal version of the author, and if the author tries to hide behind a narrator or narrators the reader will "inevitably construct a picture of the official scribe who writes in this manner." Furthermore, that scribe will "never be neutral to all values" (p. 70). That is an impossibility. The "authority" belongs to what Booth calls the "implied author."

Booth then attempts to avoid accusation that his theory is narrowly expressivistic by claiming that his implied author is a "superior" or ideal version of himself, a "second self." (This is a matter we need not go into except to remark that certain forms of phenomenological criticism would break down the distinction between the author and this idealized form, while others do not.) The "second self" is the voice of emotion and judgments, out of which great fiction is made (p. 86). It is not always the narrator, indeed is not likely to be. Booth finds two sorts of narrators, the reliable and the unreliable. It is not merely a matter of first- or third-person narration, but one of "how the particular qualities of the narrators relate to specific effects" (p. 150). A reliable narrator "speaks for or acts in accordance with the norms of the work (which is to say, the implied author's norms)" (p. 159). An unreliable narrator does not. Certainly for interpreting Cary—and many other writers—we have entered a circle, because in order to check reliability we must know the norms, but (unless we are to import information from the outside and trust it) our way to the norms is only through the narrator. This is a version of the old hermeneutic circle, in which the whole, which is composed of the parts, determines how we are to take the parts. Of course, narrators can be supported or unsupported by other narrators, but there is no breaking out of the circle here, only enlargement and combination.

Booth is more worried about the sacrifice a novelist makes under these conditions than he is pleased with the gains possible. The author runs the danger of surrendering to the limitations of a narrator's view. The narrator can "take over" (p. 341). Cary was well aware of this problem and chose to risk the loss: "in order to get the life of the character, Sara herself, I chose a means of presentation which because that character was simple and had to be simple, active, unreflective, could not show the character in depth, as aware of itself, or its significance in the world" (*SE*, 126). He was less worried about a second problem, Booth's concern that the author will no longer have any means of showing what the facts are from which the speaker's interpretation diverges (p. 175). When this occurs, dramatic irony is lost, because author and audience cannot share knowledge that the narrator does not have. (In a trilogy, of course, the divergent interpretations of three narrators can all be suspect. The reason this does not bother Cary very much is that for him the facts are not the fundamental question.)

Booth does not very much like what he sees in the history of unreliable narrators, which has produced numerous traps for unsuspecting readers. One of the most insidious traps, Booth obviously thinks, is the decreasing emotional distance that inevitably results from a situation like that in Camus's *The Fall*, where the reader is locked in the consciousness of a narrator. Booth finds the affirmative side of Camus's message so submerged that one is driven to seek it outside the novel in Camus's other works (p. 296). Further, since Henry James, unintentional ambiguity has appeared more and more often in fiction—to no good end, of course. It is quite all right, Booth argues (p. 353), to be presented with the complexity of things, "but it is at the same time clear that a story can hold together only if such perplexities are kept within certain boundaries—wide as they may be."

This is the issue that confronts us with Cary. Are the boundaries there? Is it possible that Cary is deliberately playing at maximum enlargement of those boundaries without breaking them down? Is he constantly testing not only himself but also the reader in this matter? Questions of this sort are better addressed after a close look at particulars. Here it is well to observe Booth's list of difficulties (pp. 316ff.) that contribute to the reader's confusion about authority. There are essentially three: lack of adequate warning of irony; excessive subtlety, complexity, or privacy of norms to be inferred; and vivid psychological realism that makes the reader identify too much with the character against his better judgment. These warnings are made especially interesting to us because of Booth's example of Defoe's *Moll Flanders*, which some critics (to Cary's annoyance) have compared to *Herself Surprised*. (Cary was quite right to complain that Sara and Moll are two quite different kinds of people.) Booth's view is that we are uncertain as to how Defoe judges Moll, and we are also uncertain as to how many of Moll's inconsistencies were actually intended by Defoe. With respect to the third difficulty above, Booth observes (p. 323) that many readers of Thackeray's *Barry Lyndon* found themselves against their better judgment excusing Lyndon's crimes and then complaining about Thackeray's immorality! These same accusations have been made against Cary's work.

Booth remarks (p. 340) on the large number of works into which he thinks unreliable narrators have actually been imported "after the original conception of the subject has been formulated." This is not an accusation that can be made against Cary's trilogies, which obviously are conceived as putting a premium on characterization via the device of narration. Booth's concern is fundamentally that the old standards of proof don't work any longer, and we have "looked for so long at foggy landscapes reflected in misty mirrors that we have come to like fog" (p. 372). His play here on the discourse of Vivian in Oscar Wilde's *Decay of Lying* is to the opposite purpose. Wilde's Vivian was claiming great social powers for the artist, who can change our worlds for us. Booth sees an example of such change that he does not like.

Both authorial objectivity and the unreliable narrator raise, therefore, moral issues. There is the possibility of their using indiscriminate compassion and indiscriminate irony. Given the tendency to identify with the narrator, how is the reader to distinguish the narrator's judgment from the author's? Is this not dangerous? In Camus's *Voyeur* Booth offers us an example of our experiencing the emotions of a homicidal maniac and questions whether that is what we really go to literature for (p. 384).

Certainly Cary's use of his narrators is not designed to such ends, even though two of his narrators are killers. He is not merely trying to put us in someone else's position, and a case could be made that in the *Second Trilogy* the narrators are sometimes their own worst enemies. There does not *have* to be something suspect in the choice of an unreliable narrator. Once again we are thrown back on examining what is really going on in Cary's novels, not to some external law of technique.

Booth raises one more point to be considered here. He remarks that we have been told often enough that the novelist has been driven back into a world of private values because the outer world has disappeared. The unreliable narrator, locked in his own consciousness, is a reflection of this condition. One thinks of Pater's famous conclusion to *The Renaissance*. Both Yeats and Eliot lamented that Blake suffered from this breakdown of an external world and the consequent disappearance of a communal myth of concern. Booth argues that even if that is the case, writers should be trying to mold a new consensus by appealing to universal values about which there can be no dispute. Cary did think he was appealing to universal values. If he is not so interpreted, either he has failed or the critic has missed the point.

How does Cary communicate an authority through or behind his narrator? Booth offers a list of normal devices: scenes created specifically for this purpose, selection of detail, the "facts," the way patterns are completed to appeal to our sense of aesthetic order, those denouements that appeal to our sense of the appropriate, and various emphases. To this list I add a list of questions that Cary's trilogies invite us to ponder: How do things turn out and what is the degree of personal responsibility of the narrator? How deeply do the narrators see into things? What is the capacity of each for sympathy? How self-disciplined, how mature is each? Finally, what is supposed to happen to the reader of Cary's text? I believe that Cary displaces the moral issue to the reader, who learns to revise his or her views, to look again, to be prepared to see the "real" anew as a new possibility presents itself.

Now a radical skepticism can easily make a shambles of these criteria, given Cary's technique of presentation; but that misses the point. Cary attempts to bring us to what I call *balances* of awareness, which must include as fundamental a strong appreciation of the uniqueness of every situation of moral judgment. The reason that a critic like Robert Bloom does not like this, and the reason that Wayne Booth, though with far greater sophistication, is edgy is that they try to press too quickly from the technical to the moral issue. The danger here is to evoke a moral law that is too abstracted from the real. Cary was a great admirer of Tolstoy, but *The Kreutzer Sonata*, for all its strengths, bothered him. Why?

> [Tolstoy's] theory was never drawn down into his nature to become a conflicting belief, a tension, an experience which was part of his artist's soul. It remained a dogma, a canon, something dry, stiff, and formal, outside the man. (*SE*, 163)

4
First Trilogy

Herself Surprised

One of the concerns about the *First Trilogy* has been that it has seemed to have no moral center. Cary had early imagined the three narrators as recounting the same events and even to have engaged in a colloquy on art together. But the trilogy contains neither of these elements. Instead, there is a center of character, not plot; and that center is Sara Monday, the narrator of *Herself Surprised*. The question is to what extent we can consider her a dependable narrator. It is clear that she is unreliable in Booth's sense: She does not represent the author's views, though she has some views that I think the author does sympathize with. Her dependability presents a more complicated problem, because it involves our determining her honesty, deviousness, naïveté, and self-consciousness. There is no question that the Sara whom Sara reveals for us colors the facts, and she knows herself to have done so. On occasion she lets us know that the Sara she is telling about had done so. On occasion the narrating Sara even tries it with her reader, only to draw back in a curious way and reveal her deception. Chapter 65 is an important example. Sara tells of Jimson visiting her to recover some drawings that he is certain she possesses:

> Now Gulley had written of the drawings, the time he asked for the three pounds, but, of course, I knew nothing of them. (*HS*, 167)

Within a page Sara has revealed that this is an untruth. Sara had kept some of Jimson's drawings. She lies to us, just as she had lied to Jimson, offering two excuses for the lies to Jimson, but none for the lie to us. After all this, she reveals:

> for the truth was I had a few of his drawings at the bottom of my box. (*HS*, 168)

76

This is a quite astonishing turnabout, unparalleled, as far as I know, in fiction. We have the spectacle before us of Sara being dependable after being undependable. We are put on our guard even as we recognize an *eventual* dependability. Sara's past deviousness has flowed over into her relations with her reader, as if it were a habit. But the narrator Sara oddly contradicts this undependable Sara, as if she cannot help letting the facts shine through her habits. We must read her alert to her tendency to self-contradiction, the underplaying of certain events, and the coloration of fact. Yet in some deeper sense we must trust her *eventually* to reveal things as they are.

Cary needs a sort of dependability in Sara because she is the central figure of the *First Trilogy*, the center around which Cary constructed its events. And she is the first narrator. But hers is an undependable honesty. The narrative is one that *comes around* to truths. One imagines that if she thought about it, Sara would be as surprised at the coming around as she claims to be about her past subterfuges. That she reverses herself about the drawings within two pages would surprise her if it were pointed out.

Quite early in *Herself Surprised*, Sara recalls being surprised at her acceptance of Matt Monday's proposal. At the time she imagined she could get out of it when she wanted to and that it was all a game. The later reasons for her surprise at herself, a repeated theme, are more complicated, and her comments on her surprise become part of her "confession" of sinfulness. Her "evil deeds . . . always took her by surprise" (*HS*, 36), but rather than really acknowledging their "evil," she "could only think it was [her] own nature coming out" (*HS*, 73).

In the usual so-called plot of character, to which the novels of Cary's trilogies surely belong, the protagonist undergoes a change either through maturation or moral revelation, or by some other means, perhaps fall and redemption. I do not intend here to offer a conspectus of plots of character, of which there are many, except to suggest that in the *First Trilogy* Cary performs a twist on the character plot's most common form. Sara claims to have learned from her fall, and she vows to do better. She has listened piously to the prison chaplain, but in fact she has not fundamentally changed, and fundamentals *are* Sara's character. The plot of character is here treated ironically. As I have already remarked, Sara is not one to be surprised—and now I add disturbed—at surprising herself; for fundamentally her nature survives these surprises intact. In a letter Cary says of Sara's surprise: "The essence of Sara is the revelation of herself to herself—she is surprised at herself but also she is 'surprised,' for us, in her nakedness, which is her naïve surprise" (Foster, p. 382). However, though she protests in her nakedness, she is never really embarrassed by it.

The framework of Sara's tale is the confession, a form that Cary offers ironically in two ways: First, it is a "true confession" in the women's magazines sense—hardly a confession at all—for a sensation-mongering newspaper. Second, Sara's motivation is not to confess guilt or sin but to make money. To any reader who, from only a few pages into the book, looks back on her early statements, her hope that her story will be a warning to others has the ring of the obligatory formality of its occasion. It is proper, and Sara has a strong sense of the proper—in certain situations. This is fortified by her sense of what a story should be, derived from her literary experience. On the other hand, Sara does not claim she is innocent of wrongdoing any more than she believes she is guilty. Judith Brawer (p. 631) is wrong when she remarks, "Sara believes, and the sympathetic reader must agree, that she has given everything of herself and that what she takes pales to insignificance by comparison." Some of us may think that, but Sara does not think that way about herself. This is something Tom Wilcher understands about her.

The information that she is writing for the newspapers and money Sara withholds until the last paragraph of the book, where she completes the framework that she began to construct on the first page. It comes to us as a marvelously appropriate motivation; it endorses our sense of her:

> I deserved no less, as the chaplain said, for no one had better chances and more warnings. Neither had my luck left me, for just when I was fretting for our quarter-day at Gulley's and Tommy's bills on top of that, this kind gentleman came from the news agency and offered me a hundred pounds in advance for my story in the newspapers, when I come out. Paid as I like. So that will pay the school bills, at least, till I'm free, and I've no fear then. A good cook will always find work, even without a character, and can get a new character in twelve months, and better herself, which God helping me, I shall do, and keep a more watchful eye, next time, on my flesh, now I know it better. (*HS*, 220)

Sara completes the didactic form of her story, but it is an ironic form, the implications of which she does not herself consciously grasp. She writes as she *is* rather than as she *thinks*. Andrew Wright (p. 119) made this point early about Sara (along with other important ones), but he goes too far when he says "she cannot think." Sara calls herself a "criminal," but she does not feel the moral force of this word, because she thinks that her actions attested to at her trial only *appeared* to be criminal. The judge called her a "woman without any moral sense" and was angry because she smiled during the revelation of her frauds. But Sara was smiling at the strangeness of the woman the testimony purported to describe. At the time she felt it was all somehow not right, though she admits that the individual facts were true "or nearly true; and . . . some things they did not know were worse" (*HS*, 9). Earlier in her life when she barely escaped prosecution, a remark by a woman in a registry office made her feel like a criminal. The woman recommended her to Wilcher's Tolbrook, to which she could not, she said, recommend any "respectable girl" (*HS*, 137). Yet the moral force of the notion of "criminal" doesn't come through to her. She takes it as a humiliation rather than a moral judgment, though she quickly adds the piety that she was due for a reminder.

In fact, Sara has no faith in confession. When poor Wilcher confesses his sins to her at her bedside, she thinks:

> [T]here were as many traps in humility as pride, and that the Devil's best hook was baited with confession. For I had found out even as a child that a quick confession could save me a slapping and a bad conscience too. (*HS*, 194)

Michael Echeruo's slant on this (p. 63) is right enough, though it is somewhat different from the point I want to make. He says, "[S]he knows enough of herself and human nature to suspect that a confession, if not circumspect, only serves to overwhelm the conscience either with its pride or humility." I read the first phrase of Sara's remark as one of her maxims, about which I have spoken in chapter 2. Her primary attention is to the practical results of any single act. Wilcher is in an agitated state, unable to enter her bed without confessing to her, and he is freezing cold. So she humors him in order to get him into bed before his sciatica acts up. But it is too late. So much for the value of confession in Sara's eyes.

Sara is "confessing" to the journalist in order to continue her support of Gulley Jimson and to pay his son Tom's school bills. If she does not believe in confession except to some end, we recognize that in its motive this confession is different from her childhood ones; it is a practical effort of sympathetic giving. One might say that Sara believes in sympathy, giving, and forgiveness; but this would not be as precise as it might be. Sara never finds in others anything that needs to be forgiven—excused perhaps, but not forgiven. "Belief," itself, would not be—did she use it—a word of any particular significance to her, for it involves abstracted reflection, and Sara is defined by her actions, not her abstract thought. Her sympathy is in her nature and habits. Thus she is sympathetic to Matt Monday, whom she knows to be weak; to Tom Wilcher, who is lonely and emotionally isolated; and to Gulley Jimson, who has beaten her: "I don't know how it is but when you have lived with a man, and cooked and cleaned for him and missed him and been through troubles with him, he gets into your blood, whoever he is, and you can't get him out" (*HS*, 166). She goes on to excuse Jimson:

> Besides, there was no doubt Gulley was the most of a man I ever knew. For he carried his own burden, which was a heavy one; and even if he was cruel, it was only when driven mad. (*HS*, 166–67)

Wilcher's pestering of girls in the park is excused because of his "boils and hot blood." She sees him "so worried and pestered by everything in his life" that it was no wonder he took advantage of her and didn't pay her enough. The poor man was "like three men tied up in one bag." She sees the good in him after all: "I liked him for trying to do his duty by the house" (*HS*, 167). Even towards her "enemy" Blanche, Wilcher's niece by marriage who dismisses her and presses for her prosecution and steals her own sister's boyfriend, Sara has no malice. In other words, she believes that the assessment of blame is futile. This is the reason that she is so shocked at the bitterness of the two servants, the Felbys, against Wilcher and the world, more shocked than by any couple she can remember: "You wondered they did not die of the poison" (*HS*, 149). In an important way, as we shall see, Sara actually *lives* the role that Jimson tries to play—without the irony necessary to the more intellectually sophisticated Jimson.

Sara would not understand the notion of determinism or fate, but she does understand "nature," a word on which she unconsciously plays. It is her view that nature works in people; it is something beyond their control, and she excuses it, though she also credits those who fight against their natures, even though they lose. But the exact location of this nature is uncertain. Is the nature that works on Matt Monday *in* him, or is it in fact Sara? How are we to read the line: "I could not be too angry, for I saw it was Nature working in him" (*HS*, 15)? The confusion of causes in the following appears at first deliberate, but we feel finally that it is simply in *her* nature to see it this way:

> The worst battle with Miss Maul was when she told me, in anger, because I would not change my style of dressing, that I had set my cap at Matt and caught him. This made me angry, too, and I was going to tell her how I had fought against him, when it came upon me that perhaps it was true. For though I had run away from him and told him to let me be, and kept out of his way too, all these could be for leading on as much as putting off. (*HS*, 21)

She continues to see it this way. Even when her children have become young women, she sees herself reverting to her "nature" and embarrassing them before their boyfriends with her broad talk (*HS*, 73). This is not merely to excuse herself. She excuses others much more readily. Jimson, she observes, is "chosen" to be an artist. But, of course, this also excuses her supporting him.

One's nature, which frees one from accusation in Sara's eyes, is also, however, an imprisonment. Sara is writing from prison, into which the mistakes of following her nature are supposed to have put her. But she seems to be astonishingly free of all that the prison represents. This freedom is connected with her nature. Jimson, a shrewd observer, once one pierces his hyperbole, is remembered by her as saying that her true home was in a kitchen and she was, in her soul, a born servant (*HS*, 149). She says of herself that she liked to cook only for others, not for herself (*HS*, 127), and this information parallels her notion that it is bad to dwell too much upon oneself. It is not sinful, it is simply not good for one and unproductive; of Hickson she says, "he thought too much about himself, and what was due to him in joy, to get any" (*HS*, 39).

When Sara casts blame, it is upon herself; but again it is not an accusation of sin but a homemade device not to blame others or to create scapegoats. On the one hand, she thinks that what a wife may "lose in justice comes back ten times in kindness" (*HS*, 37), and that in any case it is unproductive to lay blame elsewhere. Jimson's violence, by this code, is unproductive; and, in fact, it always is. Sara's remark ("So I came to see that if I had been done by

81

Wilcher, it was my own fault") (*HS*, 161) is not self-accusation but the expression of willingness to take on responsibility for one's own fate.

There are other reasons. Sara thinks that wrong is not a "steady thing" (*HS*, 37). It takes different forms in different situations. Further, she thinks it is difficult to get to the truth, which becomes tied up with words and shifts around as words shift around. When truth is put into evidence, she complains, it changes. She has little faith in words, and one of her characteristics, expressed several times in her story, is at critical moments avoidance of using words. Often this avoidance seems to work against her better interests, but she thinks things would have been worse had she spoken out:

> So all was as before, and I forgave Hickson; not, I mean, by words, for words would have brought it all up for talk, and talk is dangerous in such a case. But it was understood. (*HS*, 32)

One wonders about this and other incidents, which we shall look at shortly, where words might conceivably have changed the flow of events. But her silence here does make her relation to Hickson renew itself and continue as before. That is Sara's "nature." Her suspicion of words, in any case, goes deep into moral questions:

> [P]eople use words so that you can never be sure what they mean. When the preachers used to speak of adulteries, it would turn out after all, in the thirdly or fourthly, that they were thinking of silk stockings, or women's bicycles, or mixed bathing. (*HS*, 61)

This passage constitutes a recovery from self-accusation, in which she has momentarily seen herself as others might: a philanderer. Confused for a moment, she compounds the confusion but in the end draws from the experience the insight that Matt's jealousy of Hickson is self-destructive, that discussion of the whole matter made things even worse, and that it was better to let Matt "believe what he liked" and go on to rebuild from there.

Her recognitions are not, then, moral recognitions in the sense in which events are recognized by reference to a verbalized moral code. She admits to self-indulgence (*HS*, 143); but even as she utters this remark it is clear that she is unconvinced of her sinfulness or even that there is any such thing. Her detachment of mind and action from our usual language of morality has made it difficult for some critics to put their fingers on her nature. It doesn't seem quite right, even with qualifications, to claim that Sara is "basically a religious person" (p. 73) or that "by the end of *Herself Surprised* Sara is revealed as a woman with a high moral sense" (p. 71), as Charles Hoffman does. However, neither are we inclined to say that she is immoral and irreligious. In spite of her language, she is unique.

In the end she makes a statement that articulates perhaps not what she has *known* but what she has acted on all along, that a good cook can get a new character after twelve months of service. When she was sent to Tolbrook, the woman at the registry had made her feel, we remember, like a criminal and "to know what it is not to have a character" (*HS*, 137). I have already observed that to think of herself as a criminal was for Sara a humiliation which included a sense of lost security but not a moral self-accusation. Sara never comes to think otherwise, and it saves her. Her deepest instincts are endorsed in her realization at the end that in *service*, with all the meanings the word has, she can easily regain the character that she has lost only in the world's eyes.

All of this is true in spite of the pious framework of her story. One of its devices is that of the protagonist's learning from and changing because of moral types met along the way, as in an allegorical journey. Rozzie, her friend, and Nina, Jimson's "wife," she treats as types in a morality. After describing them, she concludes: "If my poor Nina made me remember God and brought up my soul when it had fallen flat, Rozzie was one to make me thank Him for being alive" (*HS*, 85). From what we learn in the trilogy as a whole, however, it is clear that Sara is stronger than either. In any case, the moral lessons Sara claims to glean here are part of Cary's ironic frame because this is a novel in which the protagonist may be reminded of things by Rozzie and Nina, but not changed. Sara comes to assert what she has always felt—that she can renew her "character"—not what the law implies that she should learn; and she distributes sympathy as she goes. The plot is a demonstration of how she is able to survive her fortune.

It is therefore not surprising that Cary constructs the novel by repetitions and parallels. Sara's behavior as she reports it naturally repeats itself. For example, she does not like Tolbrook at first, but then does not want to leave it. The same thing happens when she moves to 15 Craven Gardens. Finally, after Craven Gardens burns, she comes to like Rann Park. The pattern is always the same. To go to any one of these places is reluctantly to leave a nest; but, for Sara, to be anywhere for any length of time is to make a new one. Establishment of a nest involves a kitchen at its center. Sara discourses more than once on the virtues of a good kitchen and kitchen garden. Some of these statements are close to being rapturous, especially her hymn to the kitchen in chapter 58. She has just been surprised to come upon Wilcher naked in the upstairs hall and then shocked by Mrs. Felby's bitter rage at Wilcher and the world. She expresses thanks to be in a kitchen. This long passage—perhaps the most heartfelt in the book—is supposed to express Sara's thoughts at a certain time in the past, but it clearly reflects her constant attitude. The kitchen is a place of peace where there are no enemies. "Providence Himself" has led her back to her kitchen: "Then it came back to me what poor Jimson had said about my true home being in a kitchen and that I was a born servant in my soul and my heart gave a turnover and I felt the true joy of my life as clear and strong as if the big round clock over the chimney-mouth was ticking inside me" (*HS*, 148). The passage continues as Sara surveys her domain. If the clock is inside her like a heart, so is she spread through the kitchen's environs like the body of "a king or queen whose flesh is brought up to be the father of all his countries, and not to forget the little bye-lands even when they are on the dark side of the sun" (*HS*, 150). The whole passage is quite unsophisticated, even made crude by Cary in its mixed use of figures and capacity for slight irrelevance or tenuous pertinacity. It begins with Sara observing objects around her, for each of which she constructs one of her characteristic homely similes. The theme is brightness, whiteness, and warmth. The notion of royalty is introduced by a cliché: "I call it a treat for queens to sink your hands in new wheaten flour" (*HS*, 150). This is left undeveloped for a few sentences in which some rather detached comparisons of objects in the kitchen to the front of the British Museum and to Aladdin's lamp appear. These similes have little relation to each other or to the whole except as bits and pieces from Sara's sightseeing and reading bundled together. They and their odd juxtaposition reflect the limits of her experience. Then the royalty motif reappears, and she imagines herself as king or queen in the passage I have quoted above, only to follow it with a more characteristic homely image. It is as if her romantic notion of her own royalty is not something she can maintain seriously for long against her more fundamental nature, which she expresses as follows: "You would say I was putting out in buds like a shallot with my big kitchen heart in the middle and my little hearts all round in the empire of those good faithful offices, all fitted up as they were, even the cupboards, in the best of country materials" (*HS*, 150). This, in turn, with the notion of empire, ends in a vision of utensils and pots as soldiers lined up in regiments—a toy soldier figure virtually out of a child's book.

Then quite suddenly there comes a homely expression, in which Carl Jung would have found an archetypal world navel or womb. It is connected to the earlier figure of the clock heart and the king's body distributed throughout his empire, but at the same time only crudely, for its actual contents are quite different from anything that has gone before; and Sara is not conscious of the connections: "'Well,' I thought, 'if you tied a knot of all the roads and railways and pipes and wires in the world it would come to a kitchen in the middle of it'" (*HS*, 150). This image, in which the complexity of the modern technological world begins and ends in the domesticity of the kitchen, reflects Sara's sense of what true order is. It is as a whole a touching passage, an effort to express deep feeling. The inadequacy of her literary powers is appropriately revealed at this moment in the chaos, the lack of firm control of her imagery. An impression of non sequitur is countered by the unity of the feeling "behind" the words, created by the context. The passage is one of Cary's *tours de force*. Its eloquence is that of someone who feels that language is severely limited and is herself limited in her capacity to use it.

Sara finds in the old idea of the kitchen a marriage of beauty and utility that has been the modern desire:

> And so close and neat, there wouldn't be room for a single piece of useless nonsense or vain furniture. For the great beauty of my jewels was that every one of them was needed. (*HS*, 150)

Further, beauty and utility are endorsed by their moralistic simplicity. Though not particularly religious, Sara finds in the kitchen, then, a symbol of a traditional Protestant ethic. Sara's whole treatment of her kitchen deflects a violence that could be latent there. The imagery is of not very violent toy soldiers. It culminates in a vision of peace: Her treasure chests contain not the gold of conquest but flour and cakes, and armor is the silver plate. In the imagistic chaos typical of this passage, the bayonets go into steaks and chops, and the only glory is "conquering hungry stomachs and bad tempers" (*HS*, 150). After a good dinner, she says, the lion and the lamb lie down together. One of the interesting things about this passage is the primitive archetypal nature of much of its imagery, as if we were indeed hearing the speech of nature. It is an innocent speech, its military figures as disarming as a children's pantomime. It would be a critical impropriety and psychological naïveté to read solemnly into the war imagery an unconscious violence in her attitude.

Even with her language's tendency toward figurative confusion, Sara has a certain consistency of feeling that overcomes the surface chaos by means of the homely utterance. The passage I have discussed is curiously eloquent in spite of its very limited literary sophistication because it tries to go beyond what its speaker is capable of controlling. But at times Cary is not so successful, and the reader finds Sara's kitchen similes overdone and unlikely when Cary seems to force consistency on them. The following passage describing Hickson's house begins by catching Sara's voice most effectively in the simplicity of its opening description, the phrases "were a wonder" and "beat Babylon." But a little later the domestic similes begin to troop by us, and we sense a mechanical principle of selection present:

> The house outside was not so much, though big and old; a great square block like a box, with stone railing round the top and statues all along; as if someone had opened the box and left the nails sticking up. But the gardens were a wonder; and to beat Babylon, falling down by terraces, and fountains in every one, to a lake, and on the other side of the lake, rising grounds with woods and single trees and Jersey cows as fine as deer, and pale as lemon, grazing and drinking. It was about sunset with a sky like a kitchen fire, all sparkles below and blue ash on top; meaning perhaps a storm tomorrow. But the air as warm as new milk and still as water in a goldfish bowl. The water was as soft and bright as sweet oil, it seemed that you could have put it on your tongue and tasted its luxury. (*HS*, 29–30)

Obviously, Cary is making the point that Sara's mind is centered on the kitchen, which produces figures and food, indeed figures of food. She is constantly reaching out to connect things to the hearth, but this and other passages overdo the device of simile. One can perhaps defend each alone. It is the whole that calls attention to the author trying too hard. When the homely simile comes along with a bit of a surprise, it is more successful: "Oh, that joy, to feel the open again and to see the lovely world and know that your nine months are over, when you felt like a parcel coming out of its string" (*HS*, 29). Sara's hackneyed maxims are more effective than her heaps of more original similes. The similes have always the same form and usually make the same point, whereas the maxims are each different, and she amuses us by seeming to have one in store for any occasion. This resourcefulness reflects effectively her capacity for survival. The maxim is a way of putting a situation behind her and going on to the next, and it is appropriate to the limitations of her mind. This is why I say it is her *characteristic* device. The maxim is not a lesson in moral law but in what to expect in life and how to survive it. Indeed, it is not so much a lesson as an ounce of prevention already known to her: "A kitchen fire is just the right height to look at, without going to sleep, and then it is a useful fire and not just a luxury; and it is so made that it drops its coals and tells you, with every fall, that life burns away, and it has the stove top for a kettle to remind you that, at the worst, there is always tea" (*HS*, 71–72).

Even the country maxims stated as warnings, which seem to be about sin, turn out to be about survival and how to avoid creating needless burdens for oneself. The warning against jealousy that she offers to us—the moral she finds in Hickson's behavior when he betrayed her to Matt—is that to do a "trifling thing" is to hurt oneself. She invokes the old saying "the worse the grief, the better the heart to bear it" to remind herself of her own strength. She preserves the color of the country in her language, constantly surprising us when out of her simplicity comes a common phrase made especially apt by the context: "[Miss Slaughter] was a sly one and meant Jimson to have me, like meat to a lion" (*HS*, 91). (The phrase is hers. Cary is responsible for the pun on the lady's name.) There is consistency to these phrases. They cluster together without self-consciousness. Looking in a mirror as a young married woman, she thinks that she is nothing but "maiden meat" (*HS*, 10), and she recalls how the boys used to call at the girls, "Beef to the ankle" (*HS*, 140). Her description of herself when newly married is characteristic: "I did not know how to manage myself, any more than a filly foal running about with her tail in the air and pretending to bite the trees, and to kick at her own mother" (*HS*, 20). The invocation of the filly here would please Gulley Jimson, because for him the adult Sara is real horse meat.

Sara's prose contains several references to the novels of Charlotte M. Yonge, who provides for her the model of what a piece of writing ought to be. Sara is a great reader of Yonge and mentions several of her novels: *Young Stepmother, The Pillars of the House, Heartsease, The Heir of Redclyffe,* and *Mrs. Ewing.* A piece of writing ought to prepare one to face the "real trials and sorrows of life, for God knows there are enough in every life, and every one of us wants help to face them" (*HS,* 13–14). Sara's way is to imagine how a young heroine or hero would face her adversity. Sara's own book does this, but not in the way its pious frame indicates; for what she offers is not how she went wrong but how her sympathetic spirit survives.

The real structure of Sara's story is based on her relation to her men, especially Gulley Jimson, and to the making of her homes and kitchens. Her attitude toward men in general is that they require management (in this sense she is a politician), that their behavior is irrational (nature works on them), and that they have certain rights. In practice, the principal right is to be provided a home by a woman and to be domesticated and managed by one. In marriage, with this go sexual rights. Except for Gulley Jimson, the men Sara would domesticate she regards as naturally weak. Even Jimson she sees as unable to put himself forward, and she tends to press him or to manage his affairs. (It seems to me that Charles Hoffman [p. 73] is mistaken in stating that "she understood intuitively that in a real sense society owed Gulley a living as an artist." That is a notion, intuitive or otherwise, quite foreign to her idea of life.) Sara thinks it quite natural for a man to need a woman, not only sexually but as protection and support. Her men are all, it seems, rather ugly, or at least certainly not handsome, and the story she tells of her initial sexual relationship with each of them always begins with a description designed to help us believe she is rather sorry for them or at least finds little that is attractive in them. Of Matt, she writes: "I thought him a poor thing, with his long neck and long nose, his bulgy eyes and his bald head" (*HS,* 15). Of Jimson:

> Mr. Jimson was a little bald man with a flat nose and a big chin. His head was big and hung over so that his face was hollow in the middle. (*HS,* 41)

Of Wilcher:

> He was a little man with a bald head and round black spectacles. His nose was very short, just like a baby's, and he had a long blue upper

lip, like a priest which made me say: "You're one of the arguers." He had long thin red lips and the under one stuck out and curled over. (*HS*, 142)

Whatever Sara sees in them, and she doesn't see much—except in Jimson—it is not their looks.

What they see in her is various, but clearly her relation to all her men is sexual. Though she never says that she deliberately attracts men, it is clear enough that, if it is not deliberate, it is in her nature and she does nothing to combat it. There are hints of this in her brief mention of flirtations with the bank manager and her daughter's dentist.

Her story divides fairly neatly into four parts. Chapters 1 to 30 are about her marriage to Matt Monday. Chapters 31 to 50 recount her life with Gulley Jimson. Chapters 51 to 78 tell of her life at Tolbrook and at 15 Craven Gardens as housekeeper and eventually mistress to Tom Wilcher. Then there is a final section of denouement. The interesting thing about this structure is Jimson's intrusion squarely into the middle of the sections devoted to Sara's life with the other men. Jimson appears in the first part in chapter 15 and in the third part in chapter 65. Jimson and his "family" dominate the concluding section. Indeed, the conflict which dominates Sara's story is that between her making of and attachment to homes and her attraction to Jimson. When she introduces Jimson to us, she does it with an ominous flourish very different from her treatment of the other men: "Now I come to the time of my meeting with Gulley Jimson, who was the turning-point in my downfall, and, I dare say it, the instrument of Providence, to punish my prosperity and forgetfulness" (*HS*, 40). This is one of those statements that in Sara's mode seems an obligatory pious formality. Sara would be hard pressed to *demonstrate* Jimson's role in these terms. Yet Jimson's appearance in her life is as important as the *tone* of this statement insists. Jimson is "the most of a man she ever knew" (*HS*, 166), and her relationship to him takes precedence over all others.

In many of Cary's novels there are what we call key scenes. The most important one in *Herself Surprised* comes exactly at the middle of the novel. (There is an interesting parallel to and contrast with a scene in *Prisoner of Grace* that I shall discuss later.) The scene constitutes chapter 43, and its aftermath is the substance of chapter 44. Sara and Jimson have been to Oldport Fair, and Sara muses that when she was a girl it was "only my mother chasing me home that saved me, on fair days, from my nature" (*HS*, 107). Returning, they are confronted by Miss Slaughter, who wants Sara to put up some of her money to keep the builder at work on the hall at Ancombe that is to house Jimson's picture. At first, Sara is reluctant, but she gives in, losing her money (if not her virtue) on this fair day. (There is later in the novel a play on the relation of money, religion, and duty.) The whole chapter describes Sara's happiness. To her, giving in to Miss Slaughter did not "seem a weakness at the time." This phrase is somewhat foreboding; her happiness with Jimson apparently established, we come to the crisis of chapter 43.

The story is plainly told, with very little ornament or even Sara's homely comments and maxims. When Sara writes in this way we recognize that her report is dependable. It is here that she learns of what she calls Jimson's "flaw." She has been pushing him to do the portrait of a General Foley, and to have an exhibition. He has resisted. Now he has become what Sara calls "stuck" in his work on the wallpainting, and he is "mooning about again and doing nothing" (*HS*, 109). Inactivity of this sort in anyone bothers Sara. She does not grasp the rhythm of Jimson's work, and she is concerned about how they are going to make ends meet. Sara discovers, when she broaches the subjects of the portrait and the exhibition, that in this state Jimson will pick a quarrel, while at the same time accusing her of starting it. She realizes suddenly that this is what must have happened to his previous "wife" Nina, who had warned her that he had better not be interfered with. Sara staunchly insists to us that she has not interfered and that Jimson is merely "determined to have his quarrel" (*HS*, 110). Sara tells him that she has no time for quarrels over nothing, particularly when Miss Slaughter's cook has gone off. She proceeds to the kitchen, followed by Jimson, who now looks for other things to complain about: She should not have to do the cooking, etc. She says she likes cooking and doesn't mind Miss Slaughter's taking small advantage. Perhaps because he is now in Sara's territory, Jimson changes his behavior. He begins to consider doing the portrait and speaks enthusiastically. He builds up the fiction of making fifteen hundred pounds a year by devoting one week a month to portraits. He concludes with a self-description quite far off the mark:

> I'm not one of those half-baked amateurs who thinks he has to wait for inspiration. Inspiration is another name for knowing your job

and getting down to it. I can paint anything you like any time, and why not. I've learnt my job. I'm a painter, a workingman, a trades-man. Do you know, Sall, I wish the very name of artist were abol-ished. (*HS*, 110)

It is not that he doesn't have the technical capacity to do what he proposes; he doesn't have the will.

This and the rest of his speech Sara comments on, saying that she thought Jimson had talked himself around. Jimson has not de-livered the speech ironically. He really has been trying to talk him-self around, but we see that he can't make it hold. Saying at last that he will write to General Foley about the portrait, he is sud-denly irritated by Sara's quick offer to get Foley's letter for him, and he can no longer hold back:

> My dear Sall, you've never had any other idea but to turn me into a money-maker with a balance at the bank and two motor cars. Well, I give you warning—stop it and stop it now. That's all I ask. Not to be nagged. (*HS*, 111)

This is not a quarrel over nothing. Jimson's whole notion of himself is at stake. In their subsequent bickering it is a matter of two dif-ferent perspectives. In his unproductive state, Jimson is extremely sensitive. On the other hand, Sara reveals that she has pushed him, and she feels no guilt, because she thinks he needs a push. Early, before Matt's death, he had joked about her ambition for him:

> You're like a train—nothing will turn you when you get started. It's a good thing you're not my wife or I should have murdered you long ago. (*HS*, 54)

At this point we don't know how *The Horse's Mouth* ends. The state-ment foreshadows the conflict between them, and here our sympa-thy is partly with Sara, since she does not seem to be demanding anything for herself. She is right about Jimson's need to have a suc-cess. But in the later scene, she doesn't grasp that Jimson's genius condemns him to periods of unproductivity or, better, waiting. She also doesn't understand that Jimson simply can't bring himself to paint General Foley. The result in chapter 43 is Jimson's rage and Sara's bleeding nose. Even more important, she doesn't grasp that though Jimson does want worldly success, he hates his desire for it. Her actions remind him of this.

Sara insists that she never interfered with Jimson, because he did want these things. He wanted to be famous, to make money, and to be in the Academy. What she fails to see is that he wants these things on his terms only, and he becomes violent when forced to recognize this fact. Early she also naïvely misunderstands Jimson's capacity to survive, thinking that Jimson's whole life depends on his winning the Bradnall competition (*HS*, 59). Later she recognizes more: that his whole attitude was "not to trouble about his ups and downs. But to get on with his work" (*HS*, 72). That he can't always live up to this discipline she also finds out. His exuberant imagination and irony make it possible to stave off rage and depression most of the time, but not all of the time.

The conflict in Jimson is parallel to the conflict in Sara which Cary expresses in chapter 44. Sara walks out on Jimson, and she is disoriented. Her "home" has been disrupted, and she anticipates missing his enormous appreciation of her cooking. The following establishes the motive for her return:

> But the worst of that terrible day was walking about and wondering what I would do. Every minute my mind was hopping back to the kitchen at Rose Cottage, saying: Now's my chance to get a new colander, or, Perhaps they will have a *bain-marie* in this place, or I must try Jimson with salmon in pastry. For though Jimson was the kind of man who could live on happiness and moldy crusts if you let him, he had a great taste for good food. (*HS*, 113)

This passage goes on to describe Jimson as the perfect devourer—the perfect critic—of Sara's art, but it ends with her reminding herself that she has "left the brute" (*HS*, 113).

But, in fact, she has not. We observe her leaving a trail, so that Miss Slaughter can apprehend her and convince her that she should return. She recognizes that she had as good as sent for Miss Slaughter and that she longed to be home. At the same time, however, she felt she was leaving behind her the "last of her youth." She was a "martyr going to the torturer" (*HS*, 115). She had given herself up to "a bad, uneasy life" (*HS*, 118). But when she returns, Jimson refers to her in laughter as the "business partner," and he has already caused her to lose her money ("virtue") to Miss Slaughter in his support. She is incapable of dealing with this bold behavior. The whole episode ends with her pleasing him on the very next evening with a Scotch salmon in pastry, after which he writes off the letter to General Foley. But he never does the portrait.

Although Sara describes her perplexity at Jimson's behavior, she manages to clarify the conflict in him and the conflict between them. Their attraction to each other is in conflict with the struggle between her nature and his freedom.

Sara had intended to go to her friend Rozzie Balmforth when she left Jimson, and she compares herself to Rozzie by way of epilog to this episode: "I never had Rozzie's art not to care for anything and to keep myself going on, like a horse, without any kind of happiness or hope or proper object in life" (*HS*, 118). Sara misjudges Rozzie here. It is she, not Rozzie, who is the survivor. Rozzie lives on bitterness, Sara on life itself. If Rozzie plods on like a horse, Sara races on with spirit. She does have the capacity to go on—in her spirited way. The problem is that the man who most attracts her will not be domesticated without periodic violence. As for the matter of "going on, like a horse," this is a virtue endorsed from the horse's mouth, but one ought not to go on like an old nag harnessed to a treadmill, and Sara does not.

Sara's sense of martyrdom to Jimson's rages is partly the emotion of the moment, but by no means entirely. She chooses the martyrdom. At the same time, his beating of her forever separates her from such innocence as remained to her. But even here, Sara sees typically a silver lining: Perhaps, to have taken up with Rozzie would have destroyed her entirely. Sara never entirely rejects Jimson in spirit. From the moment she meets him, despite his appearance, she is taken by him: "You're not one to care what the world thinks" is her thought on first seeing him, and the thought appeals to her. At the same time, we have to recognize that Jimson does care what the world thinks, and so does Sara, but in each case what they want the world to think is different.

Sara is in love with Jimson's laughter. In spite of her failure to develop any sophisticated sense of painting, she and Matt learn from Jimson to see things more clearly and deeply. (Unfortunately for Matt, what he comes to see is the accuracy of Jimson's portrait of him. Sara sees it too, though she protests against the painting.) Jimson is a new world to Sara, and he is the only lover about whom she seems to be curious. Nina tells her about one of his paintings, and she wants to see it because she thinks, quite naïvely of course, that it will reveal his religion (*HS*, 37). She is entertained by his imagination and the stories that are never told the same way twice or even sometimes with the same characters (*HS*, 125). She even picks up some of his language. He stimulates her imagination. She recalls in a number of places the happiness she and Jimson had, and she remembers that he was capable of enjoying his peace when he had it (the reservation is important) and never pitied himself: "If I ever loved Gulley, it was for his never grousing and never spoiling a joy in hand with yesterday's grief or to-morrow's fear" (*HS*, 139). Without knowing it, Sara has adopted from Jimson certain lines from Blake:

> He who bends to himself a joy
> Does the winged life destroy;
> But he who kisses the joy as it flies
> Lives in eternity's sun rise. (*Notebook*, p. 105)

and

> If you trap the moment before it's ripe,
> The tears of repentance you'll surely wipe;
> But if once you let the moment go
> You can never wipe off the tears of woe. (*Notebook*, p. 105)

These are lines which Sara's life may actually follow more closely than Jimson's, whose joy is so often cut with irony. One notes that Blake is speaking maxims here, like Sara.

Jimson's exhibition, which she finally brings off, reminds one of Blake's in 1809. It is equally a disaster, though the outcome of it has an irony—the actual sale of some pictures—that Blake's apparently did not have. Jimson makes light of it to protect himself from despair. Sara knows he is suffering, and his remark to her is double-edged: "Come on, you're in the profession now, you must learn to take it on the nose" (*HS*, 121). He takes it figuratively, and she takes it from him literally on the nose when she tries to encourage him to patch the wrecked wall picture at Ancombe. She wants him to fight for his picture, but he fights instead with her and then leaves her. So though Gulley laughs off the exhibition and the loss of his painting, Sara suffers for it. He laughs at human nature but strikes out at Sara's nature as a relief.

A month after Sara goes to Tolbrook, Jimson wants her back, but she does not want to leave, because she is nest-building, cleaning house, and generally fixing the old place up. She puts him off with money, which apparently satisfies him. However, there is little doubt she would have gone to Jimson had he pressed her. Tolbrook attracts her as a home to be made, but Tom Wilcher does not. Sara feels sorry for Jimson at times, but she never pities him. Wilcher she pities, though she says piously toward the end that he was worth three Jimsons. In articulating worth Sara supports the weak and the guilt-ridden, as if guilt were a sign of integrity; but she loves Jimson's strength. Wilcher she accepts sexually for reasons that go beneath what she is willing to say. Fundamentally, to take him to her bed is to complete, or nearly complete, the home she has restored at 15 Craven Gardens. To do this is also to protect the home and its nominal head; though her description of their relationship leaves doubt as to whether Wilcher can be said to be in charge. Wilcher proposes that they sleep together, but Sara disposes. Sara is able to manage Wilcher up to a point marked out by their class differences. She manages both him and his houses with great tact, but Wilcher is incapable of true sexual understanding and familiarity with her. He is closed in by his notions of both sexual and class relations, and they prevent Sara's complete triumph as homemaker.

The relationship with Wilcher is sharply contrasted to that with Jimson, whom Sara is not so successful in managing. With Jimson she is not so tactful, and in any case tact is not something that works with Jimson. The tact Sara exhibits with Wilcher depends on the class structure. In her relationship with Wilcher, there are rules. She understands these rules by intuition. But Jimson is classless, except in his resentment against class. Sara attempts to apply certain middle-class rules to his life, or at least Jimson thinks she does, and he will have none of them. Their relationship does not develop any tact because Jimson will not play.

Sara's downfall is also tied to class. Without the action of Blanche Wilcher, it is unlikely that Sara would have been dismissed and prosecuted for theft. Wilcher was content with her and would have accepted a certain amount of her sort of larceny had there not been interference. Blanche, of course, took advantage of his fear that Sara would expose him, as her predecessor Mrs. Frewen threatened to do. (We learn in *To Be a Pilgrim* that perhaps Blanche's failing is an excess of earnestness.) Blanche does not understand that Sara would never do what Mrs. Frewen did. She is loyal. She goes to prison not because Wilcher really wants to send her there but because he is too locked into his position, too cowardly to speak up after the first shock of learning that she had stolen and that he might be exposed. Too late he sees his mistake. Blanche acts on middle-class values. Though the following passage refers to her sister Clarissa, who is quite different from Blanche in many ways and friendly to Sara, it applies to Blanche as well:

> For one minute you would think it was all religion with them, and money nothing; in the next, money was all and religion nothing. But, of course, money for them often comes out as duty, and so religion, while for the poor, money is always money only, because there is not enough of it to be duty. (*HS*, 180)

This is one of Sara's most penetrating remarks and shows that indeed she can think, in her own way. It is not surprising that the remark is about class, which by virtue of her position as a cook she understands very well.

By her account Wilcher is shocked that she has accumulated 237 pounds and 23 gold sovereigns in his service. She does not record his response to her appropriation of his trinkets and objects. (In *To Be a Pilgrim*, he seems to imply that he was not shocked, and Sara does not see him after Blanche's accusation, so she hears of his response second-hand. On the other hand, his hindsight is probably defensive, since by this time he glorifies Sara.) What we certainly do know is that, mixing morality and money in a convenient way that protects him, he pays for Sara's defense, but makes no effort to clear her. Clarissa calls him an "old fool" who should have married Sara, and we can believe that his shock is more heartbreak at her loss than at the thievery. Clarissa's views are unusually liberated from those of the family, partly as a result of her having lost Loftus Wilcher to Blanche. Still, as Sara remarks, "Mr. W. had always a great opinion of the law, and he did not like to interfere with it just because it didn't suit him" (*HS*, 220). Money, religion, law, duty: It is the way Blanche Wilcher connects them and Wilcher's inability to grasp the moment because of fear and guilt that become the real that Sara must face. Sara is, as usual, charitable to Wilcher; she does not remark that his respect for the law does not make him always obey it. (To say that would be disloyal.) Sara actually protects him from arrest at one time, and the case is dropped through the machinations of influence. (Sara, as servant, is not, of course, told what actually happened.)

From the time of Wilcher's evasion of arrest, he connects Sara with his secular security and religious salvation. Indeed, he confesses his sins with young girls to her before he will enter her bed. He even speaks of making public confession. But he never does that. Instead, we have the pathetic picture of him being carried downstairs by Sara like a baby, "master or no master." A little later he speaks to her of the need to return to the communism of the early Christians, for religion has become corrupt: It seems to be its connection with money that has corrupted it. Though Wilcher is pathetic here, we recognize that his response to his experience, though histrionic, is an advance for him. When we look back on this scene from the perspective of *To Be a Pilgrim*, we develop a new understanding of it that goes beyond Sara's, even though Sara has a very workable attitude toward Wilcher and surely does better in *practice* with him than we could.

Sara plays the role of servant to the end. She has a warning from Clarissa that Blanche is going to have her turned out. She advises Sara to marry Wilcher, but Sara doesn't act, and Wilcher doesn't ask her. Sara's silence here is characteristic. It is part of her tact in her relationship with the class above her, but that is not all. I have already mentioned that Cary gives to Sara a distrust of words. They are unstable; their meanings shift, expand, and contract. Also, they are often responsible for distinctions that, in context, mislead, as for example when Blanche, threatening Sara, says that Sara had already served a prison sentence. This is not strictly true, but Sara knows that it could have been true and remains silent. She allows Wilcher to talk on about her religious views while recognizing that he does not really know her soul. This is a particularly interesting passage because Sara believes Wilcher's description of her nature strange. It is not the Sara she recognizes. Later on, we come to see that Wilcher's language does, with a certain art, get some part of Sara—in his terms. We grasp this even as we feel somewhat embarrassed by that style and the falsity with which it sometimes blankets things.

Sara appears totally passive in the face of Blanche's final successful attack on her. Sara works silently for the most part like nature, or behind a screen of language. She believes that explanation compounds confusion and won't reach truth. Also, what's done is done. She looks to the future. Finally, for her there is something potentially self-serving about the use of language, as there is about confession; and Sara would rather serve others than serve herself. Her own "confession" does not have a selfish motive. Its proceeds will go to maintaining a home and schooling for others.

There is a passage toward the end of the novel where Sara summarizes her happiness at Rann's Park after 15 Craven Gardens has been destroyed by fire:

> Now it was made out at the trial that I was only playing with Mr. W. and that my real mind was with Gulley at his shed. But this was not so. For fond as I was of Gulley, in his old peaceful age and busy gaiety, and pretty Lizzie who hung upon me like a daughter, and Tommy writing to me every week, by his father, for sweets and sixpences; yet I know Mr. W. was worth three Gulleys, a better and a deeper man, and a more tried. I knew myself honoured by him and I meant to make him a good wife. (*HS*, 215)

This is true, as far as it goes, and by Sara's very own law of language. By the conventional class standard Wilcher, in his torment and to some extent because of it, surpasses Jimson. Sara tactfully honors that standard in her relation to Wilcher. But by the classless standard that goes deeper than the words of the tribe, her heart is with Jimson. The law, which always operates by the first standard, will not understand the language of the second, and Sara is silent in its face. It is as if language were structured by class and her feeling for Jimson were outside it.

Yet we cannot leave her in her passivity, for she is naturally aggressive for others. If her aggression fails to push Jimson forward, it is principally because it is expressed in the language of class values and because Jimson will not play. If it works in a curious way with Matt Monday, it is because he is brought up to those values and can respond to encouragement couched in its terms, albeit passively.

What is Cary's authority here? It is an authority that understands class differences, values sympathy, and appreciates the power of survival and fortitude of the novel's speaker. It also recognizes the conflict that her strength creates when she meets a piece of the real called Gulley Jimson. Cary offers her to us as someone not sophisticated enough to solve all the problems of that conflict or to express it directly. For Sara, Gulley is rightly attractive. He is a liberator of her imagination, a bringer of joy, but he frustrates her creative impulse to manage and to make. Cary opts neither for sophistication nor against it. This would be, for him, an immoral act against imaginative power in those uneducated or in some way less fortunate, as we say. He tells us all along not to underestimate the "virtue" of Sara's plainness and *home*liness of style. Also, he tells us not to be captured by any one language.

At this point we remember with anticipation that *Herself Surprised* is the first part of an extended work. Cary has been laying the ground for two more novels. It is not so much events that overlap as the characters, but when events do overlap they are revealing. Such is the case with the one time that Gulley Jimson and Tom Wilcher meet. We shall remember Sara's account when we read *The Horse's Mouth* in part for what Jimson does *not* tell us—that his meeting with the ferocious Wilcher follows immediately his having punched Sara on the nose. Jimson has come to 15 Craven Gardens to get some of his drawings away from her, and she recognizes that he is in a "wicked mood" (*HS*, 168). Sara's account here is again plain, direct, and dependable. He asks her whether she is coming back to him, and she replies, although she knew it was her death, that she had always been ready to. But then they argue, and she makes the mistake of saying that he wants her only because he is "stuck." This word always infuriates him.

Just after he has hit her, Wilcher returns home, and Sara flies from the hall. What took place subsequently Sara gets from Wilcher. He reports that the two discussed art, that he had asked Jimson to stay, and had even walked down the street with him. Sara suspects that more was said—about her. In fact, Wilcher has kept something back, and Jimson reveals it. Their talk was not friendly. Wilcher called him a blackguard and agreed after haggling to pay Jimson a stipend if he would stay away from Sara. Sara, of course, never learns of this, and from this time on is also sending Jimson money, unknown to Wilcher. She confesses that she does not know whether she did this to salve her conscience and keep herself free of Jimson or to keep him in comfort. The reason for this is, of course, the conflict between her homemaking and her attraction to him.

To Be a Pilgrim

A stanza of John Bunyan's well-known hymn is quoted in chapter 27 of *To Be a Pilgrim*:

> Who would true valor see,
> Let him come hither.
> All here will constant be
>   Come wind, come weather.
> There's no discouragement
> Shall make him once repent

His first avowed intent
To be a pilgrim.

(*TBP*, 66)

The Benjamites, a sect which Tom Wilcher's sister Lucy has joined, sing it. It is part of an experience Wilcher remembers as a "dangerous contagion." He both fears and is attracted to the Benjamites' power. But that is not the first mention of the hymn. Wilcher tells us without explanation that the phrase, "to be a pilgrim," was a private one between him and Lucy when they were children (*TBP*, 16). He does not explain the significance it had for them. In fact, he says that he did not understand the phrase for many years. That is the reason he does not tell us what it meant to him as a child. He did not and still does not really know. Only in the writing of his journal does he come to a true realization of its meaning. One of the things he never quite faces is his own failure to join the clergy—a pilgrimage he kept refusing, though a strong part of him desired it.

Lucy's decision to be a pilgrim involves her eloping with the evangelist Brown and joining the Benjamites. In his journal Wilcher imagines hearing Lucy's voice speaking the words of Bunyan's hymn to him, the voice of Lucy as a young woman. For him it is a message that this time he must construe correctly. He begins the process of learning not only to *understand* the definition of pilgrimage as the capacity ever to move onward, but also to *feel* its meaning. The capacity to be a pilgrim he believes is not really his. At the beginning of his journal he thinks he can develop it by going to Sara when she is released from prison; this will be his salvation. It involves divesting himself of commitments to money, property, and the past:

> "Yes," I thought, "that was the clue to Lucy, to my father, to Sara Jimson, it is the clue to all that English genius which bore them and cherished them, clever and simple. Did not my father say of Tolbrook which he had loved so much, 'Not a bad billet,' or 'not a bad camp'"; and Sara? Was not her view of life as 'places' as 'situations' the very thought of the wanderer and the very strength of her soul. She put down no roots into the ground; she belonged with the spirit; her goods and possessions were all in her own heart and mind, her skill and courage. (*TBP*, 16)

Later, Wilcher returns to his father's remark, recalling that late in life, tormented by his politician son Edward's debts, the father sold property to pay them—property that had always been a worry to him. In his failing health he said of Tolbrook, "Not a bad billet, but I've been here too long" (*TBP*, 150). Just before his death, unable to speak because of a stroke, he writes the words, "Too long in same camp" (*TBP*, 158). Wilcher tells us that he did not understand them at the time, thinking his father's mind was wandering back to military days. The dying man urges his son to go into the church: "God's work—quite right, go into church. Set heart on God's things. Other things go from you" (*TBP*, 158). This is a decision that Wilcher was never able to make and one reason he does not believe he is a pilgrim.

When Wilcher hears his father's last words, he misunderstands them. He thinks the old man is speaking about the loss of his land and of anxiety about Tolbrook. He projects his own anxiety on the old man's words, and he tries to comfort him: "But you have pulled the property together. Tolbrook is saved for the family." These are just the wrong sentiments. The old man makes a desperate effort to speak, only to be sedated by a nurse. Upon the father's death, it is learned that the codicil he had made leaving his estate to several children had been revoked. Edward inherits Tolbrook after all. Wilcher never analyzes his father's motive, but to us it appears that the old man, sensing Wilcher's anxiety about Tolbrook and his inability to follow out his plan to go into the church, has decided to relieve him of the burden of ownership so that he might after all be a pilgrim. For it was virtually certain on his past record of spending that Edward would sell or lose Tolbrook. And for a while it looks as if this would happen. In his last act the father had tried to tell his son the meaning of pilgrimage.

But Tolbrook is not lost. Tom Wilcher unknowingly foils his dead father and takes it over in return for paying Edward's debts. Tolbrook becomes his to care for and to worry about; he does not enter the church. His religious zeal is displaced to the effort to preserve ownership of the family home. He becomes a lawyer specializing in the management of money and property. So we find him still trying to learn how to be a pilgrim near the end of his life. There are many false starts in this matter, and the novel takes us through them. Indeed, toward its conclusion, when Wilcher has achieved or almost achieved the freedom of pilgrimage in his soul, he continues to speak as if he has not even come close. He claims instead that it is England itself that is the pilgrim, carrying him along on its journey. This insistence in the end on his own passivity is not quite accurate, and I shall take it up later.

The structure of *To Be a Pilgrim* is more complicated than that of *Herself Surprised* and, in certain but not all ways, *The Horse's Mouth*. It takes the form of a journal kept by Tom Wilcher at Tolbrook while he is under the care of his niece Ann (except for a period of her absence) from some time in 1936 to autumn of 1938. Wilcher begins his journal one month after Sara goes to jail. The first 131 of Cary's characteristically short chapters mix "present" events (actually the events at Tolbrook that Wilcher recounts from day to day) with remembrances of past events and his family. In chapter 132 Ann leaves him in the care of a nurse at Tolbrook, and after chapter 133 there is a hiatus in the keeping of the journal, for at this point Wilcher begins to describe his escape to London to find Sara. This account (chapters 134–44) is written some time later after he has been returned to Tolbrook. Ann and her husband Robert have retrieved him from Sara, who alerted them. After six weeks in a nursing home, he is back at home. It is September 1938, and he is writing again. He brings his journal up to date in chapter 145, and the remaining chapters, with certain remembrances, deal with a "present" in which Ann and Robert are back at Tolbrook and he is in their charge.

The episode in London is thus a departure from the dominating structure, since it is not constituted as a "present." What we have there is a sustained straight narrative of recent events. There are earlier sustained narratives that extend over several chapters, but they are remembrances of much earlier events—part of Wilcher's saga of his family. The effect of the narrative in London is to speed up the movement of the novel as it reaches its conclusion.

However, the temporal structure of the novel is much more complicated than these remarks have indicated. In the journal's duration—a continuing present—there are the following different temporal situations:

1. Immediate thoughts offered in the present tense, reflecting Wilcher's opinions at the moment of writing. This, of course, includes the whole work, but by it I mean particularly things like the following: "I do not like this girl. I prefer my other nieces and several of my honorary nieces" (*TBP*, 9).
2. Quite recent events (shortly before writing) treated in the present tense: "I open my eyes, but it is still dark. There is silence throughout the house, but it is like a threat" (*TBP*, 35).
3. Quite recent events (hours before writing) treated in the past

tense: "Robert came to-day, as always unannounced, and as usual at an awkward moment" (*TBP*, 16).

4. Quite recent events (hours before writing) treated in the present tense: "Then he looks at me and Ann looks at me as if I had said something quite beside the point" (*TBP*, 37). These are usually descriptions of events that typify a relationship or a character.

5. Remembrances of distant past events made immediate by the present tense: "We are in the nursery and Lucy is holding my hand" (*TBP*, 27). These passages, often mixed with descriptions of a general nature in the past tense, are usually triggered by Wilcher's entering a room at Tolbrook or, as below, imagining a voice from the past:

> "What an extraordinary boy you are, Tommy." Her voice flies at me out of the dark like a snake out of ambush. Devil's words. For Lucy did not believe them; she meant them to stab me, to destroy my faith in myself, and to increase her own importance.
> "Let me alone, Lucy," I say.
> "Well, I'm only being nice."
> We are in the nursery, and Lucy is holding my hand. But already I feel from the hand a kind of electricity which secretly alarms me. I want to be at peace, and to think out something which puzzles me. (*TBP*, 27)

It is to be noticed that the line "Let me alone," is temporally ambiguous. It can be a response to Lucy in the "present" of number 4 above. Or it can be a response remembered from a distant past (5). In fact, it is deliberately ambiguous, a transition from an immediate experience of Lucy's haunting voice to a remembrance treated as a "present." Of course, Wilcher can hardly be writing it *as* the voice of Lucy comes to him. Or can he be? Or is he writing at all? Different answers have been offered to the second question, one being that there are really two Wilcher voices, that of the writer and that of the thinker. Ingvar Söderskog finds, for example, an author, a virtual narrator, who is reliable, and a dramatized speaker. His claim is that we listen to two voices, one less reliable, one authoritative. Söderskog's discourse is unfortunately marred by inconsistency of terminology that confuses his argument: narrator-actor, author-narrator, speaker (general), objectified actor, virtual speaker, privileged speaker, dramatizing narrator, anonymous speaker, nominal narrator, and implied author. His argument, as I follow it through this maze, draws a distinction between the actual written diary and soliloquies: "In the course of writing, memories of the past surface to be inter-foliated in monologue form. Still this is not strictly true, . . . the narration often enough evidences no clear line of demarcation between the present and the past" (p. 27). The argument is not clear. Söderskog claims that the narrator has a varying consciousness of his narrative role, "from complete unconsciousness of any reader's attention to passages of an indisputably epic character" (p. 57). Söderskog also argues that certain shifts raise questions about the narrator's identity "when his vision seems more privileged than the fiction can reasonably allow of" (p. 57). I see nothing in Söderskog's long argument or in Cary's text to convince me that Wilcher has not written every line of the novel and that he has not written it principally for himself. But he knows very well it will survive him and be read, probably by Ann and perhaps by others. This is not to say that Söderskog's conjectures are not interesting. Cary's text tempts us to ask such questions but in the end answers them differently and in so doing grants Wilcher a great deal more than we first think we can or even want to. We are surprised, for example, at Wilcher's sophisticated shifting temporal treatment of his materials. But in the end we must grant him his literary talents and conclude that his use of present-tense scenes does not mean that they are not composed after the fact. At the end of the novel, when we are most tempted to think that Wilcher is not writing, Cary goes to some trouble to have Wilcher indicate that his niece has just come into the room and taken his notebook from his bed. But it is clear, and strictly in character, that Wilcher has retrieved it to write his last chapter. In any case, the shifting tenses and continuous play between the events taking place at Tolbrook (and in Wilcher's mind) in the duration of his journal and the remembrances of his family occur in such a way as to represent the state of mind of this old man, whose past is indeed sometimes very near to being his present.

6. Remembrances from the distant past treated in the past tense. Some of these are quite extensive, though often interrupted by 1, 3, or 4.

7. Extended accounting of events that have taken place since the journal was put down for a fairly long period: chapters 134–44, discussed above.

8. The "present" voice from the past, as in the case of Lucy in the quotation in 5 above.

If there are ambiguities in the way Cary has Wilcher present his journal, these are by design. Some are consciously constituted by Wilcher as appropriate to his theme. Some are designed by Cary to convey a real ambiguity in the old man's state of mind. The sorting out of this is meant to be stimulating to the reader. Does Wilcher believe in Lucy's "present" presence? The point, I think, is that it does not matter for Wilcher. In his musing state, the difference between a metaphysical and a factual presence collapses. They merge into a much more important moral presence. It is the moral world which is meant by Wilcher to be the real one.

There is, of course, the question of senility. Wilcher describes himself as an old man "suspected of being insane" (*TBP*, 10). "Senility" is not a word he uses, but he clearly suspects that his niece thinks him senile, and some of his actions seem to demonstrate lapses of memory of quite recent events, though his account of the family past is detailed and articulate, even if the characters sometimes float up from that past into a hallucinatory present. Still, we must be careful about this, because although Wilcher feels on occasion that there is treachery afoot against him and is suspicious of those like Ann who are taking care of him, he sometimes deliberately fosters the impression of senility or madness in order to speak out with the urgency he feels. In one episode Ann intrudes into an illusion that Wilcher has had (or fostered) that a picture of his sister-in-law Amy has spoken to him. He desires to keep this contact alive and writes about it as follows:

> I took care not to answer her in case Amy should disappear from my memory, and I remained silent while Ann decided that I ought to go to bed, and put me to bed. I can tell that she thinks me madder, and she is even anxious about me, perhaps in case I am about to become violent and murder her. But I can't waste time upon this hypocrisy of trying to appear rational. I leave that to younger people.
> I am an old man, and I have not much longer at Tolbrook. (*TBP*, 114)

Ann breaks the spell, but in his waking and dozing through the night, "I felt as if she [Amy] were in the house" (*TBP*, p. 114). A chapter follows in which Wilcher speaks to Amy, but he says that he "thought" he saw her, not that he did. This means that by the time of writing the illusion of presence is gone, and that even *at the time* it was an "as if" situation. But, as I have indicated, the difference between "as if" and fact has dissolved in the "madness" of an old man's mind and his intense emphasis on a *moral* rather than an empirical reality.

There is another side to this. I have spoken already of Wilcher's language tending toward the allegorical. It is a language which does not give to both sides of a metaphor equal authority, the abstract meaning always privileged over the particular image, Wilcher always sensing the meaning that transcends the appearance. In those moments of vision where the ghosts of Lucy and Amy are *present*, Wilcher tries to make them momentary miraculous symbols, that is, figures from another realm incarnate in their appearances. But Wilcher cannot for long sustain these illusions. By the time of writing he equivocates on the matter of their presence, and in the end presence collapses back to allegory, just as Sara's illusory future presence must be exchanged for an absent Sara who becomes in the mind a model of how to live. When this happens, Wilcher's moral world takes over, and the moral meaning, not the appearance, becomes his reality.

When in the morning Wilcher wakes from a state somewhere between dream and reality, he discovers that he has been locked in his room. This fills him with anxiety. Will his captors send him to an asylum? But then he feels peace, thinking that everything is settled and there is nothing he can do. This is a false peace and the wrong sort of abdication, based in part on a misapprehension of Ann; and it does not last long—this freedom from responsibility in abdication of freedom. Wilcher is soon meddling in the question of what to name Ann and Robert's child. The struggle between a vision of peace and a desire to act has always been Wilcher's problem. In some ways his failure to go into the church is tied up with his mistaken notion of what constitutes peace of mind. There is a part of him that rejects a life of inaction even as he feels desire for it. In the case of his feeling peace above, we see that in his deepest being he is not content to pay the price of giving up activity for it.

Wilcher occasionally makes clear that he takes advantage of his "madness" to speak frankly, but he also tells of situations he "finds himself" in that give Robert and Ann good reason to regard him as incapable of taking care of himself. In a long passage Wilcher recalls his dalliance with a housemaid at Tolbrook when he was young, and he now prowls the hall to locate where, on the day after, he met her and "she pressed herself against the wall and looked at the floor." Robert discovers him at this very spot. His behavior in the hall appears odd, though harmless enough, and in any case he has written a plausible explanation of it:

> I found the place, just opposite the newel of the stairs, and leant against it. It was, of course, an illusion that the wall was still warm. . . .
>
> "Hello, uncle, I was wondering where you'd got to." Robert stood before me, but his eyes did not look at me. He did not wish to show any surprise at my position, with outstretched arms against the wall. (*TBP*, 78)

One does not want to make too much of phrases like "I found myself," because they occur in Wilcher's descriptions of events that took place years before when Wilcher was certainly clear-minded and about which he has clear memory. Rather, this usage in the remembrances describes a split he recognizes in himself between reason and feeling, which plays a very large part, he believes, in his actions as a young man. True, it is introduced by him as a problem of an old man, rather than a young one. He has just spoken of how petty worries have "wrecked" his whole life; then he proceeds to make an oblique confession that he is now (as we say today) "programmed" to be anxious. Early in the book he suspects that Robert is sleeping with Ann in secret. As much as he desires to sleep, he cannot:

> I cover my head with the bedclothes, but still my ears strain, my heart beats; I catch myself holding my breath.
>
> It is the misfortune of an old man that though he can put things out of his head he can't put them out of his feelings. (*TBP*, 23–24)

If we recognize compulsiveness here, we recognize that it is something Wilcher tries to overcome. We shall note that in *The Horse's Mouth* Jimson's compulsive irony *results from* his trying to overcome the threat of despair.

When Robert takes down the trees at Tenacre, Wilcher's response is similar: "It was all very well to philosophize, but there was a great swelling pain in my breast which I could not get rid of" (*TBP*, 119). These passages of psychological insight have much to do with establishing our sympathy for the narrator, wrenching us from our notion of Wilcher as it was supplied by Sara. This wrenching is clearly part of Cary's intent. Michael Echeruo is wrong (p. 61) to suggest that we should read the three novels in a different order, with Wilcher's first. In the first place, that would violate the chronology of the "writing" of the novels by their narrators (as well as by Cary). Second, Cary designed the trilogy so that we must revise our ideas in a certain direction as we go along, and that is part of his moral intent. Echeruo wants the clarifications afforded by *To Be a Pilgrim* in advance. But much of the trilogy's ethical intent lies in the process it puts the reader through, and that requires a certain order.

The indeterminateness of Wilcher's grasp on the real is also deliberate, and the temporal play in the novel contributes to it. In addition to providing a subtle representation of Wilcher's mind, it throws emphasis on the real pilgrimage Wilcher is making. Wilcher's pilgrimage is an effort to discover the meaning of the lives and deaths of his relatives and to work out the appropriate relationship with his surviving nephew and niece.

For purposes of discussion, it is convenient to regard the "present" of Wilcher's writing (1936–38) as the novel's outer structure and his saga of the family as its inner structure. The outer structure contains a fantasy future, a present that Wilcher attempts to construe, and a past which he must come to accept as past. This acceptance involves, of course, the acceptance of change. Wilcher's fantasy future is his hoped-for life with Sara, free of the encumbrance of his characteristic anxiety and wishful thinking. Charles Hoffman (p. 80) says that Wilcher's plan to marry Sara is "only a gesture." This is not so; it is a real intention; but it is also a hope that, in order for him to be truly free, he must renounce. The reason is that there is something escapist in the whole idea. In his idea of Sara, Wilcher is seeking the security of an innocence that cannot be recaptured. While not entirely inaccurate by any means, Wilcher's early extravagantly phrased praise of Sara is an example of misguided enthusiasm, not because of Sara, but because of the escapism in it. It is not so much what he says as the importance he puts on what he says, his insistence on glorifying her in a way that makes him pathetic because he wants to lean on her undoubted strength. This false future, it turns out, must be exorcised and Sara seen, in Wilcher's characteristic allegorical way, only as a *model* of behavior.

Wilcher must also accept the past as past. The central image of the novel in this respect is Tolbrook. Wilcher is himself ambivalent in an interesting way about Tolbrook. When Ann suggests that they go to Tolbrook, he is reluctant, but they do go. This act is like many others in his life. His reluctance has to do with his sense that Tolbrook has always been a trial to him, though he loves it profoundly. He speaks of himself as having suffered the curse of possessions (*TBP*, 16); yet much of his anxiety has been about preserving Tolbrook for the family. His anxiety makes him think of Tolbrook as having been preserved by a "succession of miracles" (*TBP*, 160). His mistress, Julie Eeles, remarked that he needed Tolbrook to torment him (*TBP*, 177–78), and he very much feared that Edward would sell it, to the extent that he found a way to acquire it for Edward's debts. It was this act that took him into the practice of law and away from his plan to enter the church (*TBP*, 180). Lucy torments him about having made a fortune out of Edward's debts. Though he resents these remarks, he confesses them to be true, and more: He also appropriated the London house and finally even Edward's mistress. Yet he defends himself, too:

> If I had not done so they would almost certainly have drifted together again. And Julie did always encourage Edward and help him in his career. She gave him a refuge; she gave him absolute loyalty. Yet, if I had not arranged the separation, Edward would have probably been ruined, and if I had not saved Tolbrook it would have been lost to the family.
>
> And my reward for years of heavy soul-destroying worries is to be thought and called a usurer. (*TBP*, 219)

Tolbrook has been his life, but it is also his death, as long as he regards it as something that must be preserved against all change. Toward the end of the novel, Wilcher has a nightmare about it in which it becomes his coffin and his body expresses bitterness against him, "as if every cell were complaining, 'What has he done with us? We are betrayed'" (*TBP*, 299). Wilcher's unconscious pilgrimage is a gradual release of his anxious hold on Tolbrook, and on the past as a past. He reconstructs his family as a living presence of moral meaning, and he is content in his soul, where they dwell ideally.

The "present" or outer structure of Wilcher's writing involves principally his relation to Ann and Robert. That drama is played out in his developing affection for his niece. As the novel proceeds, she moves toward him and he toward her. The former movement begins to worry him, and in the end we find him concerned about her seriousness. At the beginning he says outright that he does not like her and that he prefers his niece by marriage, Blanche. This is one of the reasons why Wilcher's meeting with Blanche, in which he torments her, is important in the outer structure (more of that later). He is irritated by Ann's "patient and bored manner" (*TBP*, 18), or what he takes to be a bored manner. He is irritated at Ann's apparent misunderstanding of the earlier generation. When she asks him whether it was true that his father beat Aunt Lucy, he quickly interprets this as the unfairness of one generation to another, without questioning Ann's reasons for asking. He is irritated to think that she probably considers him a "period piece," and he thinks that she is treating his brother Edward, her father, as a period piece in her book about him. When he gives her a piece of inspirational writing of World War I to read, hoping it will help her spirits, she irritates him by observing that it gave "a new angle on the period" (*TBP*, 254). He is irritated by her skepticism and what he calls her "German boxes," that is, her modern psychologizing. He regards her as an example of the faithless scientific mind characteristic of modern life.

Golden Larsen speaks of the panorama of history in *To Be a Pilgrim*:

> [The] eighteenth century was characterized in *To Be a Pilgrim* by social confidence and clarity of thought, the first part of the nineteenth century by ambivalence of thought and intense social tension; the last part of the nineteenth century by decadence; and the twentieth by primitivism. Barbarity of culture became more manifest as the Protestant will in its anarchic forms—religious, political, and social—shattered the container of the wonderfully civilized old order and drove toward a reunion with nature. . . . The tragic consequence of that social upheaval, according to Cary, was the destruction of those richly human values represented by Sara and the waste of genius (Edward, Julie, John). (p. 157)

Wilcher sees it this way. (One suspects that he overrates the genius of his relatives.) Whether Cary sees it this way is a question. In a note for *To Be a Pilgrim*, he wrote: "W speaks of the political disintegration, as he sees it, of the time, which affects his spirits and Edward's because he has lost touch with the reality of growth" (*OC*, Box 289). To my mind, Cary himself is less interested in the evaluation of vast social and cultural movements than is Wilcher. Cary thinks each age unique in its problems and solutions, not judicable in terms of other ages. Each age offers its tragedies and successes, and in every unique age it is the unique individual who counts. Thus it is *Wilcher's* attitude that is supposed to interest us at this point.

Some of Wilcher's irritation at Ann, including his suspicion of her, leads actually to engagement.

> "You didn't take your medicine." She looks embarrassed. And I am angry at being watched.
> "No, I forgot."
> "You don't really think I am trying to poison you, uncle?"
> In my astonishment I jumped to an unlucky conclusion. I said that she had no business to read my note-books. (*TBP*, 89)

Gradually their sense of each other changes. He knows her "unexpected power" to divine his feelings (*TBP*, 82), and he comes to moments where this insight does not result in paranoia. His reason struggles with his feelings, and he concludes that she is "at bottom, a good creature, spoiled only by a bad education" (*TBP*, 92). All of these steps, Cary makes us understand (by arranging Wilcher's backslidings), are tentative gropings in the unfamiliar territory of the young and of the present.

Meanwhile Ann begins to take an interest in Tolbrook, restoring the wallpaper. On occasion they seem to change places. When Wilcher attempts to convince himself of his relief that Robert has pulled down the trees at Tenacre, he does so in his characteristically enthusiastic style:

> And I thought, "In fact, I have been ungrateful to these young people, especially to Robert. For he has at least set me free. I need worry no more about those old tottering relics in the fields. Let him respect only the house, for his own son's sake, and I shall be a fortunate man."
> And I hastened down, after supper, to congratulate him. "You're quite right," I said, "about my father's changes. Revolutionary. I have been looking at the plans. And my grandfather actually pulled down the ruins of the old chapel to build a byre."
> "What a pity," Ann said.
> "But—what an act of courage." (*TBP*, 136)

At this point, Wilcher has rationalized loss of the trees at Tenacre, but he is still anxious about the house. Ann's response is clear enough. Robert's later words indicate that he lives in a language quite different from Wilcher's. Ann, on the other hand, has been studying her father's life and has developed a feeling for Tolbrook, as it used to be. In fact, Ann has become concerned about the apparent lack of stability in modern life. Wilcher discovers that he must defend the idea of progress against her anxiety about the stability of her marriage. He recognizes that something has changed in her, and that she and Robert are growing apart (*TBP*, 193). Though he has grown closer to her, and though he is in part responsible for the change, it bothers him, because he sees their son as his eventual heir and, in any case, wishes to protect the sanctity of marriage. Wilcher is put in the familiar position of arguing against his own feelings.

Wilcher's relations with other people have always been characterized by a combination of love, anxiety, and irritation at them. As he comes to value Ann more, so does she give him more reason for agitation, even as he declares that she has brought him peace. Nevertheless, he is still puzzled by her:

> Probably, of course, her patience is merely contempt for my opinions. Be it so, I enjoy now, because of that patience, whether from the heart or the mind; because of that efficiency, whether devoted or merely professional; because of that tolerance, whether due to charity or indifference, a happiness that I have never known before. So that often I feel guilty and ask myself, "Can this go on? How have I deserved such peace, at Tolbrook of all places? And with this painted chit from the laboratories." (*TBP*, 238–39)

Yet in another mood later on he will state that she is one of the most difficult girls he has ever known (*TBP*, 273). He admits, however, to a "prejudice" against her and confesses then to fondness (*TBP*, 332).

At the very end, as Michael Echeruo has pointed out (p. 51), he sees, perhaps unconsciously, in her his own excessive youthful seriousness, his own curious sense of duty; and he warns her against it. The relationship between them is one of the major threads in the book's pattern. It is one that obsesses Wilcher, surprises him in its changes, and plays a major role in his redemption. It is his link with the present. Just the fact of his enduring interest in Ann speaks for a place among Blake's "redeemed." This is a view of Wilcher that not all critics have held. Cornelia Cook (p. 109 and elsewhere) is much harder on him, seeing him as "lacking faith" and behaving hypocritically. This is true in its way, but it seems to ignore the text as a difficult process toward self-knowledge.

THE WILCHER FAMILY

Father Wilcher = Mother Wilcher
(d. 1902)   (1839–1920)

Edward = Mrs. Tirrit   Bill = Amy   Lucy = Robert Brown   Tom   Dorothy
(1857–1920) (d. 1926) (1860–1919) (1871–192?) (1863–1922)   (1867–)   (d. young)

= Lottie

William   John = Gladys   Loftus = Blanche Hipper   A daughter
(1890–1918)   (1900–1922)   (1904–)   (d. young)

Ann Wilcher ———————————— = ———————————— Robert Brown
(1912–)   (1910–)

Edward John Wilcher Brown
(1937–)

There is a true as well as a false future that is Wilcher's proper concern. That is his death, which is imminent at the conclusion of the novel, where he speaks words of life to Ann. Wilcher prepares for death by confronting the lives and deaths of his family in the remembrances that constitute the inner structure of the book. This contains two interrelated strands.

The first involves meditations on the lives and deaths of Wilcher's relatives, of which there are quite a few. Each death provides a key scene. That of Wilcher's father I have already mentioned. In addition, there are those of Bill, his mother, Edward, Lucy, and Amy—all dwelt on in some detail—plus those of his nephews, William and John. Wilcher always seeks meaning, and each of the deaths offers something because he makes each into something. Each also is connected in the narrative to the meaning of the life of that person. Wilcher's brother Bill, the army officer, dies slowly of cancer, having bought a home carelessly, knowing that his time was short. At the time this very much troubled Wilcher. It seemed imprudent, but the lesson he constructs from this is Bill's ability to live in the present without anxiety. In Wilcher's last conversation with him (or at least the last he records), Bill makes clear that he does not expect even his wife Amy to stay in the house after his death. After all, they rarely agreed on anything. He had fixed up the garden because it seemed a good thing to do, not to pass it on.

It is only very late in the book that Wilcher comes to express the value of Bill and Amy, his dowdy wife. When he comes to Amy's deathbed, he learns she has already made arrangements for the undertaker and ordered veal for his lunch. She has asked for nothing from him since Bill's death, refused a loan, and lived quietly and alone. He, for his part, has never asked her to Tolbrook. Now he believes Amy was a true pilgrim:

> I know why Amy sent away that curate and why she would not let me talk to her about the consolations of religion. She did not want them; perhaps she did not altogether like them. (*TBP*, 339)

In life the family laughed at Amy and Bill, but in death they are a wonder to Wilcher. If he allegorizes and glorifies them, it can also be said that his report of Amy's dying has the ring of authenticity in the way that Sara's account of Jimson's beating is direct. It is in such moments also that Wilcher seems to forget about allegorizing and speaks directly.

Of the other deaths, much the most important is the rebellious Lucy's. She is a powerful, headstrong personality even to the moment of her death, refusing a doctor, arguing with Wilcher, defying death up to the last moment, and then making Wilcher pledge to see that her son Robert is properly educated. This is a feat that Wilcher does not manage to bring off.

The second strand is the panorama of England in Wilcher's lifetime that his remembrances construct. The pilgrimage of England is a theme that gains momentum as the book proceeds, for Wilcher is fond of it. The conclusion of chapter 47 is the first extended example, where the idea is of England as a great ship on an endless voyage, carrying its crew of forty million souls, meeting a new morning daily. This figure for England is one of the devices Wilcher employs to convince himself of the inevitability and acceptability of change—and of his need, against his feelings, to embrace it. What Golden Larsen misses when he says (p. 126) that Wilcher's peroration on England is "not well prepared for" is that it is meant to embody the tension in Wilcher, that it is one of his typical exuberances, a shout of self-encouragement present in much of his spiritual rhetoric. Whenever the metaphor appears, it is accompanied by strained enthusiasm designed to work on Wilcher himself:

> When I look back again at the window the three clouds have jumped up towards the left-hand bow of the frame and the house seems to rock beneath me like a ship. I, eating breakfast in bed, and always the worst of sailors, feel as if I were at sea, as if England itself were afloat beneath me on its four waves, and making the voyage of its history through a perpetual sea spring.
>
> Faithful to ancient ways, the English crew
> Spread old patched sails, to seek for something new.
>
> The monk in his sleepy routine, who seduced my weakness just now, where is he? A vigorous generation snatched his peace away; the generation of my ancestors, who made a farm-shed of his chapel and bore their half-pagan children in his holy cell. Who once more pulled up England's anchor and set her afloat on the unmapped oceans of the West. (*TBP,* 108–9)

The couplet is by his brother Edward; the sentiment Wilcher repeats later on: England is a wanderer; his father and his brother

Bill, both soldiers, and Lucy, the Benjamite, were wanderers of the spirit. Finally, on the last page of his journal, Wilcher offers the figure of the wanderer and pilgrim once again. He regards himself as someone carried along on England's pilgrimage, a true pilgrim only by race. This turns out no longer to be quite true. It is only one more of Wilcher's misinterpretations. Wilcher has become a pilgrim without realizing it.

The panorama Wilcher constructs is of several cultural phases. His mother and father are for him the true Victorians, but the father dies rejecting the idea of ownership, warning Wilcher against anxieties he sees developing in his son. The mother lives on into the next generation, losing spiritual touch with her eldest son Edward. The next generation seems to Wilcher representative of various phases of the "transition," as it has been called, from Victorianism to modernism. Wilcher himself is its battleground. Bill, a soldier, and his wife Amy simply *live* without cultural anxiety. The others regard them as not very bright, and in truth from what we can tell they are not; but Wilcher perceives an important strength and serenity in their existence. They seem to know, without articulating it, their purpose. Wilcher thinks of them as thoughtless, but with faith deeper than thought or speech. In a conversation with Bill, he recognizes a power he had not seen. As is his wont, Bill has just misunderstood what someone has said, and Wilcher tries to correct him.

> "But what he means, Bill, is that in the face of death a man gets a new scale of values."
> "I don't see that. Besides, it isn't true. When you're up against it you get the same kind of values, only more so." (*TBP*, 252)

When the conversation took place, Bill knew he was dying. Bill and Amy are the last of the Empire, and their lives are devoted, each in his own way, to service.

On the other hand, Edward, the politician older brother, represents for Wilcher corruption by *fin de siècle* decadence. His mistress, Julie Eeles, plays a parallel part. She is the actress who makes a hit of playing Hedda Gabler and fails to develop her art further. Her Beardsley rooms embody the decadence. Edward is, according to Wilcher, brilliant, but he is erratic and makes little of his political career. He also loses Tolbrook and Julie to Wilcher, who in turn leaves her when, her husband dead, she proposes marriage to him. Wilcher contrasts all of this brilliant instability to the plodding steadiness of Bill and Amy. The former are attractive, beautiful people, but there is something corrupted in them. She is unhappily married—a Catholic. He is from an old Protestant family. Both end pathetically, he dying almost from lack of will, she attempting suicide and, failing in that, gradually disappearing into her own darkness.

Lucy and her evangelist husband Brown stand in Wilcher's panorama for the later phases of the English evangelical movement. The tendency of Protestantism to split off from itself Wilcher finds well expressed in the eccentric Benjamite sect and the personality of Lucy. One of the most critical scenes in the book is the one in which Lucy by her headstrong behavior compels her upright Victorian father to punish her with beatings twice in the same day. She is the victor over this perplexed father, but it is a dangerous victory. It sets her at sea alone. It is a defiance of a fixed code of behavior. Wilcher values that fixed code in retrospect because he believes that as children they all knew where they were. Golden Larsen (p. 131) points out the importance of this scene as indicating the break-up of Victorianism: "through it Cary gave his version of the process by which a cohesive myth—a fabric of religious and moral values 'universally felt' was destroyed." Larsen later points out:

> [L]ike Lucy [Wilcher] senses his isolation from his parents [that earlier culture] . . . and moves to re-establish the relationship. . . . he is at once better educated . . . and endowed with less natural genius. The result is that his commitment to getting back to the *source*, the essential substance, is less complete, seeking its resolution within the established framework of social convention and social machinery. (p. 150)

It is also true that Lucy's substitute discipline and order with the Benjamites doesn't work very well for her, or at least only sporadically.

Wilcher's fear of the Benjamites is opposed by his fascination, as if he recognizes the break-up of Victorianism and sees the attractiveness of commitment. Yet he does not succumb to the lure of the Benjamite emphasis on pure feeling. In their bitter arguments, Wilcher calls Lucy a hypocrite, and she calls him a pettifogger:

> [B]oth words came so close to the truth of our natures that they took its light and cast a shadow on our souls. To Lucy, fighting pride with

pride, it was easy to think that humility was pretence; and for me, clinging to order and rule in the turmoil of the world, it was easy to think that the word was greater than the spirit; that I valued not my father's memory but a piece of property. (*TBP*, 161)

The confusion embodies some of the fundamental problems of the history of English Protestantism, divided against itself. Yet Lucy arouses in her brother something deeper than their arguments generate:

[E]very word she said, however unexpected, found in me a response, some secret nerve within me was excited. To what? I was going to write, to the love of God, of religion, to some grandeur of thought. But now, as I pace restlessly through the lower rooms, I feel it as something deeper, more passionate. The life of the spirit. (*TBP*, 89)

This is to claim that the life of the spirit is deeper than anything that can be named. It is perhaps this particular insight that makes Wilcher ultimately a pilgrim on an allegorical journey.

Wilcher's nephew William is a sacrifice to the war, dying in a battle fought after the armistice had actually occurred. Wilcher's nephew John is a casualty of the peace. Badly wounded, he comes to regard the world as so unsettled that he is perpetually unsettled himself. His flapper wife, Gladys, is the survivor of the peace, a brassy tart who faithfully cared for John in his last days but then, after sleeping around, marries his business partner. Wilcher dislikes her but comes to a grudging respect for her capacity to survive. One of the things she survives is the weakness of her husband. Another is Wilcher's meddling.

Robert and Ann, of course, are for Wilcher the perplexing modern world. The principal symbols of this world are what Wilcher interprets as Ann's life-killing skepticism and Robert's appropriation of the great Adam room of Tolbrook for the huge reaping machine. Though Wilcher hates his destruction of the beauty of the old order, he tries mightily to rationalize it. In the end, once his dream of Sara is gone, once he relaxes by necessity his anxious hold, he succeeds, even as he complains that he has surrendered:

I sit in the armchair, a tattered bergère in white and gilt, last of the drawing-room furniture; and the very ruin of this beautiful room is become a part of my happiness. I say no longer, "Change must come, and this change, so bitter to me, is a necessary ransom for what I keep." I have surrendered because I cannot fight and now it seems to me that not change but life has lifted me and carried me forward on the stream. It is but a new life which flows through the old house; and like all life, part of that sustaining power which is the oldest thing in the world. (*TBP*, 328)

Finally, in this panorama there is Wilcher himself, who, spanning the whole period, is the most tried and tested of all. He is, to be sure, a bit of an outsider, or so feels in his family. He is apparently the least physically attractive, perhaps the least loved; he plays an auxiliary part in the war as a stretcher-bearer; by profession, he is a lawyer, but he had always meant to enter the church. He is a bachelor. Sara has already told us of the oddness of his relations with women, and his liaison with Julie Eeles was clearly unsatisfactory. He is, by his own telling admission, "Mr. Facing-both-ways" (*TBP*, 74).

In the outer structure of the novel, his immediate concern is his own ambivalence toward Tolbrook. He early declares that he never had any peace or comfort there. He has been "too fond" of it (*TBP*, 34). He speaks of the danger of loving anything, especially things. But Julie Eeles is right that he needs Tolbrook or needs to save it, and Edward is right that when he took Tolbrook for Edward's debts, he got what he wanted. He is ambivalent about what Robert is doing with it, as he was ambivalent about what Robert's father, the evangelist, did with Protestant religion. There is a split all the way through him between his thoughts and his feeling, and yet he also *feels* that he must do justice, as an old man, to what he *feels* opposed to. So his feelings war with each other. He shifts ground to save himself from his own feelings. Some of these efforts are quaint enough, as in chapter 40, where he devises a sort of balance sheet sorting out his attitudes, adding up moral accounts only to reach the conclusion that though he is not a good man, neither is he a monster.

In his own lifetime he has frequently expressed anxiety about civilization and order, but he supported the radical liberals even when he was terrified that revolution was around the corner. He clothed his anxiety in wishful thinking, which often made him wrong about the future, when his brother Edward would be right. This wishfulness is connected with a learned religious optimism. Yet his anxiety is such that he adopts quite rigid theological views. He is, nevertheless, susceptible to the religious arguments of others, the more dogmatic and self-assured the better. This pattern is continuous in his account from the time of his nearly succumbing to the Benjamite spirit through his argument with a friend on revelation to the writing of his own book on "the need for a new statement of the Christian belief, with special regard to the positive power of evil; and the real existence of the devil" (*TBP*, 262). The theme of the devil, first apprehended in Lucy's behavior, runs through the whole book. Clearly, Wilcher is the transitional figure in his own panorama.

Out of anxiety Wilcher often misunderstands. On two occasions he misreads Edward's couplets (*TBP*, 71–72), principally out of a deep fear of cynicism. Even the birth of a child to Robert and Ann causes him a combination of joy and suffering, and he is aware of this to the extent of observing that it is "as if there were something incurable in the world's suffering which was also its secret root of joy" (*TBP*, 217).

In the past Wilcher has avoided certain responsibilities, pleading an excess of burdens and anxiety over money. His treatment of Amy after Bill's death is a case in point, but so is the emphasis on money throughout his remembrances. He connects money with identity: "What is a man without cash?" (*TBP*, 19). He tries to emphasize the importance of money to Robert (*TBP*, 181–82), and Lucy teases him maliciously about his having made money out of Edward's failings (*TBP*, 219). This, as we have seen, he resents, and yet he defends himself:

> The love of possessions. It is spoken for a reproach, and I feel it like shame. But what are these possessions which have so burdened my soul? Creatures that have loved. The most helpless of dependents. For their very soul, their meaning, is in my care. (*TBP*, 219–20)

One is reminded of Sara's remark that with people of a certain class, money and religion become mixed up together. Such mixtures are insistences on certain meanings. Wilcher himself is someone not content unless he can find meaning in appearances; he does not think that he is a *maker* of meanings.

Finally, Wilcher is inept with women, shy and lacking confidence in himself as a man. He is passive in certain ways and then aggressive, as in his accosting young women. As we saw, Sara remarks of his skittishness, and he himself unconsciously reveals that he wanted Julie Eeles as a possession, and then pays her off to get rid of his responsibility toward her. His timidity with women is paralleled in other aspects of his behavior—in his attitude toward Edward, for example. He thinks that Edward's weakness was also his strength, but he doesn't want it to be that way because it frustrates his allegorizing Edward, which in turn frustrates his efforts at enthusiasm, which is at the base of his religion.

That brings us back to the way Wilcher tells his story. His ambivalence is present in his manner of narration. Past and present shift in and out of his consciousness throughout, the present treated as *just then*, the past as *now*. There is an extension of his ambivalence into the way he treats the characters of his remembrance. He is an allegorist. He constantly looks for meanings to reveal behind people and events. His tendency is toward enthusiastic inflation of the characters of his story. Our sense, however, is that his people are (or were) not that inflatable, and his ambivalence is his honesty insisting on a hearing. He heroizes Edward, but we learn from him that Edward was a failure (he is most certainly a failed poet or at least a dilettantish one). He giganticizes Lucy, making her virtually possessed of the devil, but we know, too, from what he tells us, that she is a much troubled, confused, and wounded person. The dullness of Bill and Amy, which actually annoyed him, he turns into a glorious intrepidity.

Cary makes Wilcher's enthusiasm infuriating to us even as he convinces us that it is a vehicle of his self-redemption. But Cary never lets us forget that to the end he is an old meddler. Indeed, the meddling is a result of his enthused spirit, the result of the same quality that renews his life. This meddling is characteristic of the inner structure of remembrance as well as the outer "present." He manipulates the relationship of Edward and Julie, manages (as best he can) Edward's finances, intrigues against Gladys, and tries to manage Amy, who evades him. Julie Eeles is moved to attack him for his meddling (*TBP*, 285). In the outer "present" he is deceptive about this matter. He vows not to meddle, but enters Ann's room deliberately to find out whether she is sleeping with Robert. He tries to affect the religious education of their children. Ann herself points out to him his manipulations:

> "You think me mad."
> "Never, uncle, you are much too clever at getting your own way."
> I was astonished. "So you think me cunning. Lunatics are famous for their cunning."

"Well, look. Robert meant to go back to Brazil, but here he is tied to Tolbrook, and I meant to be a distinguished pathologist, and here I am, a silly little wife with a big tummy, also tied to Tolbrook."

"And I did all this—why, it's perfectly ridiculous."

"Perhaps you didn't know you were doing it. You only suggested that I should see Robert again if we came to Tolbrook. And you knew I had fallen for his nice eyes. And then you happened to catch us together. And then you gave Robert all these new toys to play with—a little at a time. Like giving cut wool to a kitten till it's quite tied up. And now you have got the baby you wanted and you have decided that it's going to be an Edward or a Lucy."

"What nonsense, what nonsense. Though these are good English names, and I suppose if you have a son he will be in the eldest line, and they are all Edwards."

For it was true that I had sometimes hoped for another Lucy or Edward. And I had perhaps showed my preference to Ann. (*TBP*, 104–5)

More than sometimes and perhaps. He even uses his alleged senility to absolve himself of some of the guilt he feels about meddling. Indeed, meddling is compulsive with him. He fusses at Tolbrook over matters that are out of his control, thinking that he has duties there that in truth he does not have (*TBP*, 211). Robert finally confronts him over his influence on Ann, and he expresses shock that he could possibly have any influence; yet he is always after her only to discover at the end, in a moving scene, that her seriousness is too much like his was at her age—in spite of the difference of generation—and he appeals to her to live. Her answer suggests that, indeed, after winning her over to Tolbrook, he must now release her.

"You look as if you'd swallowed a safety pin," I said to her, making her look at me with Edward's eyes, which should be gay. "You take life too seriously."

"Don't you think it is rather serious?"

"My dear child, you're not thirty yet. You have forty, forty-five years in front of you."

"Yes." (*TBP*, 342)

This last word of the novel is potentially her redemption. It is certainly his.

Seen uncharitably, Wilcher's struggle is between his meddling and his escapism. Seen charitably, it is between his sense of duty and his reticence. Both views are true, and they are not in conflict in his character, only in my description. They are one, particularly in Wilcher the old man, whose feelings or habitual responses defy his reason. To be redeemed Wilcher must transcend his conflict because the opposition is unproductive, or what Blake called a "negation." What Wilcher must come to is an opposition which puts the conflict between reason and feeling on one side, and their union in gaiety on the other. This he does only at the end, oddly enough in his effort to "redeem" Ann from a similar conflict. In this act he escapes from himself or the Blakean "selfhood." There is even a hint of the Blakean "reprobate" in him at this point.

When we look back into the book from the conclusion, we see that his redemption has really been in the making all along, sudden as it seems in the end. We see it in his struggle to accept Robert's innovations and in his developing understanding of and feeling for Ann. (He never does quite understand her, but his feelings take him in the right direction in the end.) We even see it developing in his scene with Blanche, who in her dealings with Sara, matches him for intrepid meddling: At the outset, he says that he prefers her to Ann, though this is more an attack on Ann than it is a particularly affectionate statement about Blanche. Blanche has tried to manage him, has driven Sara into prison, and expresses all the anxieties about the future ownership of Tolbrook that Wilcher showed years before. Blanche's behavior is a living reminder to him of his own possibly self-serving meddling. His meeting with Blanche is a tour de force of reporting that rivals those of Gulley Jimson in *The Horse's Mouth*. Blanche is warning him against Ann as she apparently did against Sara, making the same accusations against Ann that he has secretly made.

But Wilcher torments Blanche as if he were taking revenge on his former self. He knows that he must protect himself against her, and he does it with a combination of faked senility and irony, even to the extent of hinting to her that he had burned down 15 Craven Gardens and that he still plans to marry Sara. He does this in an impishly malicious way:

> "Uncle, you don't say this kind of thing to other people, do you?"
> "Oh, no, it's just between ourselves. If Ann suspected anything like that, she would send for the asylum van to-morrow. And then I couldn't marry Mrs. Jimson."
> Blanche was quite taken aback, and I could see in her face the reflection of a terrible struggle. (*TBP*, 134)

123

In the end, he cannot "bear her kindly feelings" (*TBP*, 134). He recognizes all the things he and Blanche have in common, but with irony:

> I felt such an attack of sympathy for her, so near me in my deepest feelings, in my love of Tolbrook and the old grace of life, in her Christianity, which is that of a country-woman, the simple calm faith of the village church, that I knew it put me in danger of a serious attack. I therefore removed her quickly out of mind and reflected on the charm of the evening. (*TBP*, 134)

Here Wilcher begins to giganticize Blanche into one of his allegorical types, but changes course abruptly. It is too close to allegorizing himself, which is to make one's particularity disappear. So Blanche is simply dismissed in irony, though with (indeed, because of) grudging affection. This scene is one of the most important of the book, for it offers us a Wilcher that either did not exist until recently or has succeeded in hiding completely in the inner structure of his text. There is no need for Cary to tell us which. It is unimportant. It would certainly not be in character for Wilcher to do it. Wilcher's view of his early self is not that of an ironist, let alone an impish one. It would not fit if he had such a view. The earnest younger man is necessary to Wilcher's stance in the "present."

The treatment of Blanche is appropriately tempered in the end when Wilcher decides to leave no will and assumes that she and Loftus will share in the estate. To have carried out his earlier treatment of her would have been a meanness that Wilcher transcends. In the end, he recognizes that like him she really did have the "best claim" on Tolbrook—precisely because of an honest concern about it. But he recognizes also that other sorts of concerns are of equal value on their own terms.

The renouncing of the dream of marriage with Sara is the single major step that Wilcher takes. It can be said, of course, that this step is taken for him, and that is partly true; but involved in it is how Wilcher responds to the shattering of his dream. Going to Sara's bosom is like going to his mother's as a child in a time of terror when he was locked in a clothes hamper by the terrible Lucy. Wilcher *was* to leave the coffin of Tolbrook for the comfort of Sara. The excuse was that Sara was a true pilgrim. But a true pilgrimage into the perilous future is made on one's own. Once this becomes clear, Wilcher makes Sara an allegorical figure like the dead members of his family. She now has *meaning*, and she offers a message of active faith, but she is no longer a future hope for escape. Wilcher has been, he thinks, different from Sara, Amy, and Bill. He has been a seeker after meaning, not an actor who makes it:

> Amy and Sara, countrywomen both. They didn't submit themselves to any belief. They used it. They made it. They had the courage of the simple, which is not to be surprised. They had the penetration of innocence, which can see the force of a platitude. Amy's "got to die sometime" has been on the lips of every private soldier since the first army went into battle. For her it was still profound. (*TBP*, 339)

At the end in his attempt to liberate Ann, he reaches something like this state.

When we first meet Wilcher in Sara's account, it is difficult to find anything in him to sympathize with or admire. *To Be a Pilgrim* is meant to turn the tables—part way. Wayne Booth (p. 378) remarks that both the strength and the weakness of such a form of personal narration are that we almost inevitably sympathize even though we might not approve. This is exactly what Cary wants of us, and he wants us to give sympathy with some reluctance and full knowledge of how Wilcher appeared to Sara. Though Sara is sympathetic to Wilcher, it is noticeable that it is not through her that our sympathy is evoked. Why does Cary want this initial reluctance in us? I think it is to press home the idea that the possibility of redemption is universal, not an exclusive possession of any class, profession, point of view, or intellectual authority. To confuse it with any of these things is likely to be an act of pride. Wilcher gains redemption in spite of our sense, strongest at the outset, that we are superior to him in many ways; to see this via our growing sympathy, which he earns, is a step in our redemption. Neither redemption is a religious one, at least in any conventional sense. It is a redemption achieved by honoring life in its great variety.

Wilcher's redemption comes through his writing out his situation. In his allegorical brand of artistry, he comes to transcend allegory and return to the particular. His relatives are dead and subjected to being made into abstract meanings and representative types of modern English history. However, while Wilcher is gathering them into their significances, they keep slipping away to assert their individualities. For his purposes he succeeds in glorifying them into allegorical types, but we feel that these people are not the epic characters he makes them. They are real in a particular way in spite of their idealization.

In his dealing with Ann and Robert, he is a better artist than he knows. They are real, living people; and his failure, by his own admission, quite to understand them, as he tries to make them into types of the modern, is a process which actually reveals their particular life to us. It is amusing that Wilcher should complain about Ann's tendency to put all actions into "German boxes" when he puts all actions into the boxes of Bunyanesque pilgrimage. Toward the end he recognizes Ann's similarity to him. The allegorical type of the modern that he had made her he almost erases in that act of sympathetic identification. Ann, Robert, and John, the baby, are alive and in the real present. As long as they are alive their meanings are never fixed; this is Wilcher's urgent message to Ann, answered by the simple affirmation "yes." The moment marks Wilcher's abdication from sentimental anxiety, of which his allegorizing tendency is one characteristic. One might conclude that his tendency turns inside out in the end. All the ghosts called up he exorcizes by distancing them into abstractions. When that is accomplished, Wilcher is alone with Ann, Robert, John, and the present.

Wilcher's reflections on the other speakers of the trilogy are worth special mention here. It is revealing of Wilcher's nature that he speaks hardly at all of Gulley Jimson, and in the most distant terms, though we know from Sara's description of their meeting that he knows more about Jimson than he states. Indeed, he dwells hardly at all on any of Sara's men. His relation to Sara he glorifies, and all else around her recedes.

And Sara is glorified beyond anything Sara recognizes in herself, even though Wilcher does have real insight into her particular nature. His first remarks about her have an element of self-serving. He is attempting to absolve himself by confession. Though he is partly accurate, he does understate the amount she has stolen:

> It was I who was the unfaithful servant, and Sara, the victim. It was because I did not give Sara enough pay and because she did not like to ask me for money that she ran into debt and was tempted to take some useless trifles from the attic. (*TBP*, 9)

Wilcher's interpretation is in a way more accurate than the facts as they came out at the trial, yet not perfectly true. He glorifies Sara as a pilgrim wanderer who puts down no roots, but we know that Sara does put down roots. Fate and luck intervene to pull them up again. Sara's talent is homemaking, not wandering. She always takes the opportunity to nest; so Wilcher is inaccurate in the impression he gives here; but he manages to get at something in Sara's nature, nevertheless. He is right that Sara does wander, that her true possessions are in her heart, and this enables her to rebuild.

Wilcher also recognizes that Blanche's interpretation of Sara has factual accuracy. He is charitable toward her as long as he does not have to face her directly. But to his mind the facts add up to a spiritual lie that conflicts with the allegorical Sara:

> All of them, including, I suppose, Ann, accept the vulgar story that I was a wicked old bachelor who lived with his cook-housekeeper. They see Sara as a fat red-faced cook of forty-six, and they believe that this cook, a cunning and insinuating countrywoman, who had deceived two men before, swindled me and robbed me, and so enslaved me, by her sensual arts and smooth tongue, that I promised to marry her. They flatter themselves that by employing a detective, they stopped Sara's wicked plot, found her out in her robberies, and sent her to prison for eighteen months. This is what they believe, and the facts are true; yet they believe a lie. The truth is that when Sara came to me I was a lost soul. (*TBP*, 35)

The chapter from which this passage comes is devoted entirely to the matter of Sara. It ends with an unconsciously ironic remark that in its irony reveals Wilcher's tendency to glorify Sara:

> We say of such a one as Sara "a good servant," and think no more of it. But how strange and mysterious is that power, in one owning nothing of her own, to cherish the things belonging to another. (*TBP*, 36)

Wilcher intends the term "servant" to have two meanings—the domestic and the religious. But he does not intend us to be amused and to respond that, yes, indeed, Sara has cherished his belongings. Sara will not stay in Wilcher's allegorical box. Even Wilcher cannot keep her there, extravagant as his praise of her is.

It is in the ten chapters devoted to Wilcher's escape from Tolbrook and attempt to go to Sara permanently that we see the older, contemporary Sara, who tricks him and arranges his return to the care of Ann and Robert. It is here that Wilcher comes to accept (under duress) a different role for Sara in his life. She can no longer be an enveloping protector in a fantasy future but must take her place in Wilcher's pantheon of allegorical personages who offer to him models for the life of the spirit. In fact, he must go further: He cannot tell the story of his pilgrimage without revealing a Sara too particular to be boxed by allegory. Sitting in her parlor, he recognizes objects from Tolbrook and Craven Gardens:

> Four years ago I was shocked to find that some of my trifles had passed into Sara's keeping. But now I was not only amused; I felt a secret exultation in Sara's impudence, and more than impudence. Something far deeper. Something that had come to me also from Lucy. A freedom. An enterprise. And looking round, I saw a dozen more objects from forgotten corners of Tolbrook and Craven Gardens: An engraving of Wellington at Waterloo; a glass picture, cracked in four places, of Cherry Ripe; a little tripod table with one foot broken short. Apparently Sara had permitted herself to take nothing that was in use, or in good order. A woman of principle. And by this strange route, I pierced again into the living Sara, with her peculiar attitude to life. As one who faces a powerful but stupid enemy with the ready invention of a free lance, and the subtlety of a diplomat. (*TBP*, 316)

The admission of shock and the use of the word "trifles" here are important because we know that Wilcher has deeply valued possessions. To call them trifles at this point displays, I think, a slight exaggeration that reveals his determination to struggle out of his possessiveness. The passage through that word to exultation in Sara's impudence is an achievement. Wilcher's sexual relationship with Sara was, by Sara's account, oddly reticent and distant. But now he believes he has really come to know her spiritually—he "pierces" the "living Sara" again, but this time by a spiritually strange route. This is an achievement perhaps possible to Wilcher only as an old man who has come to grasp the nature of the "real" as a "powerful but stupid enemy."

While sitting in Sara's parlor, Wilcher goes on to recall various examples of her diplomacy from the past. He recognizes her obstinacy and cunning. Then, in a moment of supreme anger, suspecting that she is betraying him (as she is) by calling Ann, he attempts to assault her. It is a pathetically ineffective parallel to Jimson's assault in *Herself Surprised*:

I shouted out, "You are deceiving me, Sara. I thought you so good and religious, and wise, but you are nothing but a cunning greedy creature, a regular peasant. I suppose you have caught this boy Fred just now, as you caught me, and catch everyone—yes, that's what you do. You pretend to be so religious and modest and respectable, and all the time you're leading a man on, and heading him off."

And I rushed at her. I had never hit anyone in my life, much less a woman; but at that moment, so had Sara maddened me with her talk and her honest look that I believe I should have hit her. I meant to hit her on the nose. (*TBP*, 332)

Wilcher loses his balance; Sara catches him and carries him "like a child" to the sofa. But the ineffectiveness is only physical. In another sense, Wilcher makes a very belated and saving pilgrimage away from an innocence held far too long. He faces the real, and though he collapses physically and has to be carried like a child (as he was after he confessed to her years before), though he is irritated at Sara's treachery and observes to himself, "this is the end of me" (*TBP*, 323), it is not the end of him. He is physically weakened but begins to learn to walk in the spirit. It is a new, though muted, beginning.

Sara has exceeded the role planned for her in Wilcher's fantasy future. He now creates for her a larger, distanced, allegorical role to play. One recognizes that in doing this he has moved along, freeing himself from the fantasy of innocent protection. He will always be an allegorist; that is his way. But it is a way. It is, of course, a perilous one, as Cornelia Cook seems to point out (p. 125) when she remarks that even Wilcher's notion of pilgrimage vacillates between that of wandering free of "materialist preoccupations" and that of "purposeful journey." Wilcher is attracted and repelled by both. By finding another and different place for Sara in his pantheon, Wilcher frees himself. That is why I say that in the end his allegorizing is a sort of exorcism after all. In such a view, his allegorizing of Lucy is an exorcism of the devil, his remembrance of his father's last words an exorcism of his own failure to understand them, his treatment of his family members as representative types an exorcism of their failures. When Wilcher finds a new place for Sara, he offers the second half of the paradox of her. She has the "courage of the simple, which is not to be surprised" (*TBP*, 339). This seems at first wrong again, if we consider how many times Sara has claimed in her own account to be surprised. But it is the other half of a truth about her. As I have already said, Sara is never surprised to be surprised. Her innocence contains her cunning and vice versa.

There are still some things that Wilcher does not know. He does not know that Sara was stealing from him to help Jimson. There are still some things he neglects to mention: He does not write of his sexual relationship with Sara. It is right for the trilogy that Sara should deceive him. A natural person allegorized is bound to hide some not entirely pleasant facts. The allegorizer is likely to purge away his natural (including sexual) relationship to the idealized figure. Both omissions enhance our sense of the characters of the natural figures. We know what Wilcher doesn't know or won't tell.

There are also some things that we do not ourselves know. For example, did Wilcher burn down 15 Craven Gardens? Perhaps Wilcher is himself not certain. The important point, emphasized by leaving the fact undetermined, is that Wilcher certainly burned it down in spirit. Much of the indeterminateness of fact in the trilogy (and there is less than might be imagined on cursory reading) is there to throw emphasis on some other aspect of the issue, as if to say: "Don't look there, look elsewhere."

Before leaving *To Be a Pilgrim*, one ought to say something about power and freedom. What one can say is abstract: One can point to the ambiguities of power and freedom in the book and in Wilcher's mind. His freedom of spirit is greatest at the end when he is most physically weakened and most bereft of all possessions except his newly discovered sympathy for Ann. Before, Wilcher had only *preached* freedom, but by his own admission it terrified him, just as its efforts to break loose in Lucy terrified him.

The Horse's Mouth

Of the three narrators of the trilogy, the voice of Gulley Jimson asserts its presence and domination over its materials most strongly. We must constantly take into account Jimson's tone, his devices, shapings, and modes of assertion. Sara and Wilcher have their own definite voices and devices, but Jimson's are more self-consciously the artist's than Sara's, which are natural to her "nature," or Wilcher's. His, though by no means artless, partly express a failing physical and mental condition. Finally, of the three narrators only Jimson makes a conscious pact with his reader, who is as close to identical with us as a fictive reader can be. Sara writes for the newspaper and cash. Wilcher writes for himself and spiritual redemption. Jimson writes from the horse's mouth, the truth as he sees it; and he conveys it to posterity. It is a gratuitous act; he makes us feel that we are in on things by sharing his ironies with us. He compliments us by letting us know that he knows we know.

Jimson's memoir covers a relatively short space of time from some time in 1938 until early summer of 1939. No account is given of six of these months, which Jimson has spent in jail. Unlike Wilcher, Jimson reveals no changes in his attitude as he writes. Unlike Sara, he does make change of fortune a theme. Fortune for him is always from bad to worse. There is little recourse to events before 1938. What we learn of Jimson's past is incidental to the inner structure of his narrative, which is enclosed in a relatively brief space of time. As for the outer structure, it plays a role similar to that in Sara's narrative. We learn that Sara is writing in prison, that Jimson is dictating to his "honorary secretary" in the hospital, where he is bedridden, unable to paint any longer because of a stroke. In both instances the place and conditions of writing are important. In contrast, however, to Wilcher's attention to the present of writing, Jimson mentions it only at the beginning and ending of chapter 13. The ending of that chapter is the only place where Jimson seems momentarily to lose heart and even rationality; the situation of dictating is clearly a tragic one that emphasizes Jimson's power of ebullience. Here, for only a moment, it fails him:

> And to-night it seems that I can't paint at all. I've lost sight of the maiden altogether. I wander weeping far away, until some other take me in [the sentence is an adaptation of two lines from Blake's "Mental Traveller"]. The police. It's quite time. I'm getting too old for this rackety life. (*HM*, 65)

Andrew Wright observes (p. 124) that Jimson wouldn't be writing (or dictating) at all if he could paint. It is true that for Jimson painting is the only satisfactory art, but Jimson needs to create, and so he does what he can with the materials at hand. Indeed, this is the principal motive for Jimson's memoir—to continue creating. Even after the lapse of spirit at the end of chapter 13, Jimson recovers and begins chapter 14 full of energy as if nothing had happened. The capacity to recover spirit is typical of Cary's most powerful characters—particularly Jimson and Chester Nimmo.

The reason that Jimson does not change in the course of his narrative is, first, that he is speaking out of the sum of his experience compressed into the events of only a few months, and, second, that he believes so completely in change that he is unchanging in his view of it. For him, change is not, past one's apprenticeship, necessarily growth or purposive quest. It is creation and then creation again. This is the reason that Blake's cyclical "Mental Traveller" appeals to Jimson, and it is the reason that the triumph over the cycle in Blake's poetry is not emphasized by Jimson.

Jimson tells *how it is* for an old artist. The critic Alabaster would, no doubt, have entitled Jimson's memoir, at posthumous publication, something like *The Wit and Wisdom of Gulley Jimson*—if he could have brought himself to a grasp of either the wit or the wisdom. Jimson assumes that he has truth and that as an artist he achieves its expression cyclically. This speaking of Jimson from the horse's mouth presents some problems for Cary that he doesn't fully solve. It explains, but does not defend some rather stilted, fixed, and discursive set pieces. Chapter 13, already mentioned, is one. It is a brilliant *tour de force*, but it sits uneasily in the text. There Jimson uncharacteristically goes back beyond 1938 to treat his career as a microcosm of the history of modern British art. Into it is woven Blake's "Mental Traveller." But the chapter resists the movement of the narrative in ways that Wilcher's panorama of English history, woven into the whole of that novel, does not. Critics have been drawn to this chapter because of the Blake parallel, but it is one of the times that Jimson's (and Cary's) art slips. The whole chapter is mechanically shaped in order to *bear significance*. (It is, in fact, a late addition to Cary's text.) There are other problems: In chapter 20, Jimson's (and Cary's) cleverness runs on in straight descriptive passages like a little travelogue. In chapter 22, Jimson is observing the Beeders' paintings:

> Usual modern collection. Wilson Steer, water in watercolour; Matthew Smith, victim of the crime in slaughtercolour; Utrillo, whitewashed wall in mortarcolour; Matisse, odalisque in scortacolour; Picasso, spatchcock horse in tortacolour. (*HM*, 146)

And on and on. It is overdone. It is saying more than need be said for the sake of the narrative. It is rather like the piling up of Sara's kitchen figures in *Herself Surprised*. Here the attempt is to give a contemporary flavor to the scene, but it is only flavor, really Cary at play. Jimson's long comparison of Sara and Rozzie Balmforth in chapter 38, though interesting enough, halts the narration to a purpose that could be accomplished in other ways. The book, in fact, bears marks of awkward revision. Chapter 15, for example, begins with the statement: "Plant has two rooms down an area in Ellam Street" (*HM*, 73), but by the time Jimson is writing he no longer has those rooms. Cary should have changed the verb to "had." The same problem comes up with the sentence in chapter 16: "Hickson lives in Portland Place" (*HM*, 97). At the time of writing, Hickson is dead.

If these sorts of problems occurred in Wilcher's discourse, we might pass them off as confused garrulousness, but Jimson is clearly meant to be in command of his materials. It is Cary who is confused or tempted by the situation he has created, in which the narrator, speaking from the horse's mouth, is occasionally a bit pontifical.

It is fortunate that in the overwhelming majority of pages Jimson and Cary are in far better control. In spite of the passages I have mentioned, I disagree with James Hall, who claims (p. 96) that this novel is difficult to reread because Cary is sometimes dull. Jimson is usually quite tricky about avoiding the dullness of mechanical contrivance. Take, for example, the figure of the horse. When we see it we might conclude: Oh, a repeated motif; truth is about to come forth. But this is not quite the way Jimson handles it. For Jimson, the horse is complex and variable, appearing in wonderful individual forms. It is always so individual that we cannot always pin the same significance on it. There is, for example, the old work horse about to drop. This is the way Jimson thinks he himself appears to the "wolves" crouching around his old boathouse. Elsewhere he is a horse for an entirely different reason:

> I'm not a wild ass of the desert. I'm an old hoss. I know something. I've been ridden by the nobility and gentry. Millionaires have cut an important figure on my back. Hickson kept me in the stable for years and trotted me out for his visitors. His Gulley Jimsons, his pride and his joy. My stomach has had two kicks a day for sixty years, one to put the saddle on and one to take it off. It can take anything. And eat its own hay. And organize its own kicks. And save up a bite that will take the bloody pants off the seat of government. If it likes. (*HM*, 114)

This is the horse who knows from experience like the deceased "old horse" Rozzie (*HS*, 205). Often the "horse" is instinctive knowledge, as in the case of Coker late in the book: "No one knows how she knows what she does know. But it's definitely horse meat" (*HM*, 288).

Horselike behavior is also connected comically with dawning understanding or anticipation. The latter characterizes Alabaster upon being asked if he is married: "The professor looked like a horse about to receive the nosebag" (*HM*, 177). The former characterizes its use in a passage on Nosy Barbon: "It was drizzling rain and Nosy stood on one foot like a young horse, with drops sticking to his nose and his ears flapped, meditating" (*HM*, 223). In addition to being descriptions "straight from the horse" (*HM*, 29), these passages illustrate the variety of the horse's true being to an active imagination. One gets the sense of a sort of magical horse that keeps turning up in the faces and movements of characters throughout the novel. This seems to make the point that the artist who sees the horse in the picture is getting at truth. We have no sense that this figure from the book's title has been fixed by some abstract principle.

The Horse's Mouth aims at cleverness, as befits its narrator. Jimson's is a flexible, inventive intellect. The result of this is a structure that evades fixity, is deliberately multifarious, and controls itself just this side of wildness. *The Horse's Mouth* takes more chances than the other novels, and Jimson does not hang his narrative on a single, easily traceable thread.

Or at least almost not. For there is the matter of Blake. The Blake theme has been seized upon by Cary scholars and made more solemn in the telling than it really is. It has been mentioned by nearly everyone, but rarely studied as to its actual tonal function in the work. Rather, it has been made an abstract principle on which everything has been hung like a formula. But that is not the way Jimson works. He tries to evade formulas. We must remember to see everything as it flows through his transforming voice, the tone of which is the dominating element.

Jimson is clearly enough an independent Blakean rather than an enthusiastic Bunyanite, or a sentimental Yongeian. Like everyone else, he picks and chooses from his Blake. The most obvious choice, as I indicated in chapter 2, is his appropriation to his own purposes of Blake's "Mental Traveller" to illustrate the cyclical process of growth, decline of inspiration, and renewal in the artist. But this appropriation has a certain capricious ebullience, like the many appearances in his memoir of the horse. It keeps turning up in different shapes. The question is, how does it really work in Jimson's narrative?

Quotation from "The Mental Traveller" begins in chapter 11, where, irritated by the preachers Mr. Plant has brought to see his painting, Jimson explicitly warns himself against being Blake in his "Mental Traveller" mood:

> "Come," I said, "you're not one of those asses who takes himself seriously. You're not like poor Billy." (*HM*, 48)

Well, we know that Jimson tries not to be an ass. He thinks of himself as an old horse, and to speak horse is to speak irony. Actually, though, he *is* like Blake crying out. Blake's vision of the world of endless cyclical generation and dissolution dominates "The Mental Traveller," but the poem exists inside Blake's larger vision of triumph over the natural cycle into higher forms of creative life. We shall see that Jimson recasts this aspect of Blake to make the creative moment itself cyclical. This is partly because of the notion in Cary (and Jimson) of the moment of inspiration followed by the loss of some of it in expression.

However, it is important not to become too schematic about Jimson's treatment of all this, or too solemn. Obviously, Jimson sees the poem as Blake's serious cry against the same sort of world that he thinks he is up against. But consistent with his belief that one should not be an ass, but an ironic, worldly horse, Jimson softens his attack on Blake and claims that after all Blake's poem probably has as its real subject the same mundane irritations that torment him. This is comforting, since it helps him to solidify his identification with Blake after all. So he quotes stanza one of "The Mental Traveller" and interprets it mundanely as follows: "Which probably means only that when Billy had a good idea, a real tip, a babe, some blue-nose came in and asked him why he drew his females in nightgowns" (*HM*, 48). The situation distressing Jimson is thereby brought down to the comedy of everyday life via Blake.

The interpretation of the third stanza (he does not quote stanza two) does not speak directly of Blake but generalizes in such a way as to take it for granted that his and Blake's problems are the same: "Which means that some old woman of a blue nose [interpretive critic] nails your work of imagination to the rock of law and why and what; and submits him to a logical analysis" (*HM*, 48). The poem is employed quite specifically as a means of communication between Jimson and Blake's spirit. The temper of quotation has changed. Blake is not an ass, but knows it all. Jimson is not an ass for crying out the poem.

In chapter 12 the second mention of Blake's poem has to do with Jimson's relation to Sara. It is triggered by observing two young lovers walking arm in arm, whom Jimson imagines to be playing the roles of the male and female figures of the poem. He reflects that she is both herself and a product of the young man's imagination. He considers the danger of the vision turning into "a frow, who spends all her life thinking of what the neighbors think"—in other words, "A woman old/who nails him down upon a rock." By a process of association he comes to his own relation to Sara. "The Mental Traveller" shows us a male figure born into domination by a female crone, mother nature, the surrounding natural world. From this point the male grows older as the crone grows younger until they are lovers, thence to a point where the male is an "aged shadow," the female a babe. Jimson applies this pattern to his life with Sara, who in his view mothered and attempted to envelop him. The male's rising up and revolting against this matronly female love has its parallel for Jimson in his attack on Sara when he thought her meddling had gone too far.

At this point there is a subtle shift from consideration of their domestic relations to the relation of model and painter, to which Jimson makes the poem equally apply. He rises up also to put Sara on canvas:

> Yes. I found out how to get Sara on the canvas. Some of her anyhow. And I was always at her, one way or another. The flesh was made word; every day. Till he, that is, Gulley Jimson, became a bleeding youth. And she, that is, Sara, becomes a virgin bright. (*HM*, 52)

A problem swept under the rug here is the conflict between Sara as model and Sara as homemaker. Jimson makes the two the same and subject to the same pattern. But we already know from *Herself Surprised* that Sara the enveloping homemaker is not exorcized so easily as Jimson's interpretive equation makes out. That is the problem with all interpretive equations. Sara won't be merely a tractable "virgin bright" model though for a while Jimson manages the feat of both painting her and making love to her. "What a time that was" (*HM*, 52). A balance is momentarily achieved. But inspiration wanes as the male becomes figuratively an "aged shadow," and his lover is reborn as a female babe, only to run off with a new lover. We note that this is not quite what happened between Sara and Jimson though Jimson tries to remember it that way. It was

Jimson who went off after smashing Sara's nose in a fit of anger. Of course, Jimson feels he was driven to do this by her attempt to chain down his inspiration in attention to money and domesticity. This use of the poem to describe Jimson's relation to Sara (and also to "the old woman of the world . . . old mother necessity" [*HM*, 55]) is its second function in the memoir.

The third use is quite brief. It involves Jimson's identification of himself as the "aged shadow" after he has run from the police and feels exhausted and depressed. But Jimson does not allow himself to tolerate depression for long—at least on the outside. That is one of the lessons the old horse teaches. He speaks in summary that the trick is to "take necessity and make her do what you want; get your feet on her old bones and build your mansions out of her rock" (*HM*, 58). He almost grows younger as he says it.

The fourth and final use of the poem is in chapter 13—Jimson's capsule history of his career. Here emphasis is again on the cyclical. Jimson's account describes his movement from a classical style learned by hard labor to an impressionist style, a "resurrection," brought about by sudden experience of a Manet:

> By Gee and Jay, I said, I was dead, and I didn't know it.
>   Till from the fire on the hearth
>   A little female babe did spring.
>
> (HM, 62)

After four years of hard work, Jimson declares, he captured the maiden Blake describes as "all of solid fire and gems and gold," and he made money to boot. But then he became an "aged shadow" once again, and he had to go through the difficult process of achieving a new style. This period Jimson describes as a crisis. As a classicist he was "dead"; as an impressionist he was for a while inspired. That ended soon enough, and then he seemed to be enticed by a new female, who teased him, always beyond reach. This figure is also described in Blake's poem.

A foray into cubism offered another turn of the cycle, but it was not satisfying for long. It eventually gave him "indigestion," and soon even his patron Hickson stopped buying his work.

It has not been mentioned by critics that this career, moving from one fashion to another, is quite unlike Blake's, for Blake seemed to follow no contemporary fashion. It has also not been mentioned that Jimson does not in chapter 13 discuss his "epic" style as only another cycle. He remarks that "he got a nice girl in his eye, or perhaps she got after me," but he does not speak of having captured the maiden anew. The chapter ends with Jimson in a depressed state because he can't paint. What he has said is that all of his work up to his epic phase was derivative, including the pictures of Sara so valued by collectors. Now, in his old age, there is a Jimson truly inspired by Blake to paint large epic canvasses and walls in a new style that is apparently both ahead and behind the times; but he has no patrons for this sort of work, no adequate materials, and no public except apparently the young art students. Without these things he has a hard time maintaining his certainty that he has captured a maiden. Perhaps she is a will o' the wisp. Now, speaking from a hospital bed (though we do not know this yet), he knows it is unlikely he will ever find out. The importance of the conclusion of this chapter is that it reminds us, when we recall it after completing the book, of the situation in which Jimson is speaking his memoir and his struggle to maintain gaiety. It is certainly implied here, though Jimson would never admit it, that any artist needs approbation and intelligent criticism in order to know where he is.

Jimson does not think of his or perhaps any artist's career, past apprenticeship, as development, but instead as movement from inspiration to inspiration, with no comparisons of value among these moments possible. Jimson's interpretation of the movement through generation to regeneration is that this movement comes and comes again uniquely and there can be no stopping place, only new beginnings.

Blake's poem is certainly cryptic, but one can read it in the context of his other works as a description of a fallen condition redeemable by commitment to eternal work, a discipline of gaiety that escapes the cycle. The figure of Los comes to this in his struggle with his spectre in Blake's great poem, *Jerusalem*. Jimson lays his emphasis on the cyclical pattern of creativity, which explains his constant search from style to style. It also explains the pattern of getting "stuck" (though he hates to admit being stuck) and unstuck that occurs in the Jimsonian process of creative activity. This is one of the reasons for the introduction into the memoir of the incident of the sculptor Abel and his stone. That Abel's work takes the same pattern Jimson finds symbolized in "The Mental Traveller" objectifies Jimson's theory for us and invites us to regard Jimson as not eccentric to the point of absurd uniqueness. At the outset Abel seems to be faced with simply a huge block of meaningless stone, but soon the stone demands the artist's respect. It has its own nature, though not as difficult to deal with as Jimson's Sara. (The stone and Sara are, of course, not parallel; Sara is the model, like Abel's Lolie, but both are "nature.") The artist must begin to see things potential in the stone; his work becomes a kind of conversation with it.

It is worth noting that at one point Abel seems to lose inspiration and, as Blake's poem says, "wanders far away." At another point Abel and Jimson go off together—stuck. There is a lot of wandering far away in *The Horse's Mouth*. Jimson's "Raising of Lazarus" on the Beeders' wall is interrupted by their return, and he must wander far away, "an aged shadow," into the wilderness of Sussex, "dark as the inside of a Cabinet Minister" (*HM*, 219).

At this point there is an amusing submerged parallel to Blake's career. Blake spent three years at Felpham on the sea in West Sussex doing commissions for William Hayley, who tried to interest him in the relatively lucrative profession of miniature painting. It was a difficult time for Blake. He had to leave familiar surroundings, his wife did not take to the climate, and he struggled in his mind with the well-intentioned Hayley's plans for him. On the other hand, he managed to get started on his great long poems, *Milton* and *Jerusalem*.

Jimson and Nosy Barbon end up in a town Cary calls Burlington-on-sea, which we can imagine to be near Felpham. There is actually a Middleton-on-sea nearby. On the way, Jimson quotes to a busload of strangers Blake's description of Satan from *Milton*, written out of his Felpham experience, with Hayley as Satan. On the next morning he is reminded of Blake's visionary poem to Thomas Butts, written from Felpham, and the wonderful lark's song passage from *Milton*. He is on the verge of inspiration again. But he needs cash, so he peddles some postcards as if they were pornography. They are an ironic version of Blake's miniatures. But he is beaten up by a racketeer and put into hospital (Blake had an altercation with a soldier in his garden at Felpham that landed him in court with a charge of treason). Jimson's incarceration produces his idea for "The Creation." Blake's "incarceration" at Felpham produced *Milton* and parts of *Jerusalem*. This parallel has a capricious humor that fits very well into the narrative intent. One doesn't want to make too much of it allegorically. It is there primarily, I think, to point up Jimsonian ebullience.

The incident at the Beeders' involving the sculptor Abel has an-other aspect that connects with Jimson's use of "The Mental Trav-eller" to describe his life with Sara. Quite a lot is made of Abel's relationship with his model Lolie, who is also his wife. Poor Lolie really has been reduced to "spiritual fodder" by Abel's activity as a sculptor. The marriage is one of convenience. According to Abel, she wanted security, and she was practically made for him—as a model. This is told to Jimson by Abel in a voice so matter-of-fact as to convey the sensibility of someone who has only his art in mind. Lolie tries to act the wife and fusses that Abel has not eaten prop-erly, but Abel ignores her and works on and on. She tells Jimson she can manage Abel as long as he does not have insomnia. But Abel treats her wretchedly, and after the stone is finished she has to go to the hospital, suffering from overexposure and malnutri-tion. Lolie is not Abel's first wife or only wife. He seems to have another one elsewhere just as Jimson does, or did.

The parallel is clear enough. So is the contrast. Abel says:

> "Yes, she said she wanted to be settled. . . . It's been a great suc-cess. . . . Yes, there's nothing like marriage for an artist—if he can find the right woman, of course."
> "I found her once," I said. "And what a woman, Rubens and cream." (*HM*, 205)

But Sara was not Lolie. She had more of a mind of her own. She had her own domestic creative powers, and this meant that for Jim-son she was two Saras—the model and the old domesticator. This makes Sara the perfect vehicle for Jimson's Blakean allegory of the creative artist. She is artistic material that has its own existence.

This reveals what might have been an irresolution in the so-called artistic theory of the novel itself. Though the theory we ab-stract from *The Horse's Mouth*, as I tried to show in chapter 2, is su-perior to that in *Art and Reality*, the latter notion seems to creep back into the novel in the form of Jimson's attitude toward Sara. Because she is intractable in her own purposes, Jimson loses pa-tience with her. But Jimson *does* paint Sara and make a masterpiece of the job; nevertheless, what his assault on Sara indicates is his need to go on to something else, as his "Mental Traveller" inter-pretation of the cycle of creativity insists. Rightly or wrongly, he interprets Sara's behavior as a serious threat to his freedom. Thus, though Sara was his greatest model and greatest love, her very power made their staying together impossible for him. Sara is just a lot more woman than Lolie, and that is the problem. It is a serious oversimplification to see Abel, as T. James Bridge (p. 52) does, successful in art and love, and Jimson unsuccessful. Abel is the more conventional artist and Jimson the more imaginative. But need all this be the problem Jimson apparently makes it? For Jimson, yes; for some artists, no.

The work in Blake next most often quoted in *The Horse's Mouth* is *Visions of the Daughters of Albion*, which is given an interesting interpretation by Jimson. Blake's story is that of the virgin Oothoon, who is raped by Bromion and rejected by her friend Theotormon, whereupon she utters a passionate lament about true purity and freedom. The poem is in Jimson's mind during his work on "The Fall." For Jimson, the fall is a fall into freedom. After "The Fall" is destroyed, Jimson cheers up the outraged Nosy Barbon by imagining a new and better painting actually to be called "The Fall into Freedom." Jimson is particularly taken by Blake's Oothoon because she rhapsodizes over an absolute freedom in which restraint is absent. Oothoon is innocence personified, the virginity of the soul that, Jimson holds, never allows experience to grow stale because it is always new. The major passages Jimson quotes in chapter 17. Here he treats Bromion and Theotormon in an interesting way. Bromion is all passion, and Theotormon's jealousy is internalized as Oothoon's lost chastity, her jealous "touch me not." The usual way of interpreting the poem is to call Theotormon her theologically tormented lover who cannot forgive her for being raped by the arrogant Bromion. The problem with Jimson's reading is that Bromion, whom Jimson treats as her boyfriend, does rape Oothoon and seems, in addition to being a beast, a stranger by comparison to Theotormon. The problem with the usual reading is that it doesn't know what to do with the speech of Bromion that Jimson quotes in chapter 33, with an appropriate comment:

> Thou knowest, I said, that the ancient trees seen by thine eyes
>   have fruit
> But knowest thou that trees and fruits flourish upon the earth
> To gratify senses unknown [trees, beasts, and birds unknown,
> Unknown, not unperceived, spread in the infinite microscope]
> In places yet unvisited by the voyager.

> That is, until the voyager arrives. With the eye of imagination. And sees the strange thing. And throws a loop of creation around it. (*HM*, 222)

(The passage in brackets is unaccountably omitted in the Carfax edition.) This does, indeed, seem to be real horse meat and inappropriate in the mouth of as consummate a villain as Bromion. In any case, both readings show Bromion and Theotormon imprisoned by their attitudes toward Oothoon and Oothoon free in her own mind but imprisoned in the minds of the two men.

Jimson's notion of freedom is much more radical than Cary's and one that Cary elsewhere pointedly attacks. It can be described as including the old liberal idea that freedom is the absence of restraint, in which situation the imagination has free rein. Jimson's political views uttered to an audience of bus riders in chapters 32 and 33 during the night trip south to Burlington are anarchic: "The only good government is a bad one in a hell of a fright," Jimson remarks (*HM*, 217–18) to the anger of some of his fellow passengers. Jimson's attack is really on all generalizations—an attack similar to that of Blake on the *Discourses* of Joshua Reynolds. But Jimson adds to Blake's notion that only individuals exist a grim thought: "Only individuals exist—lying low in their own ratholes" (*HM*, 220). There follows Jimson's quotation from Blake's *Milton* about seeing the interior of Satan. In the southland Jimson too has his vision of Hell; it is the spectre of government, not William Hayley.

Visions of the Daughters of Albion works as an antidote in Jimson's mind to this grim vision. The poem involves the incorruptible individual woman Oothoon, and for Jimson it involves Sara. Reading *Herself Surprised*, we are driven to a crisis of decision regarding Sara. Is she corrupt? Is she innocent? Innocence in Blake's and Jimson's terms is a condition of the spirit and has nothing to do with whether one has been raped or has violated a law. Jimson, who is shrewd about Sara once we appropriately discount his rage at her power, believes she is innocent, and he quotes lines from Blake's *America* to back himself up. It is, however, a quotation amended in the last line:

> Because the soul of sweet delight can never be defiled
> Fires surround [Blake wrote "enwrap"] the earthly globe, yet man
>   is not consumed
> Amidst the lustful fires he walks, and polishes his door knob.
>   (*HM*, 41)

Blake wrote, instead of the last phrase, "His feet become like brass." The door knob polishing is Jimson's invention, remembered from a few pages earlier when, coming with Coker to Sara's house he sees the door knob "shining like rolled gold," symbol of her capacity to survive and make a new home. This is in turn connected to an earlier remembrance by Jimson where he calls Sara "solid brass to the Adams rib. The only way to touch Sara's feelings is to hit her with something." No wonder he sees her walking through lustful fires undefiled. This innocence is tied up in Jimson's mind with a naturally protective isolation that makes Sara always a little mysterious to us in her workings.

Jimson's isolation is less serene, being self-created, rather than natural. It is reflected in his persistent irony, which stretches into suspicion of nearly everyone. Even those devoted to him, like Nosy, he keeps at irony's distance out of a strong suspicion that they will make demands on him that will interfere with his compulsion to paint. Nosy is a special case in that Jimson vainly attempts to protect him from catching the compulsion.

The most important Blakeanism in *The Horse's Mouth* is none of those mentioned so far, nor is it the more abstract parallels that have been seen between Jimson's career and the plots of *Jerusalem* or *Milton*. Rather, because it embodies the notions of love, isolation, and the necessity of acknowledging one's power and responsibility, it is Blake's epigram that follows:

> The Angel that presided at my birth
> Said, "Little creature, born of joy and mirth,
> Go love without the help of anything on earth."

Jimson's use of this short poem is quite straightforward. He uses it twice, applying it once to the life of his poor sister Jenny midway in his memoir and in his rambling speech in the ambulance on the way to the hospital. It is his memoir's appropriate epitaph. As he remarks, it is "real horse meat." He does not always live up to the angel's command, but he knows that he should, if only to "avoid getting in a state" (*HM*, 297).

The other important connection between Jimson and Blake is in Jimson's championing of Blake against Plant's Spinozaism. I have already discussed the matter in chapter 2, and it has been carefully studied by Michael Echeruo, who draws a distinction (pp. 74ff.) between Blake's view of the ugly world as a subject for transcendental creativity and Spinoza's view that it is an object of transcendental contemplation. For Jimson, Spinoza's view is making the best of a bad job. The bad job is the determinism inherent in the world.

Spinoza tries to achieve freedom through contemplation, which is supposed to reveal the meaning of things, including the justice in them. In drafts for *Power in Men*, Cary argues against the possibility of freedom in Spinoza's system:

> True freedom must be creative or it is nothing, an illusion. In Spinoza, a true creative activity would mean that God was not yet complete, and so not perfect. Therefore there is no creative activity, no freedom. (*OC*, Box 200)

Jimson does not believe in meaning inherent in things. For him the world *is* unjust, or more accurately, *a*just. Jimson asks Plant rhetorically whether a kick in the stomach from a blind horse means anything (*HM*, 127), while Plant meditates on the meaning (the hidden justice) in the loss of his hand. Jimson's motto, as T. James Bridge (p. 32) has pointed out, is a play on Tristram Shandy's unfortunate sash-window accident (V, 17): "Keep your pecker up, old cock. Here's the chopper coming" (*HM*, 86).

In his choice of creation over contemplation, Jimson goes so far as to attack language as symbols of attempt to *find* meaning. It is, in other words, Spinozaistic. It tries to articulate the hidden justice in the world. But there is, for Jimson, no meaning or hidden justice out there. A picture, on the other hand, is the "only satisfactory form of communication." It is "neither true nor false. But created" (*HM*, 88). Jimson is, of course, using language in his memoir, being reduced to it by virtue of his hospitalization. He is like old Spinoza, making the best of a bad job. But even here Jimson, in his creative persistence, tries to force language out of its Spinozaistic shape. This is the reason for the many devices Jimson employs to put meaning *into* things via language. Jimson is perhaps wrong about language and defines it too narrowly, as the success of his own memoir shows. In order to make language work he speaks hyperbolically, counts on the reader to interpret him ironically, does all he can to escape imprisonment in another man's system. As the *Tristram Shandy* motto urges, one had better be alert at all times. But the world is *a*just, and eternal vigilance is impossible. The best one can achieve is the cyclicity of creativity that Jimson finds in Blake's "Mental Traveller"—a more violent world than the idealized diapason of movement between what Blake called Eden and Beulah, the place of rest, in the later prophecies. Jimson would be suspicious of a Beulah that might become identified with a mothering figure like Sara.

Jimson's view is one that to be held at all must be strenuously held, and while there is a certain sadness in Plant's view, the gaiety of Jimson is really a deliberate discipline, even a desperate discipline, kept to at great cost and occasionally slipped away from. Below is an abyss that Jimson, unlike Blake, cannot claim is an illusion owing to an opponent's mistaken metaphysics. This is the reason that in the end, though Jimson disagrees with Plant and even at one point condescends to him a little, their disagreement is less about the nature of reality than about how to cope with it. Both men occasionally act on the other person's principle. Plant creates an imaginative way to survive in the doss house with a modicum of dignity, having gained control over the key to the water closet. Jimson's striking out against Sara and others is at least a tacit admission of the real's existence and its own purposes. The disagreement between these two old men is not really epistemological at all, but ethical. Further, it is a disagreement transcended by their formal, affectionate respect for each other. In the end they are both in the same fix, and Jimson knows this. In the darkness of night in the doss house, on his bed of chairs near Plant, Jimson watches the shapes of clouds, making strange changing patterns of them in his mind. With his admirable courtesy, Plant had pointed out to Jimson the excellent view from the chairs:

> Plantie himself did not sleep either. Whenever I looked his way I could see his little eyes glinting as he stared at the ceiling. But what he was thinking of, I don't know. An old man's thoughts are an old man's secret, and no one else would even understand them. He only once spoke to me, when he heard the chairs creak and said, "You all right, Mr. Jimson?"
>
> "I'm all right, Mr. Plant. Why aren't you asleep?"
>
> "I've had my sleep. I wondered how you were sleeping."
>
> "Like a top," I said. For it saves a lot of trouble between friends to swear that life is good, brother. It leaves more time to live. (*HM*, 236)

Jimson making images of the clouds and Plant staring at the blankness of the ceiling announce their difference. The rest announces their togetherness. James Hall has said, "Cary mutes the isolation and loneliness of anarchic individualism, and plays up its fun and warmth" (p. 89). A scene like this—a very important scene—and others make one feel such a remark is quite mistaken.

The night scene with Plant and other scenes in the trilogy indicate that for Cary Blake's is the artist's philosophy. But it is not everyone's. Cary embraces its exuberance, but he sees it not as an expression of the nature of reality so much as an ethical stance, even, I think, as the expression of a necessary cultural role. But Cary does not, as some have thought, negate the opposite stance. He sees the tragic implications of both. Jimson and Plant occupy the same place in feeling. They are alone together, and this is why it would be a mistake to say that Cary chooses Jimson at Plant's expense. Cary's God quite clearly does not, even though Cary gives to Plant a name that seems to identify him with what Blake called the "vegetative" world.

The focus is, of course, on and through Jimson and his struggle to play his particular role. All of this, by Cary's choice, has to be embodied in the way Jimson tells his story. He works in a number of interrelated ways. Much has been made of a so-called triple pattern in the novel, corresponding to Jimson's involvement with his three paintings. In order, they are "The Fall," "The Raising of Lazarus," and "The Creation." The plot does roughly divide into the periods of Jimson's concern for these works. However, these parts do not define the action nearly as well as Sara's relations with her three men do in *Herself Surprised*. Sara is complicated enough, but Jimson is not that simple. Instead, the titles of three paintings emphasize three aspects of the cyclic situation of the artist's imagination—the fall into freedom, the cyclic rebirth of imagination ("By Gee and Jay, I was dead, and didn't know it."), and new creation. However, the titles of the works do not represent phases Jimson is in, only the pattern of creativity that repeats itself with him.

There is a good deal of deliberate repetition in the novel to back up this notion. The three paintings are unfinished or destroyed or both. Indeed, more of Jimson's paintings than these three have suffered cruel fates. It is worthwhile simply to list here all the works by Jimson mentioned in the trilogy and their fates: a drawing for a wall painting at Bradnall that is never executed (fate unknown); "English drawing from the Hickson collection"; a large painting described by Nina as the interior of God, with someone who looks suspiciously like Hickson sitting in a water closet (refused by Hickson, fate unknown); "Portrait of Mrs. Bond" (Tate Gallery); "The Garden of Eden," wall picture at Ancombe, mutilated and covered over; "The Fall," used by Coker's mother to patch ceiling of boat shed; "The Living God," taken by landlord for unpaid rent (fate unknown); "The Raising of Lazarus," left unfinished on wall of Beeder's domicile (fate unknown); "The Creation," unfinished and destroyed when ruined church wall is taken down; "The Bath," left to the nation by Hickson (Tate Gallery); "Portrait of a Gentleman" (Matt Monday, fate unknown); "The Holy Innocents," lost and probably made into an awning; "Drawing for 'The Bath'," actually a copy made by Jimson at the Tate, sold to the Beeders; "Jacob and His Wives," mentioned but with no information about it; and finally the drawings possessed by Sara at her death. There is enough of a pattern here to make it a significant part of a larger order of repetition in the novel.

There are others. Jimson has done three terms in jail. He has had a succession of "wives," of whom three are named. He repeats his behavior with Hickson. He likes to recall parallel situations in his memoir. His early conversation with Coker is counterpointed by the garrulous rambling of an old seafarer. His conversation with Sara likewise takes place against the backdrop of a lecture on nature and property. Both of these juxtapositions are ironically perceived by us. The lecturer who praises the beneficence of nature and attacks private property, is doubly contrasted to Jimson, who always sees art as superior to nature, and Sara, who after hearing the attack on property remarks that the lecturer must not be married. With the three paintings there is in each case a visitation of uncomprehending people that disrupts the work. The descriptions become progressively worse.

Clearly, Jimson as narrator is fond of such repetitions. They fit with his cyclical views. Also, Jimson is quite consistent in his modes of utterance. He persists in exuberant, often hyperbolic expression, which indicates his sense of a pact with his reader. He knows *we* will understand his intent though most of those he meets in the novel he perplexes. The following exuberance describes his inner response to Plant's efforts to interest some "blue nose" visitors in his painting:

> The more he tried, the worse I felt. As if I had been a happy worm, creeping all soft and oily through the grass, imagining the blades to be great forest trees, and every little pebble a mountain overcome; and taking the glow of self-satisfaction from his own tail for the glory of the Lord shining on his path; when all at once a herd of bullocks comes trampling along, snorting tropical epochs and shitting continents; succeeded by a million hairy gorillas, as big as skyscrapers, beating on their chests with elephant drumsticks and screaming, "Give us meat; give us mates," followed modestly by ten thou-

sand walruses a thousand feet high, wearing battleships for boots, and the dome of St. Paul's for a cod-piece; armed in the one hand with shield-shaped Bibles fortified with brass spikes, and in the other with cross-headed clubs of blood rusty iron, hung with bleeding heads of infants, artists, etc., with which they beat up what is left of the grass, crying, "Come to mother, little worm, and let her pat your dear head and comb your sweet hair for you." (*HM*, 47)

This wild hyperbole with jumbled oblique allusion to Swift and King Kong has ironic overtones of Blake's *Songs of Innocence*, which treat of the sympathetic identification of children with lambs, of the benevolence of nature, of motherly protection, and of small creatures guided lovingly to their homes. The hyperbole is present to convey a complicated message: (1) I was quite depressed by this turn of events, (2) but, after all, what is one to expect from the real? Best to make a joke of it, (3) in fact, why not make it a really good joke, an artistic telling, an exuberance, (4) as a defense against, among other things, the spectral dull.

Another sort of hyperbole is present in Jimson's descriptions of other people. It is a means by which he keeps them distant from him, a learned protective device. I spoke in chapter 2 of Jimson's attitude toward Wilcher, his description of whom invokes the Blakean spectre. It goes:

A little grasshopper of a man. Five feet of shiny broadcloth and three inches of collar. Always on the jump. Inside or out. In his fifties. The hopping fifties. And fierce as a mad house. Genus Boorjwar; species Blackcotius Begoggledus Ferocissimouse. All eaten up with lawfulness and rage; ready to bite himself for being so respectable. (*HM*, 183)

Their conversation is then described in comic hyperbole, with appropriate mundane interpretation, as for example:

There was a short pause, while this news filtered through the loopholes of the blockhouse to Mr. W. within. Who then stood on one leg, put his finger in his ear and gave a loud halloo, followed by uproarious and uncontrollable laughter; that is to say, he wanted to do so; but being a respectable blackcoat, he could only place his hands together, press them so hard that they cracked, and remark, "In-deed." (*HM*, 184)

Jimson ridicules Wilcher's repressed personality by letting his own version of it out into language: "At this Mr. W. sprang clean through the ceiling, turned several somersaults in mid-air, sang a short psalm of praise and thanksgiving out of the Song of Solomon, accompanied on the shawm, and returned through the letter-box draped in celestial light" (*HM*, 184). A second "indeed."

Jimson admits that Wilcher got on his nerves. The hyperbole he employs is protection against his own rage. He decides deliberately not to bottle it up, but to give it artistic outlet. Jimson inflates many characters to these mock-epic proportions. This treatment has a parallel in his epic paintings, which in their own way seem to be efforts to overcome meaninglessness by imposition of a gigantic vision upon the real. The paintings, as described to us, are exuberances in the tradition of Blake. Jimson's activity and attitude in creating them are similar to his treatment of Wilcher. We notice, however, that Jimson tries not to exaggerate a grievance. He believes that a grievance ought to be dismissed by the discipline of hyperbolic gaiety. Even his belief that there is no meaning in the world is a sort of exaggeration contrived to justify the plight of the artist in it or, at least, his own fortunes.

I have mentioned Cary's treating Wilcher with pathos, but there is pathos here too, though masked by Jimson's voice. The relationship with Nosy Barbon is in the end touching. Jimson's usual device with people of whom he is suspicious, as in the case of Wilcher, is distancing. It is both aesthetic and defensive. The relationship with Nosy begins this way, but in the end we discover that Nosy has gotten through to Jimson and broken his defenses with a persistence as stubborn as Jimson's own. In treating this relationship, Cary humanizes Jimson, as he does also in the night scene with Plant. In the early meeting with Nosy, Jimson, who has given his career to art, is warning him against (or at least initiating him into) an artistic career. The irony is reversed here, because Jimson is actually making assertions he believes to be true, but from a point of view outside himself. Nosy's perplexity is clear in Jimson's comic descriptions of him as a horse and rabbit. A further twist is that Jimson believes nothing he can say to Nosy will deter the boy, in any case, since he regards the disease of art as irreversible.

Nosy has the disease. Yet Jimson feels that he must persist in the name of a reasonableness in which he does not believe. He does not want the appearance of responsibility for Nosy's decision. One can go on through the layers of this—to point out, for example, that Nosy's analysis of Jimson and his situation is fairly accurate and therefore insufferable to Jimson because he believes that if one dwells on it one can easily give way to a grievance.

We learn, in time, that Jimson has real affection for Nosy, though it would be a weakness, he thinks, to make a direct admission of it. Certainly it would be so against his habitual irony that we would be astonished to see it directly expressed. We might even distrust it, or Cary, if it were. Instead, we learn it indirectly when Jimson tries to calm Nosy's grief over the destruction of "The Fall," or when he comments approvingly on Nosy's having developed a talent for "commerce," i.e., Jimsonian creative larceny. One sees Jimson's capacity for affection even in his treatment of Alabaster, the critic, once he realizes Alabaster's developing talent for survival.

An early remark and a late one in Jimson's narrative provide a frame enclosing and defining all of his efforts. Their presence endorses Cornelia Cook's observation (p. 135) that Jimson's metaphor is "an extension of an inner dialogue which Gulley has carried on all his life." Early in the novel, he asserts that one must not give way to a grievance; and at the end he equates prayer with laughter. Then, almost in the center of the novel, we find, "on the whole, a man is wise to give way to gaiety, even at the expense of a grievance" (*HM*, 169). This is followed immediately by a typical reversal: "A good grievance is highly enjoyable, but like a lot of pleasures it is bad for the liver." Here Jimson tries to make over the world by claiming that gaiety is the fundamental *nature* in man. If it is not, it ought to be, and the *ought* of things is what the artist is about. Furthermore, as he tries to show, it is a *practical* belief, though not easy to hold in the face of the real.

This is the reason that Jimson's discipline is not perfect by any means. He advises us to look squarely at reality, but he makes some convenient omissions, of which we are aware from having read Sara's and Wilcher's books. He does not tell us that just before his meeting with Wilcher he has again punched Sara in the nose. He is quite oblique and secretive about his relations with women other than Sara. He tells us the minimum about his domestic past, and we discover that he has taken liberties with the truth about the past in his dealings with Sara. Finally, he is not able until the final vision of Sara to be entirely truthful with himself about his feelings for her, and even then the truth comes obliquely. Just as Sara thinks him the most of a man she ever met, so does he feel she is the most of a woman. He is faced with the same sort of dilemma Sara faces, but in reverse. As an artist, he must protect himself against her, while at the same time he desires her. He chooses his art.

But it is a perilous choice, and it ought to come as no surprise that his elaborate discipline, which includes a deliberate hyperbolic mythologizing of Sara as the terrible mother of "The Mental Traveller" (in addition to her role as the "virgin bright") breaks down at times. It breaks down in his wretched treatment of his patron Hickson, in his outrageous destruction of the Beeders' home, in his assaults on poor Nina, and finally in his fatal attack on Sara. It is not murder in the first degree. It is perhaps not quite murder in the second degree. It is probably manslaughter. It is inexcusable.

Yet it is interesting how often this attack with its terrible result is overlooked by readers and critics. Apparently many readers do not want to admit Jimson's guilt or his wrongness. They have been eager to accept Jimson's position up to this point and do not want their security jostled. One critic, M. M. Mahood, has gone so far as to find Jimson's killing of Sara gratuitous and not consistent with the novel as a whole (p. 23).

But Cary's intent is to jostle us. His whole trilogistic approach has been based on the idea of requiring us to look again, to adopt a sudden new perspective—a perspective that has been latent all along but made explicit only to hindsight. Surely Jimson's career leads to desperation. Surely, too, the violent act should not be premeditated; and surely, too, we should ask ourselves, as we so often do in tragedies, how to apportion the blame. But we should also learn here that apportioning blame is not the end of our task. Understanding is our destination, and with it a grasp of the dangers as well as the power of imagination. R. W. Noble (p. 67) says that when Jimson kills Sara, Cary shows the "moral limitations of Jimson's treating life as if it were all 'fodder' for his artist's imagination." This is part of it, but the statement is more reductive than it need be. It doesn't give attention to the specific case—to Jimson's desperation and the motive at the time. Jimson is not every artist. He is an individual with his own concerns touching individuals with theirs. He is in a fix. Jimson himself remarks, "If it wasn't for imagination . . . we shouldn't need any police or government" (*HM*, 226). This appears at first an overstatement, but it is worth a pause. Cary asserts in his own voice elsewhere that it is the existence of freedom, which he identifies with imagination, that requires government. Jimson is a sort of anarchist, but his irony is an effort at self-government. But behavior as imaginative and disciplined as Jimson's may of itself become compulsive and take itself too seriously. This is to say that although Jimson's is a more intense form of consciousness than Wilcher's, as Wilcher's is more intense than Sara's, it would be a mistake to conclude that this gets Jimson off the hook, that he is therefore a better person. *The Horse's Mouth* comes at the end of a long tradition of almost two centuries in which one of the archetypes of fiction has been the artist as hero. Indeed, Gulley Jimson may mark a turning away from this tradition; Cary is by no means debunking the artist in Jimson. He respects him, but sees his isolation and compulsions without sentiment. He sees that the imagination is always mixed up with a recalcitrant real. That mixture can be a damnation as well as a means of grace, and the imagination is implicated in both.

This mixture, which Cary treats as a tragic balance, is always perilous; and in one of Jimson's final acts, in which he carries on a dialogue with his final imaginative projection of Sara, the novel keeps that balance finely. (In the remarks I make about these acts I am in the debt of suggestions made to me by Professor James B. Meriwether.) When in the pub, near the end of the novel, Jimson hears that Sara has died in hospital, he does not yet know that Sara has given a deliberately and wildly inaccurate description of her assailant. He goes at once to his wall to paint. He believes that the police will soon come for him, so he refuses to waste a moment. Jimson's narration here begins with an admission that he is extremely upset by Sara's death, though this distress is expressed, as usual, with a sort of impudence. Here the impudence is even more full of tension than we are by now used to. Jimson's effort to make a joke of it, so to speak, has reached its limit, and it seems tasteless, thus pointing up the stress on Jimson himself:

> Boo-hoo, I cried, putting a little more cobalt on the shadow side; and I didn't know whether I was more upset about Sara or the whale. (*HM*, 288)

And:

> I'm raising up some nasty difficulties, I said, with a great sob, probably for Sara. But who cares? Boo-hoo. There's no doubt I'm damned upset about Sara. (*HM*, 288)

Finally:

> Boo-hoo, there's a tear on my palette. Who would have thought I could cry a tear as big as a halfpenny? At sixty-eight for a battered old helmet like Sara Monday. (*HM*, 289)

This is, of course, Jimson recounting the episode and, I think, struggling with his emotions as he does.

In this scene, as Jimson persists in painting, a vision of Sara comes to him—nearly a hallucination—and he engages in a dialogue with this imagined Sara. What he says himself is fully in character. The words he gives to Sara are those of a loving and loyal woman who cherishes him in her way, despite what he has done to her. What is important here is that, without yet knowing that Sara has lied to the police, his imagination has created a vision of the *real* Sara, who, it turns out, *was* loyal to him, to the real Jimson as she saw him, not the desperate and violent creature who at the end killed her. So it may be said that this last vision of Sara is the truth of Sara, or part of it, from the horse's mouth, that is to say, the creative imagination, not from the frightened fugitive bent on self-protection. Art here has discerned the actuality of love and recreated it in the imagined conversation that Jimson carries on with Sara. This is finally as much of a triumph for art over the coldly rational as Cary will allow, for art and love face always the real and face it, as the lines from Blake state, alone.

As the novel proceeds toward its conclusion, this struggle of art with the real, or more precisely this artist with the real, is expressed in a deeply ironic way by Jimson's description of his last perceptions before he is toppled from his painter's swing into a blanket held by "six art enthusiasts or friends of democracy." In that moment Jimson turns what is left of "The Creation" into a last judgment of the world upon his art. As the wall and his painting fall away from him,

> [T]here was a noise like a thousand sacks of coal falling down the Monument, and then nothing but dust; a regular fog of it. I couldn't believe it, and no doubt I was looking a little surprised with my brush in my hand, and my mouth open, because when the dust began to clear I saw through the cloud about ten thousand angels in caps, helmets, bowlers, and even one top hat, sitting on walls, dustbins, gutters, roofs, window sills and other people's cabbages, laughing. That's funny, I thought, they've all seen the same joke. (*HM*, 295)

He sees them laughing at him, and then he says, his wall destroyed, that he'll "come quietly," for he wants at once to find a new studio and a new opportunity to paint the whale right. He will never do so, of course, for he has suffered a stroke. Cary has said that you yourself are part of your own real. Surely this is shown to be true of Jimson, who, it turns out, needn't have tried to rob Sara of her drawing, for only minutes afterward the idea of copying his own painting in the Tate presented itself to him. Nor was it against the coming of the police that he had to paint recklessly that last night, for (as his own imagination was to tell him) Sara did not betray him.

Each of the speakers of the trilogy has power. Sara makes and remakes, Wilcher journeys to a sort of grace, Jimson gets on with his job. It is perhaps not too noticeable that in the very last words of his memoir Jimson uses the verbal artist's ultimate power. He employs a metaphor identifying the art of laughter with prayer and, by implication, the good. In the early parts of the novel where Jimson, walking along the Thames, experiences the real once again after imprisonment, it appears that nature is simile-prone, a heterogeneous pile of rubbish, including likenesses without meaning. As Oscar Wilde remarked, nature tries, but can't quite bring it all off. Jimson moves through simile to attempt the metaphor:

> Sun in a mist. Like an orange in a fried fish shop. All bright below. Low tide, dusty water and a crooked bar of straw, chicken-boxes, dirt and oil from mud to mud. Like a viper swimming in skim milk. The old serpent, a symbol of nature and love. (*HM*, 11)

Some of Jimson's metaphors are for the better, some for the worse. Adding it all up, and recognizing the dangers that Cary has put before us, I think his last metaphor is for the better:

> "I should laugh all round my neck at this minute if my shirt wasn't a bit on the tight side."
> "It would be better for you to pray."
> "Same thing, mother." (*HM*, 297)

Even here, though, a slyness. The real has always been a bit small and cramped—a bit on the tight side—for Jimson. So his laughter would not after all stretch quite around the neck, being the bitter gaiety of the heroic artist as that tradition reaches its culmination.

5

Second Trilogy

The *Second Trilogy* culminates in a situation in which the facts are not clear. In the case of Special Constable Maufe's attempted arrest of the communist strike leader, Pincomb, we simply do not know what the facts are. In spite of Cary's method, this is unusual in his trilogies. Sara Monday did *steal* from Tom Wilcher; Wilcher did make a nuisance of himself with young women. True, we do not know for certain whether he burned down 15 Craven Gardens, but that act does not have the importance of the outcome of the Maufe trial. We would like to know the facts with respect to Maufe's guilt or innocence, because the account of that trial has played on our emotions.

But in withholding that information Cary's design is clear enough. He forces us to look elsewhere for important issues, and he insists that we stand in relation to the facts in the same way that the narrators have to stand. They cannot all stand in the same place. Even eyewitnesses to what happened were in crucially different places vis-à-vis the actual event, and this, as well as perhaps prejudice, affected their testimony. Cary never says there are no facts, but he points up—by frustrating us—the difficulty of ascertaining them and interpreting them if we come to know what they are. We are irritated, angered, anxious, and uncertain about how to react to Maufe's conviction. This is complicated by Jim Latter's definite response, but we have ample reason not to trust Latter's judgment, even though we may be tempted to sympathize with him on this particular matter. In any case, we have our own deep feelings about justice which affect what we would like to believe; but then the whole *Second Trilogy* continually makes us draw back from easy acceptance of what we might like to believe, whatever that might be. Cary seems always to be telling us to *look again* and to question our own responses.

Prisoner of Grace

In *Herself Surprised*, Sara Monday muses on how at her trial the facts were added up in ways surprising to her, but she does not go on to deny the truth of these sums. However, they do not have the same moral meaning for her that they seem to have for the judge. In *Prisoner of Grace*, Nina Woodville Latter (formerly Nimmo) has an entirely different notion of facts and their meanings, and she has developed this different notion from her experience in politics. In a working note about the novel, Cary reminded himself (*OC*, Box 288) of "Background   the universal political position—the necessary management of human nature and human beings all different and all trying to make their own lives in their own way—not always selfishly but individually." In this complicated political world the wrong inferences are often drawn, and these wrong inferences can themselves become facts with which to deal. Also, facts become material to use to establish power. Among the complications are, first, that facts are not all available, and, second, that inferences passed on by others often corrupt knowledge.

Nina's book is an attempt to be "fair," as she says, to Chester Nimmo and to the truth as she sees it. The problem of the truth is far more difficult in the *Second Trilogy* than in the *First* because Cary is concentrating in the *Second* on politics. The three narrators of the *First Trilogy* are not self-consciously "political" people. Sara Monday has a sort of shrewd political cunning, but it is more instinctive than self-conscious. Tom Wilcher by his own admission has little political acumen, and Gulley Jimson is anarchistic and deliberately impolitic. But the political is in the forefront of the *Second Trilogy*, and the characters reflect this: Chester Nimmo is, of course, a professional politician, Jim Latter is a political naif, and Nina Latter is someone drawn into politics by marriage. The traditional triangle of love and jealousy that these three form is, of course, political at the level of marriage itself; Cary was careful to indicate in the Carfax preface to *Prisoner of Grace* that politics is not government but the "art of human relations" (*PG*, 5) and therefore includes marriage.

In spite of the self-assurance and frankness with which Nina tells of her intimate life with Nimmo and Latter, with respect to our sympathy the narrators of the *Second Trilogy* are at a greater distance from us than those of the first. In the *First Trilogy* we desire to overcome our disapproval or dislike of the narrators. Often we must look again to remind ourselves of their weaknesses because each is an engaging character in some pleasantly surprising way. (This is least true of Tom Wilcher, but true to some extent nevertheless.) In the *Second Trilogy* the situation is reversed. Much of this is due to Nina Latter's narrative, to her amazing frankness, and to the concentration in the trilogy on the dominant personality of Chester Nimmo. The *Second Trilogy* is much more concentrated on Nimmo than the *First* is on any one character, and Cary reminds himself of this in working notes (*OC*, Box 287): "Chestercentral" and "Chestercharacter central." But though Nimmo is the dominating character, and we are so often looking *through* Nina's language to get at the real Nimmo, inferring what his point of view is, Nina gets in the first word, and it is a strong one. Cary was much concerned with making her consistent, even in her inconsistency. Sara Monday's statement directs us to *To Be a Pilgrim* and *The Horse's Mouth*. There the thrust is upward toward the end. The opposite is the case in the *Second Trilogy*. From Nina's narrative the course is downward to a tragic denouement that one critic has called anticlimax, despite the enthusiasm of Nimmo's memoir. *Prisoner of Grace* has so played on our conflicting emotions that in spite of *Except the Lord* we have to remind ourselves of the good in these people. Our distaste dominates—more so than Cary in his retrospective preface allows.

Readers must be prepared to find a depressing tale, in the telling of which Cary takes immense chances with us and asks us to take immense chances with ourselves. In Nina he presents us with a narrator strictly honest with us (except that we may have reason to doubt that she is always truthful about her age). The crisis we face is that her honesty with us seems in certain ways to conflict with her treatment of Nimmo and Latter, though dishonesty is not the right word to describe this behavior. We cannot like her, but we are supposed to believe her and to understand (but not necessarily accept) her "political" behavior with her men.

Something repellent emerges from the situation she is in and envelops her or throws certain of her qualities into a harsh light. I have remarked how certain expressions of freedom in the *First Trilogy* become compulsive and imprisoning. There is at least the appearance of compulsive repetition in Nina's story. It is more complicated than the compulsive behavior in the *First Trilogy*. If we stand back far enough, Nina appears to be making the same mistake over and over. She keeps failing to leave the man she does not love and claims to have come to hate. But she herself asks us to take a closer look at this matter. Her point is that her decision is never the same decision, because the configuration of events is different every time and requires an entirely new judgment without a steady precedent. She notes that for Nimmo every day was a turning point, an entirely new situation. (For this reason they lived in perpetual tension and excitement.) It is Cary's principal rule of politics that nothing repeats itself. Nina quickly learns that she is involved in a political situation with her husband. She finds always a deeper moral choice to be made beneath the apparent one.

Her problem is a familiar one, about which tragedies have frequently been written: Her sense of commitment and fairness as a wife to Nimmo is in conflict with her long sexual and emotional attachment to Latter. The interesting aspect of Cary's approach to this conflict is that he treats it as a political problem. It is not a matter of inexorable fate or a struggle against a fixed eternal tyranny. It is a tragedy in which freedom plays its ambiguous role and responsibility rests with the actors themselves. A free choice, or at least a relatively free choice, can lead to imprisonment in the decision made. Nina is unable to make an absolutely final decisive act in one direction or the other, because for her there is at every moment a complication preventing it. So, most of the time she attempts a perilous political balance. As readers we are tormented by this from the time of the crucial scene with Nimmo in the railway station, where the issue is made clear. We want her to exert her power of freedom, and we are tempted to regard her continual return to Nimmo as masochistic compulsiveness. On the other hand, in spite of ourselves (and I think this is why one reviewer called the book an "impertinent miracle") we must give credence to the notion that her behavior arises out of commitment to fairness and the sense that her life with Nimmo is important, that his work has significance beyond them both, and that in the relationship she can exercise her power for good on a greater stage. But when we do see this we have to cope with our distaste for Nimmo. It is a distaste that she has created for us by the nature of her "defense" of him. And we are further tempted to accuse her, particularly if she does feel loyalty to Nimmo, of a depraved passion for Latter that is almost sadistic. Finally, we have to decide why, in the light of what we learn about Latter, she should be so passionately attached to him. In much of this Cary trusts to our own experience of life. People like Latter are attractive to some women, who perhaps should know better. We all know of situations of this sort. The interesting thing here is that Cary doesn't stop to examine this matter thoroughly in *Prisoner of Grace*. It would be out of character for Nina to treat the matter in the depth required. Cary asks us to assume it as a fact and look elsewhere for significance. In *Not Honour More*, however, things are made to come clearer through Latter's odd focus.

But nothing of what I have said is accurate enough. We must look closer, and the place to begin is the title. Cary brings us up sharp with his very broad use of the word "grace," as broad as his meaning for "politics." He writes about this in his retrospective preface to the novel: "[G]race is not a rare and strange visitor from the mysterious depth of things, invoked only by a special exercise, it is an influence as common as the weather and persistent as the heart muscle" (*PG*, 7). For Cary it is a quite natural thing invoking the moral dimension of experience:

> A man who thinks of himself as an agnostic or, even an atheist, will declare, "I hate cruelty," and explain his disgust by saying that he is getting rid of anything like grace by calling his feeling natural. (*PG*, 7)

But he is not. Nina is not a particularly religious person, but she does have grace in her notion of fairness. This is what lies behind her decision to write the truth about Nimmo, which of course has to become the truth about her and Latter and others—the truth about a "political" situation. Her sense of the fair is also what is behind her inability to make a final break with Nimmo, even though she knows it might mean her life. It is not Nimmo who imprisons her but her own sense of duty to fairness.

But this does not mean that she *can* be totally fair to Nimmo or fair to Latter. Nor does it mean that she has a purely altruistic motive in her decision to write. Nor does it mean that her desire to defend herself (be fair to herself) invalidates her statement. One of the things we learn from this trilogy, if we didn't already know, is that political decisions are rarely one-dimensional in motivation and that what is self-seeking may also be altruistic. Of course, the moral dangers here are also pointed up.

In particular, Nina is writing because she anticipates a hostile book about Nimmo from her daughter Sally and Sally's husband, Henry Bootham, long Nimmo's secretary. She is afraid that the anticipated attack on Nimmo's character, and on her own, "will be believed simply because nowadays everyone believes the worst of a famous man" (*PG*, 9). This sense of anxious urgency is expressed again at almost the center of the novel (*PG*, 215–16) and at the end (*PG*, 399), where the threat of Bootham and Sally is mentioned. Nina emphasizes her fear that she herself will be described as "the cause of their separation from the great man and of all the scandals which have 'fallen on his name at the end of a life which should have nothing but honors from the people to whom it was devoted'." (The quotation Nina makes is from Sally's accusatory letter to her, and it certainly seems from Sally's words that the feared attack will be more against her than against Nimmo.) Nina knows that Bootham and Sally have a point if they want to pursue it, for Nina did divorce Nimmo after it appeared certain to her that his political career was over. So Nina is also defending herself. We need not be surprised at this. The question is: Does this get in the way of her fairness as a commentator on events, which might be quite different from her fairness as an actor in those events? She would probably be the first to admit that it does, and the admission might be a self-indulgence.

But the most important statement of Nina's reason for writing is the one at the middle of the book:

> [W]hat I am trying to do in this book is not to make out that Chester was a saint (which would be stupid, after all the books and articles about him) but to show that he was, in spite of the books, a "good man"—I mean (and it is saying more than could be said of most people) as good as he could be in his special circumstances, and better than many were in much easier ones. (*PG*, 215–16)

This remark suggests that as she has written, she has become involved in her subject in a somewhat less self-serving way. All along, it turns out, she does not spare herself. She really wants to be fair to the idea of fairness, and this requires making a clean breast of the situation. Her special capability for this sort of thing has, however, its own not necessarily attractive aspect.

Normally, what we would expect here is a whitewash. The first few lines of the book look like the beginning of one, but it is never produced. Instead we have a complicated account by what Cary

himself called a "brackety" mind (*PG*, 8). It can always see a qualification and make a parenthetical addition, for the sake of fairness.
This quality, which is displayed in the quotation above, is one of
the things that generates our confidence in Nina's account; it expresses her sense of responsibility. It is also a source of annoyance
to us because she reveals her own self-indulgence and makes no
apologies for it. This itself expresses a self-confidence born of the
security of her class; there is an element of exhibitionism in it as
well. Yet her sense of fairness, expressed in her willingness to see
several sides of an issue, is also due in part to her upbringing.

As she writes, her brackety mind draws her further and further
into the most personal revelations, because that mind realizes just
how much has to be said to make a fair explanation. Everything
becomes related to everything else, but not in a paranoid way that
turns everything into a single conspiracy. Nina is the very opposite
of the paranoid.

The specific situation—the "present" in which Nina writes—is
not revealed to us until the end of her account. This is typical of
Cary's method, which is periodically to require us to revise our perspective on everything we have read to a certain point. After an
alleged heart attack, Nimmo is ensconced in a downstairs room at
Jim and Nina Latter's Palm Cottage. Sally and Henry Bootham have
fallen out with Nina and with Nimmo. Jim Latter suspects that
something is going on between Nimmo and Nina, who is acting as
his secretary in the preparation of his memoirs. Only at the beginning of the last chapter do we learn that this situation has prevailed
for a year!

Now we discover that in spite of Latter's efforts to get rid of him,
Nimmo is taking greater liberties with Nina. On the day that the
Boothams have left, Jim confronts Nina about the situation. She is
afraid to say that she will turn Nimmo out:

> And I knew then I should never get rid of Chester, that I dared not
> do so. And I saw that it was no good pretending that I merely toler-
> ated an old man's whims because he was pitiful—I did not love
> Chester and I had never loved him, but now, more than ever, at the
> end of his life, I was in his power. When he fixed his eyes on me (it
> was perhaps the only time in a week that he even thought of me as a
> human being) and I felt myself shrink, I knew that he held me still
> with a thousand ties that I should never break—ties from a marriage
> of nearly thirty years that was all the more "part of me" because I
> had suffered in it. (*PG*, 400)

This older Chester Nina clearly dislikes. She presents him to us as a lecherous conniver, and she thinks him a little mad. We are forced to revise this estimate of him somewhat when we have read *Except the Lord*, and in particular her notion that he rarely any longer thinks of her as a human being. Yet she has not lied to us. She has misunderstood the old man's behavior, and she has had every right to do so.

In the picture she has drawn she has described a commitment from which she knows she cannot honorably extract herself further than she already has. She cannot say the final "no" to a whole lifetime. She cannot drive a wedge between present and past. In the scene in which Latter confronts her, she lies, denying anything between her and Nimmo. At least it is a lie from Latter's point of view. From hers it is also a lie but with the qualification that she has no love for Nimmo and does not respond to him sexually. That, of course, is not exactly what Latter is asking her, but it is what she sees as important in the situation. Still, she knows it is a lie. It leaves Latter at a complete loss. He cannot cope with her lie; he does not want to face the situation as it is, even though his suspicions drive him to discover it. We shall remember this and the fact that he endures the situation for still another year when we read *Not Honour More*, for it is meant to affect our attitude toward him. There is something preposterous about anyone's acceptance of the situation. It reflects badly on all three people for entirely different reasons in each case.

We shall remember Nina's lie when we discover that a lie plays an important role in *Except the Lord* and that in *Not Honour More* Jim Latter believes himself surrounded by lies, indeed, one big lie. And we shall recall another lie—the fiction of parenthood upon which Nina and Nimmo's marriage is based.

Nina's reporting of Latter's tactics in dealing with her lie is perceptive; Cary has made her a reliable witness to his nature:

> [H]e often comes upon us with no warning (but you can see by his face that each time he is in terror of what he may find—he will look round with his jaw set as if expecting an ambush) and with no excuse—simply to say good morning to Chester or to remark that I am not to forget some engagement. It is as though he said to himself, "I am not going to accept happiness from that woman at the cost of my honour. I know she is lying and deceitful, but I'm not going to connive at her tricks. I shall behave exactly as if she were honest, and if I catch her out, so much the worse for all of us." (*PG*, 401–2)

That Nina is accurate about Latter here is borne out by *Not Honour More*, and this endorses our sense that she is a dependable witness, or as dependable as we can possibly expect, though not a reliable narrator in Wayne Booth's sense of someone whose position is that of the author.

However, in the "present" of writing, Nina has made her decision to perpetuate the curious relationship with both men with a show of passivity that must not deceive us. She attempts a "political" solution, which like all such solutions solves nothing permanently but is a device to let life go on. This requires a lie or something near to a lie as so often politics requires something near to a lie. In this case, she believes that, given her decision, it is a lifesaving (or prolonging) lie, for she believes that if Latter knows the truth he will kill her or Nimmo. In the past, in moments of crisis with Latter, when they have been at odds, she has become silent and passive as if she were prepared to endure his violence. In *Not Honour More*, Latter has a term for this. He calls it "going mule," and it torments him, for he has no way to respond but to assault and perhaps kill her. In the matter of the lie, however, the pattern does not hold, because she is not silent, though almost:

> "Tell me the truth," he said in quite a soft voice. "What have you been up to?"
> My mouth was so dry that I could only whisper that I had done nothing.
> "You mean absolutely nothing? You mean that Bootham is making it up?"
> I nodded my head; and Jim shook my wrists as if to bring me to myself, but without hurting me.
> "I want the truth this time," he said. "You've got to tell the truth. Do you mean that there's nothing in it—on your soul and honour?"
> I nodded again, but Jim shook my wrists and told me to say the words, "I swear—by Almighty God—that this is the truth."
> So I said the words, and then Jim, all at once, appeared at a loss.
> (*PG*, 401)

Not to "go mule" and instead to lie is a political decision here for Nina, and Latter cannot grasp what has happened. He does not have any notion of Nina's motive, he does not want to have to accept the truth, but he is suspicious of her response. I am now going to call that response only a near-lie because from her point of view she has really been up to nothing but merely enduring Nimmo's behavior without what one would call participation. This distinction would, of course, be far too fine for Latter. It is the situation in Latter's mind and Nimmo's unpredictable "attacks" on her when they work together on the memoirs that make her life more complicated than ever before.

Now, even though lies in politics are sometimes necessary, they are still lies. By her own admission, Nina hates politics. Her political solution, even to herself, has an ominous quality, as the last line of the novel indicates: "and Jim can only shoot me dead" (*PG*, 402). In one of her moods she seems to regard politics as something she has unluckily found herself in. But it didn't just happen suddenly. She has acted in response to a whole series of events individually as they have occurred. Each of these events has been unique. She has had to do the best that she could in each moment. She has now chosen a compromise that she thinks has required a lie, given the sort of reason that she is dealing with. Cary has never said that lies are right, but he has said that there are situations in which they seem to be the best of a bad choice. In an essay in which he deals with this problem, he remarks,

> Before we call any statesman a fool or a crook, we should ask what problems he faced, what kind of people he had to handle, what kind of support he got, what pressure he withstood, what risks he took.
>   But our final question will still be: "Was he an honest man?" (*SE*, 232)

Cary sees situations in which a politician decides it is his moral duty to lie. It is always a gravely dangerous decision.

We can see that Nina knows this. She more than *knows* it; she *feels* it in the dryness of her mouth. Her decision is tied to a whole series of previous free choices, not to a series of events leading inexorably in a certain direction, as in *Oedipus*. The choices all along the way have been free, and fate has engineered nothing.

We may quite reasonably ask why on earth Nina thinks she must endure Nimmo, particularly given her hatred of him; but her conscience tells her that her hatred is beside the point. It would not be fair to invoke it as a reason to break with him. She has come a long way in the understanding of politicians, what it takes to be one, and what their needs are. In an early version of *Power in Men*, Cary made a number of remarks about politicians that were designed to make the reader acknowledge certain requirements for the job. They are worth looking at here because one of the resistances to the *Second Trilogy* has been a distaste for Nimmo as a politician. If Cary is right, we have to be prepared to be more sympathetic with Nina's loyalty to Nimmo, sorely tried as it is: "The essential work of government, the making of decisions, needs a certain kind of man, the practical, the improvising, and attracts only the lover of power. And this is not a condition that will pass" (*OC*, Box 200). The Nimmo we don't know yet, the Nimmo of *Except the Lord*, knows the danger of power, learning it early in his dealings with the labor agitator, Pring, with whom he broke.

Nimmo also seems to fit the following observation:

> [T]he politician is very acutely aware of his task, which is to manage people, to persuade them if they can't be forced. He spends most of his time in the enquiry, not is it in fact true, is this act right? But is this the right time to get what I want, is this the best method of pushing my policy, who have I got to fear, and how shall I placate them, or put them in the wrong. He is a practical man aiming at certain results, which are to be obtained only by a mixture of contrivance and force, and by a close study of human nature, especially on its weaker sides.
>
> Further such men are absolutely necessary in politics. (*OC*, Box 200)

Cary goes on in another expunged remark to observe that scholars, idealists, and scientists shouldn't be entrusted with political authority.

If Nina must not abandon Nimmo, then why can she not break honestly with Latter? Robert Bloom is not alone in thinking she has been less than fair to him. The first reason is emotional: her long, passionate, stormy relationship to him and the bond of sexuality between them. The second reason is practical: He may well kill her if she does break with him, and probably Nimmo too. What would become of Latter then, or of any other survivor? Besides, she wants to live.

The penultimate paragraph of the novel is crucial and easy to misread by only half-reading it:

> But how could I make him [Jim] understand that it is because that happiness is so precious to me I dare not turn Chester out. For I should know I was committing a mean crime against something bigger than love. (*PG*, 402)

(The last phrase, "something bigger than love," we shall remember when Jim Latter utters a similar phrase with quite a different meaning in *Not Honour More*.) There are two motives in her behavior here, as there so often are in the political acts Cary presents to us. The first is not attractive. It is her desire to keep their passions at a high pitch by maintaining excitement: "Jim has never before been so much in love" (*PG*, 402). It is surely this element that causes Robert Bloom to observe: "The closing scenes grow out of an intolerable acquiescence and strike a note of authentic depravity," which for him calls in question Nina's whole "liberated ethic" (p. 128). I hope I shall be able to show that this is but one aspect of Nina's situation and character, though certainly an aspect. There is an interesting parallel here between Nina and Nimmo. She speaks of him earlier in the novel as thriving on excitement and tension and creating it when it is absent, and she describes the period of Latter's return from his regiment, when the three are much together, as a time of "special tension . . . and tension is itself exciting all round" (*PG*, 80). When we observe Nimmo at the end of the novel, tired and politically defeated, we notice that excitement and tension are still a need for him and that he seeks them compulsively— partly in the smaller political arena of the triangle with Nina and Latter. It is the form without the content of his earlier significant political acts. Suddenly, here at the end of the novel, we see that some part of Nina—a small part perhaps (for she repudiates it finally in *Not Honour More*)—requires the same tension, out of the habit of thirty years and out of a narcissistic pleasure she seems always to have had from the attention of men. She identifies this tension with Latter's love for her. It is a tragic example of freedom turning into imprisonment as it becomes habit, a situation we noticed in chapter 1 as a possibility in Cary's view. It is a curious irony, for we recall the argument that Nimmo's dreadfully unpleasant physician uses on Nina to influence her return to him earlier in the novel. He argues that a disruption in their sexual life will wreak havoc on Nimmo's uncertain health, arrogantly reducing Nina to little more than a common sexual object. The old Nimmo whom Nina describes is repulsive physically and in his compulsive, cold sexuality, which leads him to take the risks he does. We see that there is a parallel in Nina's desire to maintain excitement. The behavior of both seems to be a decadent parody of the excitement of their political career together.

The second motive, however, is admirable, though we recognize an irony in it. Nina knows that she cannot be happy with Latter if she is unfaithful to a commitment to Nimmo that is the product of a huge number of individually unique decisions made over the years. There is something admirable, and also terrible, about the honesty of her admission that it is her own happiness that is at stake here: She really wants to be alone with Jim, who excites and satisfies her sexually, while Nimmo never has. But she knows her happiness must be based on an ethical principle of fairness and loyalty.

We need not like or approve of Nina. There is ample reason to think her quite impossible, even as we recognize her wit and insight and, of course, her physical beauty. What we are expected to acknowledge and base our judgment on is that every decision she makes is a new one in a unique situation and cannot be judged by reference to previous ones, except that previous ones are part of each new unique situation. Her past with Nimmo affects all that she sees about her in the present of her writing.

Nina's earliest decisions she thinks not entirely her own in the way that the later ones are. She was young and inexperienced when she found herself pregnant, and she thinks of herself as having been manipulated into marriage with Nimmo by Aunt Latter, her guardian. But Cary allows that even these early events are products of her decisions, no matter how unprepared she was to make them. Nina speaks of Jim Latter's "coming to my room or taking me to his" when they were quite young, but she had to have acquiesced in this. Jim puts the responsibility for these early dalliances on her in *Not Honour More*. Even in *Prisoner of Grace* Nina quotes him as saying, "You were a funny kid, Nina. You did what you liked with me, didn't you?" (*PG*, 78). Neither is quite right, and neither is morally practical, because they don't accept responsibility for their free actions. Nina as a young woman accepted Nimmo even if she chose to be passive in the act. This choice was comparatively innocent, but Cary insists on freedom and responsibility even in innocence. There is no escape from the consequences, and laying blame elsewhere does no good.

The first major decisive act of the novel, which is not encumbered by the problem of innocence, occurs not when Nina passively accepts Nimmo, or even when she tries to be "a good wife," but when she decides first to leave him for Latter and then decides freely against this course of action. The scene is the one at the railway station. She treats the episode as Nimmo's "victory" over her, and she even sees him acting like a victor, but the truth is that a second victor is her sense of fairness.

The events immediately leading up to that decision begin in chapter 22. Latter has returned on leave from his regiment, and Nimmo invites him to their home. The act seems oddly impolitic to Nina (and to us); Nina explains Nimmo's behavior by saying that he had just been defeated in an election and was feeling particularly religious, as he usually did when his "ambition had been frustrated" (*PG*, 67). This is unkind and unfeeling (though partly right) because Nina does not understand or sympathize with Nimmo's religion. One of the problems some critics have had with Nimmo is the one Nina has here. Another is lack of sympathy with politicians. Charles Hoffman reveals this when he says (p. 132), "Though he married Nina knowing she was pregnant (by Jim Latter) in order to further his political ambitions, he is fond of her and needs her." Hoffman distrusts Nimmo and cannot admit Nimmo loves her, in spite of the fact that Nimmo says he does, that Nina acknowledges he does, and even Latter recognizes that he does. Some critics do not want to accept either Nimmo's language of love or the possibility that his act might have two motives. Jack Wolkenfeld (p. 183) has less trouble than most but still some, with the double motive: ". . . in Nimmo it is impossible to disentangle the sincere from the self-centered." This implies 1) that something self-centered cannot be sincere, and 2) that something sincere must be altruistic. Cary, on the other hand, accepts the double motive; something self-centered can also be sincere—and altruistic. In dwelling on this, perhaps we appreciate better why Cary says that scholars should never be trusted with political power (though this statement disappeared from *Power in Men* in revision). In any case, in his Carfax preface to *Prisoner of Grace*, he tries to point out (*PG*, 6) that Nina's selfishness does not automatically cancel out her moral sense.

Religion is a matter of embarrassed misunderstanding between Nina and Nimmo from the beginning. It is tied up with their difference in class: Nina is Church of England; Nimmo is Chapel. Nimmo becomes more religious in adversity because he believes in the appropriateness of such behavior; that is, in part, what religion is for. She suspects this sort of behavior since it seems to be a search for solace, and she suspects him of a political motive in inviting Latter to their house. But Nimmo never rejects a political act because it is both moral *and* convenient. In fact, he does what he does for multiple reasons which in his mind are one. He believes the situation between Nina and Latter must be confronted rather than avoided. Otherwise there would be a "lie in the soul." He quite rightly believes that a politician cannot evade the real. A positive act can be a moral one, an evasive act never. To invite Latter to his house was also for Nimmo an act of common kindness and family duty.

Nina treats it at first as a "confidence trick": "We are to stop Jim from doing any more damage by trusting him not to" (*PG*, 68). But Nimmo really does see it as a moral question, and he is quite consistent even at the expense of his peace of mind, in leaving Latter and Nina free to act (which they unfortunately do). Nimmo also acts on the *feeling* of what is right; Nina comes to feel it, too:

> Chester said this in his thoughtful and "convinced" manner, and the moment he spoke I *felt* how right he was, so that I was even surprised at my own small-mindedness. I was ashamed of myself. It seemed to me that Chester's "grand" gesture was only another proof of something not merely "imaginative" and "theatrical" in his character, but true, for he had seen the plain truth of Jim's unhappiness where I had simply overlooked it.
>
> And as for the "confidence trick" (so often made an accusation against Chester with his "trust the people"), what did it mean? That Chester really did believe in trusting people? Perhaps he took advantage of his faith when it seemed the best policy for him, but still it was his true faith, at least at the time. (*PG*, 68)

This unity of feeling, morality, thought, and political expediency Nina comes to understand here; but as the last phrase suggests, there is always a residue of suspicion. It is not her way. She does not hear, or thinks she does not hear, the true voice of feeling on which Nimmo's whole ethic is based. She tries as hard as she can to be fair to it as his way. Indeed, in a sense, she does hear that voice in the railway station and repeatedly thereafter, but it is a voice that speaks in a style quite unlike Nimmo's nonconformist voice, which embarrasses her when she hears Nimmo use it. For example, his mixing religion into their sexual lives is to her both laughable and vaguely repulsive, an impiety:

> I had been a little startled on our first night together to hear him murmur (but we were both so nervous at the time that I was not sure if I had heard him properly or if he knew what he was saying) some-

thing like a prayer for God's blessing on our union, which seemed to me so comical at such a moment that I had almost laughed. But luckily I was so shy of him it was only afterwards I realised that he had really meant to pray and that what he had meant by our "union" was just what I had thought so unsuitable for prayer. I was, I think, even a little shocked. (*PG*, 26–27)

Nina's response to Nimmo's explanation of why Latter should be welcome she describes as a passive acquiescence in the face of his arguments, though with foreboding; for she has little trust in either Latter or herself. She understands Nimmo's position, but she does not quite feel the tension in him over it. He *believes* that he must act as he does; the moral and practical are one for him here, but that does not mean he is naïve about the risks. His behavior is in contrast to that of Latter at the end of the novel, who does not trust anyone and keeps coming upon Nina and Nimmo suddenly, expecting the worst, but afraid to find it.

Indeed, for a time Nimmo's tactics work: "For it had seemed to us all that we had found a new kind of social being in which, simply by the exercise of Christian virtues (forgiveness, mutual sympathy, and the scorn of mean suspicion), we could all be not only happy but, as it were, exalted" (*PG*, 79–80). But it cannot last. Nina falls in love with Latter all over again. This renewed passion for Latter has a new and more strongly sexual character, and this is particularly important for two reasons. First, if Latter is incompetent in most things, he has become through his experience in India accomplished in lovemaking. Second, there is no reason to believe that Nina's sexual life with Nimmo has been satisfying. When she married him, he was sexually inexperienced and handicapped by his religious and social background. Nina's narrative leaves the impression that Nimmo, though in many ways attentive to Nina's desires, tended only to *use* her sexually and may even have been unaware of her own needs. In the passage in chapter 29 describing Latter's lovemaking to her in the garden after his return from India, Nina implies that for the first time she has received sexual fulfillment. After this, the bond between them is fundamentally strengthened. Latter, in his characteristic way, declares that after this she "belongs" to him (*PG*, 86). The contrast between the way Nina describes this experience and her reticence about her sexual relations with Nimmo makes clear a considerable difference. We can conclude that Nimmo's later "interference" with Nina, as Latter calls it

(*NHM*, 7), is an outrageous parody (as the late Nimmo is a parody of the earlier) of what has been implicit in their sexual relations from early in their marriage. That Latter's lovemaking in the garden produces a second child and Nimmo's never produces any seems to symbolize this view.

In Latter's mind it becomes a matter of honor for Nina to leave Nimmo. It is also in his mind a matter of ownership, so that although Nimmo's sexual behavior is that of a user, so to speak, Latter's eventuates in another sort of selfishness. Nina does attempt to bring herself to leave Nimmo at the railway station. In that crucial scene, Nina thinks of Nimmo, who has found her there waiting for a train, as trying to manage her. He is her "enemy." There is no doubt that Nimmo is trying to keep her with him, but she is so captured at this point by her sense of Nimmo as a conniver that she does not give any attention to the truth that Nimmo loves her and wants them both to do the right thing. Indeed, she resents this invocation of the "right":

> At this I felt a little throb of excitement or fear; I knew that there was going to be a battle. I looked at Chester and found him staring at me with that fixity which meant that he was plotting something and trying to spy out his ground—that is, the state of my mind. (*PG*, 91)

Nimmo's imagination is the enemy here, the very thing that has kept her attached to him. He appeals to her sense of what is right, to her sense of duty to their marriage—"our work together," he calls it (*PG*, 92). Nina is outraged at his remarks, which she takes as the old accusation of class difference: He says that he couldn't expect her to love him, that their differences of religion and class were too great, that her efforts to be a good wife were therefore even more admirable, that she "stooped" to him but didn't make it an insult. She hates the mention of stooping. It is a preying on her conscience, and she believes he uses the word only so it will have that effect. She understands his shrewdness, but has more trouble grasping his feelings.

In fact, Nina *has* been condescending to Nimmo, especially with respect to his religion, even as she tries to be fair to him and to it. Nimmo's remarks to her are quite accurate, from all the evidence of Nina's discourse. He believes neither she nor he can entirely escape their class upbringing, and she takes this as an accusation rather than the fact he regards it as being. Still, she has good reason to believe it is a contrivance to play on her conscience. What she doesn't grasp fully is that Nimmo thinks this is a perfectly legitimate thing to do, because he believes the conscience is free. After making his "speech" to her, he suddenly leaves her alone in the station with her own thoughts. She sees this also as a "confidence trick"—with a little trust in God added. It is perfectly in Nimmo's moral character, for even Nina remarks: "Freedom for Chester was the answer to every problem. It meant for him, Let God provide—don't get in His way" (*PG*, 83). Here it means specifically that he is allowing Nina to do what he would do—consult his own conscience, or let God provide.

So Nina stays with him. But she sees his behavior as a manipulation of her feelings; she refuses to acknowledge her own freedom. She blames fate: "It is really thoroughly unjust that I should have got mixed up with such an extraordinary person as Chester, who uses his religion to torture me and his class hatred to tie me to him till I can hardly breathe" (*PG*, 98). She remarks at this time that she saw clearly that Nimmo had destroyed "most of my happiness, and unless I was absolutely firm and rather hard he would wreck my life" (*PG*, 98).

The railway episode ends on this note. The next chapter begins with her acknowledgment that there is another view, wrong as it seems to her: "It has been said quite openly and it is passionately believed that I was Chester's ruin; that I not only 'corrupted' him morally but forced him into luxury and extravagance; that I divided him from his best friends and destroyed his religion" (*PG*, 98–99). Her own view and this one have one thing in common: They both assume that the individual is acted upon, is not an actor. In the light of the whole trilogy, both are wrong, morally mistaken. Ill fortune and the real are there to be dealt with, but it is the individual who is the responsible actor. Nimmo seizes on this notion, even to excess, and Nina finds him as a result always conniving. But he believes his impulse is right. Indeed, it is not easy to find any fault with his behavior at the railway station. It is all to his advantage (unless one thinks he is quite mistaken and would be better off without her), but it is all directed toward his conception of her own best interests as well as his. Even this is consistent with his belief in the institution of marriage, in which self-interest must be viewed jointly.

Nina has wanted to think that her feelings direct her to Latter and that her sense of duty to her marriage with Nimmo is something that Nimmo infuses in her by casuistry. Nimmo does not see it this way at all; for him duty is discovered through feeling. In her resistance Nina makes him a scapegoat for "persuading" her. But at the end of the novel she acknowledges "something bigger than love" that she never quite names, and she acknowledges that she is a prisoner of her own freedom to decide.

The moment of decision in the railway station is one of feeling. Nina observes of Nimmo elsewhere that he wrestled in prayer, that he was not acting when he did this but was in fact in a kind of agony. In the station she wrestles, but not in prayer. Nina is not particularly religious and does not pray deliberately to get help in solving a problem. But it is much the same thing. One is reminded of Cary's remark that an atheist will attribute to nature what a believer will attribute to grace.

> [W]hen I reached the door my feet stopped and turned me aside. I simply could not go out, and neither could I make up my mind to stay. I went a step to one side, and then came back to the door, but absolutely stuck there. I seemed to have no will to do anything, or rather I had two wills which were fighting inside me and tearing me apart. I can never forget the agony of that time, which must have lasted three or four minutes before the train went out. And really I think it was a kind of relief to me when at last it did so, for it made a decision for me. (*PG*, 95–96)

Of course, the train did not really make the decision.

This account may be contrasted to that of Sara Monday in *Herself Surprised* when she fails to carry out her plan to leave Gulley Jimson after Jimson's assault on her. Sara speaks of her hatred of Jimson and calls him a brute. She is saddened by the thought of returning to him. Unlike Nina, she does not return out of conscience, nor does she believe that she has been talked around by Miss Slaughter. She had, she admits, as good as sent for Miss Slaughter. Sara returns in order to try to maintain a home she has created, and she knows that she does it freely. She accepts responsibility and freedom. Cary makes this acceptance one of her attractive qualities. Also, in spite of her hatred, she is attracted to Jimson in a way that Nina never has been to Nimmo. Sara does not regard her behavior as ruled by conscience, and it is not. At once we see that the whole Nina-Nimmo relationship is much more cerebral. Nimmo's weapons, by which Nina believes he assaults her, are words. Jimson's are his fists. There is an irony in this which will come out later when Nimmo himself inveighs against the falsity of words.

The railway scene is the first major moment of unique decision for Nina, and she carefully delineates it, leading up to it for several chapters and then considering its aftermath. It is ever present thereafter as part of the real against which her later actions are taken. It has been preceded by her careful establishment of her youthful relationship with Jim Latter. A sort of enmity also existed between them from very early. As a child, when Latter beat her she would "stay limp and not say a word" (*PG*, 14), and he would burst out with invective against her which she would resent. The relation with Latter is established early in their lives, and it is one of passionate attachment that develops into a pattern of argument followed by reconciliation, complicated by growing sexual attachment. It is a "war to dominate each other or to stop being dominated" (*PG*, 12). When they are older they both bitterly resent that they did not marry, and they accuse each other of ill-treatment (*PG*, 38). One of these bouts leads to a confrontation between Latter and Nimmo in which Latter claims correctly that Nina's child is his.

This is a critical scene for a number of reasons. Before Nimmo appears, Latter behaves quite badly, accusing Nina of jilting him, only to have her respond that "he had preferred going to India and playing polo" to marrying her. Hearing Nimmo approach, he deliberately embraces Nina so that Nimmo will see them. Admittedly, this is not quite the "interference" of which Latter accuses Nimmo years later in *Not Honour More*. Nevertheless, Latter's act is deliberately impertinent and a declaration of ownership. By Nina's own account, Nimmo behaves with "great dignity" (*PG*, 39). After Latter has claimed Tom for his son, Nimmo says to Nina, "You needn't be afraid. I don't believe a word of this wild nonsense" (*PG*, 39). Latter responds with the absolute that characterizes him in *Not Honour More* that they all know the "facts." He is, of course, quite right about these facts, though he has never faced the facts of his behavior after Nina's pregnancy. Nimmo, once he is alone with Nina, will not accept the facts Latter insists on. I quote the passage at length because it is so important to the trilogy:

> Chester then looked at me with a sympathetic expression and said in an indignant tone, "I'm sure he hadn't the least excuse for such a suggestion—I mean that he had taken liberties with you."

I could only answer that, of course, he had taken "liberties"—as Chester knew.

"How could I know—no one told me. I had no reason in the world to suppose anything of the sort."

I was absolutely astonished by this declaration. I knew it had to be a lie, and if I had not I might have suspected so from the very cool way in which Chester made it.

I answered at once that, of course, he knew—he had arranged for Tom to be born abroad and for all the confusion about the announcements.

Chester had now changed his sympathetic expression for a peculiar look that I had not seen before—not so much "hard" as fierce. It seemed to say, "No nonsense, please—I won't stand it." There was a pause while he seemed actually to be letting me feel this threat.

Then he said in the same cool voice, "We both know very well that Tom was premature—the doctor himself can testify to that. And it was on the doctor's orders, too, that I took you abroad for your health." As soon as he said this he went out of the room.

I was left very angry and also rather frightened. I was quite astounded that the mild and loving Chester could dare to threaten me. (*PG*, 40–41)

Nimmo has acted quickly. He has refused to reject the fiction on which their marriage has been based and has invited Nina to refuse it as well. Then, in his view, all can go on as before. She wants the relationship clarified on the basis of a truth she has been unwilling to embrace at the outset. She thinks his attitude dishonest, though she conspired in it originally. He thinks the fiction necessary to their marriage, which he desired at the beginning in spite of her pregnancy. He desires to maintain the marriage because he thinks it is right. The fiction now has to be preserved for the sake of his career as well. Her sudden scruple about truth seems to him capricious and dangerous. The passage quoted above and what follows give Nina's view. We infer Nimmo's.

This is a classic example of the situation in which the politician—the true man of affairs—must improvise a workable solution or protect one already working. Both involve "as if" worlds. The problem is that if it is to work, everyone has to play. Suddenly Nina no longer wants to play, and Nimmo finds that he must regard her as a political problem. Their relationship changes. Aunt Latter understands some of this well enough. When Nina says she can't go on unless Nimmo acknowledges the facts, she replies: "Impossible? What's impossible?" (*PG*, 41). It is then we find out what the issue as Nina sees it is: "I mean that I can't live with a man who deliberately accuses me of the meanest kind of trick when he knows very well that I didn't deceive him at all" (*PG*, 41). But Nimmo has never accused her directly of deceiving him about her pregnancy. The truth of it was unspoken between him and Aunt Latter when the marriage was first arranged. He has always known and has never used the fact against her. He accepted the fiction when they were married, and Nina now insists on betraying it. On the other hand, Nina wants it betrayed only between them, but Nimmo's uncertainty about her, for which he has good reason, prevents him from facing that matter frankly *with* her. They have never been that close.

In the climax of this confrontation Nina accuses him of putting her in an impossible situation in which she can be accused any day of duplicity. But it is really her own conscience that accuses her. Nimmo has not and will not. He seeks to resolve the situation without destroying the fiction or at least by giving it a decent burial:

> And when he simply made no answer at all, I was so enraged by what I thought his impudence that I threw back the clothes and was trying to jump out of bed on the other side to run away from him, when he caught me by the arm and said in an anxious voice (but I thought it also sounded cunning), "I see now, of course, how you could make such a mistake. There were misunderstandings on both sides. Perhaps neither of us has been in a condition to face the truth. And as for blaming you for what had happened, that would be stupid as well as cruel." Then he went on describing my unhappiness, deserted by Jim, and how he had known that I was ill and unhappy and had taken advantage of it. This, he said, was a very great wrong, because he had done it deliberately, knowing that I did not love him. And so on. And then he excused himself on the ground that he had loved me so much. He said that if I could not forgive him, of course he could not ask me to go on as his wife, but that if I left him it would break his heart. (*PG*, 43)

At this moment, Nimmo never admits to the falseness of the fiction but does not quite deny it either. Most important, though, he is truthful about his feelings. Yet Nina thinks of it as a "speech" even as she is deeply affected by it against her own desires. She hates his "thrilling" evangelical voice, so alien to her class, though it is the vehicle of his power. She is astonished to see him, after this crisis, pray "against lies, and especially what he called the lie in the soul" (*PG*, 45). To her, the lie is his refusal to admit that Latter is Tom's father. To him, the lie is the far deeper one of only pretending to forgive. He seeks to be "born again every moment," which is to put both the lie and the truth behind them.

As we read, we discover that Cary is forcing us to look *through* Nina's account to infer Nimmo's true thoughts, feelings, motives, and actions; we discover that there is a silent novel behind Nina's that we are constructing. Our faculties are being roused to act, and the motive, beyond curiosity and abhorrence of a vacuum, is to be fair.

One has the impression of Nimmo's always being barely able to save the situation, which, one has to admit, sometimes appears not worth saving. That is from the outside, of course, and Cary wants the maximum act of sympathy from us—before we judge. In fact, Nina saves the situation as often as Nimmo does. After praying, he has praised her, and she remonstrates that he is quite wrong to call her forgiving. She is, she says, merely lazy and likes to be "comfortable in her mind." Therefore she hates mysteries. In the end she

> felt all that Aunt had said about Chester's special position and his goodness to myself; I saw why with his feeling of being surrounded by enemies (including myself) he was so careful about what he admitted even to me.
>
> It happened so suddenly that I was quite startled by my denseness before. It was, I suppose, just what Chester's chapel friends called a "conversion." (*PG*, 46–47)

But from this point onwards the situation between them is far more complicated and political, like a precarious treaty: "I knew now and could never forget that Chester, with all his affection, was playing a political game with me" (*PG*, 47). But she also recognizes that he is a man of unusual imagination who can enter into other people's feelings. Cary is asking his reader to exercise his own imagination by reading through to the real Chester Nimmo.

Nina recognizes also that he is subject to imaginary anxieties. Yet from our vantage point, Nina's behavior gives us reason to understand that to preserve his marriage Nimmo could well have thought he had to treat her more politically. In fact, he makes many concessions to her, hoping that they will improve the situation. Cary takes us through several of them to make the point: Nimmo gives in on Tom's schooling. True, it is after he is frightened by what appears to be a suicide attempt by Nina, and her death would of course hurt his career. That is the way Nina first reads it, but there is good reason to believe that he is genuinely devastated; he is clearly devoted to her. He is consistently anxious about her. He also relents and finds a way to make it possible for Latter to return from Africa, where he had to go to escape his creditors. True, he had helped to see to it that Latter left the country, but this seemed to be in everyone's interest at the time. We observe a marriage in which the early political settlements, one an unspoken fiction, are thought by Nimmo to be mutually protective. The later settlements fall into the class of treaties between forces with different interests. Nina knows that she is being treated politically and resents it; Nimmo knows he is acting politically and hopes good will come of it. What he cannot deal with fully is the intransigent real in the person of Jim Latter and Nina's even greater sexual passion for him. In the end, of course, it is everyone's nemesis.

Nimmo's involvement in politics is an education to Nina because she comes to realize, as she does about Nimmo's relation to her, that there are many ways to see a political situation. She has had to come to terms with the language of political behavior, the accusations, and the fiction that plots exist. She has observed that Nimmo's acts always seemed to have more than one explanation:

> It was at this time I began to feel among "political" people the strange and horrible feeling which afterwards became so familiar to me (but not less horrible), of living in a world without any solid objects at all, of floating day and night through clouds of words and schemes and hopes and ambitions and calculations where you could not say that this idea was obviously selfish and dangerous and that one quite false and wicked because all of them were relative to something else. The lies were mixed up with some truth (like Chester's belief in a class plot), and the selfish calculations (like Goold's planning to make trouble at Lilmouth) melted at the edges into all kinds of "noble" ideals (like Chester's passion for freedom and free speech). (*PG*, 59–60)

Nina's treatment of Nimmo's political career is defensive, that is, she emphasizes those acts that have been most questioned, not in terms of their results, but in terms of Nimmo's own avowed principles. She defends some that at the time of their occurrence she herself did not care for. The major event of this sort is Nimmo's decision not to resign from Asquith's cabinet when war was declared in 1914. (His evangelical supporters called it the "great betrayal.")

Nina recounts how she was approached by the press before she knew Nimmo's plans and stated she "had no reason to suppose that Mr. Nimmo had changed his views about resigning from a war cabinet" (*PG*, 265). She remembers that she was made to feel like the enemy for making the statement she did:

> Chester jumped up quickly and looked at me as at an enemy. "What is the position? A terrible one—and one that no one could have foretold. And my position? The P.M. says the country needs me—that I am indispensable. As Bootham says, it may be my duty—a moral duty—to change my mind and face the consequences, however irresponsible publicists like Round may make somewhat treacherous haste to compromise a situation already dangerous enough."
>
> And he went to the door. When, seeing that he was furious with my "treachery," I began to say that I had only told Round what he had said himself a week before, he stopped in the door itself and said impatiently, "What Round does not realize is that this is going to be a new kind of war—that it's going on for a long time. All this fuss will be forgotten in six months." (*PG*, 267)

It is to be noted here that Nina offers no evidence that Nimmo's anger is directed at her, though she thinks it is. This is a sign of a certain self-centeredness, but also indicative of the tension that has been built up between them. Nimmo is naturally irritated by a situation in which he is tempted to go back on his word and at the newspaper editor Round, who will go after him. This can account for his avoidance of Nina in the next few days.

But the key phrases in the passage above are "one that no one could have foretold" and "What Round does not realize is." Both emphasize the politician Nimmo's problems in dealing with an ever-changing situation and the problems of an electorate which must judge shifts of policy, past promises, and future likelihoods. In one of Cary's working notes, he writes (*OC*, Box 288): "[I]n the *new situation* his duty was to stick by. It is the *situation* that has to be faced each time and with contempt for the public opinion as a personal refutation. Every situation has to be weighed with balance of good and evil." Also, there is a draft passage for *Power in Men* (*OC*, Box 200): "the honestest man in the world could not keep his word in government." These ideas were certainly in Cary's mind in rough form when he wrote this scene. Nimmo does go back on his commitment. There is the usual multiple motive: He has been offered the important cabinet post of Minister of Production, and, by his own statement, he has been shocked by the German invasion of Belgium ("a dastardly crime"). Nina's eventual response is typically twofold:

> I can still remember my astonishment . . . for here was Chester "ratting," and not only did he make it appear quite an honest thing, but even rather noble, in owning his mistake. I was quite moved by his words—they made me feel (like thousands of his supporters who had been raging against him) short-sighted and narrow-minded, lacking in "vision."
> And I told myself Chester had really been surprised by the sudden attack on Belgium. (*PG*, 268)

And so on. But she is also uneasy because of Nimmo's remark that "all this fuss will be forgotten." This strikes her as the statement of a "calculator." But then, of course, the question becomes one of the motive for the calculation. Nimmo is right in his calculation, at any rate. Six months later, the pacifist pledge is ancient history, and Nimmo's refusal to serve would have been regarded as unpatriotic and unproductive. It would also have been the end of his political career. Mainly though, to have refused to serve would have been to misunderstand the real events.

It is clear from *Power in Men* that Cary did not intend Nimmo's decision to remain in the cabinet to be a hypocritical act:

> Pacificism of the third class, of those prepared to use all available means, including force, to end war, is the commonest and the only rational. But it does not absolve men from using their own judgement to decide whether peace, in any given case, is better secured by concession or by force. Nothing can save them from this problem, because they are real men in a real world, and their liberty is also real. (*PM*, 156–57)

This can account for Nimmo's anger, assumed by Nina to be directed at her only. It is directed at the situation of decision. But Nimmo passes through it to act on his decision. The problem for our attitude toward Nimmo is that we must read through Nina's response to construct our own. Nimmo's own statement (*EL*, 252) is more convincing about his views (it virtually repeats Cary's above). Nina does, of course, defend him but with a flaccidity that expresses her distaste. The problem many critics have had here is their expectation of greater purity or singleness of motive and, perhaps, greater political success than is likely in life. (Cf. Giles Mitchell, p. 275: "[Nimmo's] inner springs of action are basically anarchic. . . . His work is primarily ego-oriented, and it becomes progressively more so throughout his life. The subtle tension between the demands of common good and personal ambition he is never able to reconcile." This is general; Cary asks us to look deeper.) It is worth noting that both Lloyd George and Churchill were on the "pacifist" side in the crisis over naval expenditures in 1909, yet Churchill took over the Admiralty in 1911. In 1912, several cabinet members complained of having been kept in the dark about the "German menace." (I write from notes made by Cary's secretary, OC, Box 288.)

Nina's defense that politics requires decisions like Nimmo's seems rather half-hearted and plays into the hands of Nimmo's critics. Though it is accurate enough in its way, it acknowledges neither the complexity of motivation that can lie behind such an act nor a politician's possible critical detachment from his own acts: "Politics after all is a kind of war (and in many places they still shoot or even torture the defeated), and people who are fighting for their lives (at least their political lives) have quite a different view of things from those who only work and eat for them" (*PG*, 225). After a discussion along these lines, Nina does something rare in her memoir. She abruptly shifts the scene to an episode with Latter years before, and offers a didactic example. It is a scene in which Jim and Nina through Jim's foolishness are almost drowned sailing. (It also gives Cary the opportunity to put into the child Nina's thoughts the words, "So I really am going to be drowned! What a fool I was to come! Jim has killed me at last!" [*PG*, 288], which comments on her early sense of eventual violence at Jim's hands.) Nina's point is that Latter was not a hypocrite, nor would anyone have so accused him, for "pretending to himself and me, in the middle of a violent storm, that we were doing something reasonable and possible" (*PG*, 230). She then argues that politicians are never "in harbor," and she defends their shifts of position as necessary responses to events. At the same time she recognizes that Nimmo needed to be sincere. He had to believe in what he was doing. This is an extremely important point which brings Nina closer to the real situation of Nimmo from his own point of view than she often is. The didactic example which precedes this is an indication of her own sense of the importance of the point.

One of Nimmo's convenient principles, but also one of his most deeply felt, is the notion of the new beginning. The idea, deeply ingrained in him by his Adventist upbringing, directs his imagination always toward the future. Nina states that Nimmo had great imaginative power, and this means for her that he was imaginatively susceptible. He could be deeply moved by something at a chapel meeting. His strength was his ability to respond to situations, but it was also the source of accusations of hypocrisy against him.

Nina is aware of the vulnerability of politicians to attack and makes every effort to be "fair." Even the "Contract Case," which is a parallel to (but she says not to be confused with) the infamous Marconi Case, which implicated Lloyd George and other ministers, she excuses by trying to lay out the facts. (R. W. Noble remarks [p. 86] that Nina's argument is not convincing because the Marconi Case was inexcusable. That may be so, but Nina does tell us that the two cases are different.) Yet all this time Nina hates the "managing" that Nimmo does. She hates politics, even though she comes to understand and play politics herself. She wants peace, but she comes to need the tension politics provides.

The Contract Case is only one example of the parallel Cary develops between Nimmo's career and that of the Liberal Party. This parallel has been regarded as nearly exact by Fr. John Teeling, S. J. (p. 281). Teeling's view is that the glorious Liberal achievement ended miserably, and he concludes that therefore both Nimmo and the Liberals failed. I do not think Cary thought politics worked quite like that. For him, political movements have their day, make their contribution for better or worse, and then give way to new ones. In any case, Nimmo's religious background reflects the blending of evangelical religion and secular politics in the Liberal Party of his youth. In a note, Cary wrote: "I wanted a nonconformist because of importance in liberal democratic history" (*OC*, Box 288). On this point Malcolm Foster (p. 485) makes the excellent observation that Cary distinguishes between Nimmo and the character of Dolling in *Except the Lord* on the basis of the difference between the nonconformist Christian background of English labor movements and the abstractly intellectual background of European movements. It is in part over this difference that Nimmo breaks with Pring, who is going to discipline the old Christian union man Brobdribb.

Nimmo's connection with the radical liberals is another element. His support of the Boers, his participation in the land campaign, and his pacifist stand prior to 1914—all reflect some element in the party at the time. Nimmo rises to Undersecretary for Mines in the Liberal sweep of 1905. He tours the west, speaking against the war in 1914, but joins the War Cabinet when war is declared. The number of Liberals in the House of Commons in August 1914 was 261; by 1918, 165; by 1922, 116. Chester Nimmo is defeated in the 1922 election. He stands again in 1924 and is again defeated. By this time the Liberal Party is in shambles, never to regain its strength. In 1923 following the Liberal reunion the number elected was 158, but in 1924 there were only 43. Nina describes the party as attacked from without and "at last simply torn to pieces" (*PG*, 61), but much of the trouble was internal and the wounds self-inflicted, as is usually the case in a political collapse. Nina's defection from Nimmo is coincidental with the Liberal collapse. This parallel between Nimmo and his party is perfectly natural. But he is an individual. Cary does not make the mistake of representing abstractly in him all factions.

Nina's account, of course, is written at a later date in the light of Nimmo's defeats, his recent outrageous behavior toward her, and her growing alienation. She begins to think of him almost completely as a creature to be "managed," just as she thinks she became such a creature in his mind after the crisis with Latter over the paternity of Tom. Indeed, to outward appearances Nimmo is a parody of his former self and to some extent of the party's former grandeur. His behavior, formerly imaginative, seems to have turned compulsive, and his approaches to Nina are now desperate contrivances. This matter of parody is one that Cary develops through the pathetic career of Tom, whose role is false like a copy.

Nimmo's relationship to Tom is given quite a lot of space in Nina's account; it is exceedingly difficult, culminating in Tom's having to leave the country or face indictment and his eventual suicide in Germany. A parodist of Nimmo, he is also a sad copy of his true father Latter, who also had to be expatriated. Though not really Nimmo's son, Tom is molded as if he were. The relationship is very complicated. Tom is heavily influenced by Nimmo and particularly by Nimmo's imagination, but he also resists him. His career as a nightclub mime is a vehicle of many ironies. As an adolescent he hates Nimmo's "acting" and thinks it insincere. He then comes to a grasp of Nimmo's sincerity, but he cannot put the two responses together in quite the way Nina can when she defends the shifts of ground that politicians must make. He is deeply hostile to what he concludes is falseness in Nimmo. An early observation that Nina makes sets the situation. As a young boy Tom is very much, even alarmingly, stimulated by Nimmo's dramatic storytelling; it is over-whelming. Tom's hostility, which is combined with a fierce loyalty, becomes a pathetic alienation. The passage to that state is ex-pressed in a number of ways: the closeness to his mother, which becomes at times a sort of courtship; his characterization of Nim-mo's speeches as "performances"; and his unconscious parodies of Nimmo in his mime act. A key scene is the one in which Nimmo comes unannounced to see Tom perform and ends up giving his own performance, a speech from the back of a car outside the the-ater after the show. Tom treats the whole thing as if he were assess-ing an actor:

> "It's a good deal in the voice, the way he manages his pauses."
> "I couldn't stop him from coming."
> "Oh no—he was quite right to come; it was a first-class chance for a popular speech."
> "And he meant every word."
> "Oh, he's sincere enough" (Tom and I would always remind each other at such times when we felt the pressure severely that Chester, though he had to "play politics," was really a sincere good man). "Oh yes," Tom sighed, "and what he said was pretty important—it got me. I was almost in tears."
> I said hastily that he had been very good, too, but he laughed at me and said, "Thanks"; then suddenly he frowned and said, "I felt like a clown—but I suppose that's what I've got to expect." (*PG*, 257)

This parodic relationship in which Nimmo is degraded by mimicry degrades the boy, and he finally destroys himself. Much is made of the struggle that Nina sees herself having with Nimmo over Tom and her fear that Nimmo will exert undue influence over the boy. But beyond the fact that the boy is an object of struggle is their strife with each other. There is also the fact, which Nina perceives, that Nimmo is an overwhelming person.

Tom's career as a mimic is an unconscious revenge. Fr. Teeling (p. 282) sees Tom's parody as Cary's moral comment on Nimmo. But it is much more complicated than that, as I shall try to show. His mimicry is of Nimmo's acting without its sincerity. When Tom says above that Nimmo is "sincere enough," he speaks ambigu-ously with a touch of sarcasm. From an actor's point of view, which is Tom's, sincerity does not mean believing what one says but putting oneself provisionally into a character. Sincerity in acting is hypocrisy in politics, and so Tom's admission of Nimmo's sincerity is very nearly a charge of hypocrisy or at the least an evasive irony. We see this matter developed further from Nimmo's point of view in *Except the Lord*, where he tells of watching the villain of the melodrama *Maria Marten* at Lilmouth Fair.

Here it is important to remark that the later, defeated Nimmo seems outwardly to be a parody of the earlier success. His deliberate recklessness, as against his earlier tact, in his relations with Nina is a parody of his earlier imaginative behavior. It is as if he were making strenuous and unreasonable demands on his imagination, which can no longer rise to the occasion. He makes a desperate effort to reestablish a relationship with his muse, but Nina has always regarded this as a rather absurd role for herself. The more loyal she has been outwardly, the more false the role has seemed to her. Nimmo has tried to make a marriage out of this falsity. It is, of course, not quite false to him. He is not the father of her children, and she has never loved him; but he loves her and tries to elicit her love by all the political imagination he has. He recognizes her sense of fairness and tries to build a solid family situation on the slender base of his devotion and her conscience, in the face of the lie of parenthood. He is hopeful in spite of their differences of religion and class. But in the end the marriage fails. It comes up against the intransigent real, as did the Liberals, though Nina doesn't abandon him entirely.

This final situation is, however, in itself an absurd parody of the earlier marriage. Nimmo insists on declaring by his sexual approaches his ownership of her. In contrast to his earlier tactful understanding he refuses now to accept the reality of her feelings. This is a demonic expression of power, the form of imagination without its substance. The Nimmo Nina perceives is like the old man of Blake's "Mental Traveller": "An aged shadow soon he fades, / Wand'ring round an Earthly Cot." The Nimmo who pursues Nina in Palm Cottage is a desperate man, at least in his outer behavior, though we shall have to make some qualifications when we have read *Except the Lord*, since the narrator of that book seems fully in control of himself.

Nina's relation to Nimmo is balanced against her passionate, stormy affair with Jim Latter. Though in some ways Latter appears to be a typical Tory, Nina rightly regards him as apolitical. That view we endorse when we gather the evidence from *Not Honour*

More. He is impulsive and irresponsible and in many ways pathetic. Cary first establishes their relationship not so much on the basis of their natural attractiveness to each other (though both are physically attractive) as on that of their youthful intimacy, fueled in each case by loneliness. Nina is an orphan; Latter is virtually abandoned by his father, and his mother is dead. In spite of the growing sexual passion, which strongly binds them, neither seems able finally to outgrow the terms of their youthful attachment. Childishness is a quality of both. Their relationship is characterized by strife, irresponsibility to each other, and frequent inability to communicate successfully. When they were children, Nina recalls, Latter's occasional rages against her were of the sort that make people "do murder" (*PG*, 14). Rather than face these rages, her feelings made her evade them, irritating him even further:

> [H]owever he beat me and whatever he did, I would stay limp and not say a word. This, of course (because he realised that he could do nothing to me except batter me or kill me and that even then I should not care), made him still more furious, especially as he thought I was doing it on purpose; though, in fact, I could not help it. All I could do was to try to ignore the whole horrible situation, and I was quite ready to be killed if only it would stop. (*PG*, 14)

As we shall see, after reading *Not Honour More*, each regards the other as responsible for their youthful relationship and its tensions and strife, except when Nina blames Aunt Latter or, occasionally, herself for certain acts.

Latter is generally a failure because he has little political sense. Aunt Latter has a passionate interest in politics. Nimmo is a master of it. Nina comes to understand it. Latter's career is a series of impolitic acts from his first relations with Nina, including their first sexual relations, through his inability to handle money and incapacity to get along with his superiors in the army, to his failure in the matter of the natives in Dutchinluga. The final failure comes, of course, at the end of *Not Honour More*.

Nina regards herself, in hindsight, as having developed a greater understanding of politics, but in certain other respects she believes she has not changed very much. In contrast to her guardian Aunt Latter, she has little interest in politics. She is self-indulgent, and she is fond of luxury and physical well-being, just as she consciously describes herself. However, she does have a conscience, which prevents her from forsaking Nimmo at the end, though by this time she writes as if this behavior is more compulsively habitual than governed by conscience. Her problem has been the clash of opposed feelings—one based on a notion of fairness deeply ingrained in her upbringing along with her capacity to be "brackety," that is, see several sides of an issue; the other based on sexual passion grown from pre-adolescent intimacy fueled by Latter's surprising sexual prowess on his return from India, perhaps also compulsively habitual in its later stages. To grasp this conflict is exceedingly difficult, particularly if one is intent on assessing blame. Giles Mitchell makes a number of interesting remarks about Nina, but in the end he tips the balance by finding in her a "profound moral imbalance": "Her final insistence on Nimmo's greatness in the face of overwhelming evidence to the contrary reflects an almost complete loss of intellectual and moral control over irreconcilably conflicting facts" (p. 275). Nina calls Nimmo "good" (with certain qualifications) and "great." Many great politicians and poets have been quite dreadful people. In the matter of greatness, Nina does not give us so much conflicting facts as very little information enabling us to judge Nimmo's political career. One thing we do know: He is important enough for people to have written already about him.

We shall pursue this problem further. The theme of lies and truth is involved. Early in her book Nina says of something that happened, "from a nonpolitical point of view it was all lies" (*PG*, 32). She seems to be inventing here a new form of truth. It would have to be pragmatic. It would have to emphasize what is *made* rather than what simply *is*. The danger, as she well knows, is that this sort of thing sounds like a justification for any means to arrive at a desirable end. Certainly there is a serious problem here. But to be fair, she thinks, one must come to understand the situation of the politician faced with trying to make something and make it work. We see in her account that there is often a very thin line between a lie and a creative act or fiction, and we see too the dangers when a fabric of untruth grows up around a lie. This is one of Cary's reasons for making Latter and not Nimmo the father of Nina's children. This "lie," which Nina wishes Nimmo to acknowledge, Nimmo would like to treat as a fiction because it is at the base of their marriage, which he values. But the lie, if it has not corrupted the marriage, is certainly an apt symbol for its course.

Did Nimmo do enough good to be forgiven his clinging to the lie? (We must remember, of course, that the lie of parenthood was not entirely Nimmo's in the making. It was Aunt Latter's, Jim's, and Nina's as well. It is, in fact, the one thing they have in common. And we must remember that, given the original decision, there is even something honorable in their maintaining the lie.) Against all this Cary seems to assume that the parallel between Nimmo and the Liberal Party is sufficient to convey Nimmo's greatness. We know that Cary regarded the Liberal Government of that period as one of the greatest in English history. But we don't *see* Nimmo *involved* in the things that made it great. Cary seems to have left us to infer his participation.

R. W. Noble has found this inattention to government a flaw in the novel, but he does not give enough attention to the fact that what he is reading is Nina's account. She is, by her own admission, not sufficiently interested in the give and take of politics and therefore, in character, does not speak with interest or authority on such matters. Noble also does not note that we learn more about Nimmo in *Except the Lord*, but it is true that we learn nothing directly about the great political events of the time. Noble's proof of the flaw is that *Prisoner of Grace* does not bear out the intention stated in the Carfax preface to "reveal the moral basis of Nimmo's political compromises." These are Noble's words, not Cary's, but the preface can be read so as to expect something of this sort. Of course, Noble is on thin ice when he invokes Cary's prefaces as the standard, but he does put his finger on a problem Cary has to struggle with because of his narrative technique and in this case the limitations of a particular narrator. Noble writes:

> The portrayal of Chester's betrayal of pacifism in return for the post of Minister of Production in the War Cabinet also lacks insight into his moral dilemma and psychological motives. Towards the end of this novel Nimmo's character blurs; his loss of moral dynamism is not particularized. Through Nina, Cary asserts historical truisms about the causes of the post-war collapse of the Liberal Party . . . but he gives little specification of Chester's personal doctrine. (p. 86)

He further observes correctly that Cary's insights into Chester's political life are not as profound or convincing as Cary's insights into "this tension in the personal lives of Chester and Nina." This is quite true, but the reason has not been explored. It is simply that Cary has chosen Nina as the narrator. Malcolm Foster (p. 487) puts the matter more bluntly: "Some people have complained that they can find no real connection between the young Chester Nimmo of

Except the Lord and the middle-aged and then elderly politician of *Prisoner of Grace* and *Not Honour More*. The former, they say, is a dedicated young man, the latter is just a speechifying crook." Robert Bloom (p. 166) speaks of "discrepancies between the two novels." The question Cary had to face was not how much he could say but how much Nina would be likely to say. In any case, Foster's readers have not read carefully enough. Nimmo himself is critical of the "dedicated young man" of *Except the Lord*. The old writer is, by his account at least, more dedicated than the young man. That is in part the point of his memoir. The evidence to convict the Nimmo of *Prisoner of Grace* for being a "speechifying crook" is not in the novel. That is only what Jim Latter thinks in *Not Honour More*, but he is not a reliable judge.

The choice of narrators and what they are to narrate is an imposition of limits that Cary cannot escape once he commits himself. What Nina says cannot be out of character. Furthermore, she must be allowed to express her hatred, muffled as it is by her intention to show that Nimmo is a good man. In short, in spite of the dominating character of Nimmo, *Prisoner of Grace* is Nina's book, and in the end fundamentally her self-expression. If we look back on *Prisoner of Grace* from the perspective of the whole trilogy, we see how much this is so and how isolated her view is, despite its brackety thought.

One of the aspects of this trilogy, indeed, both trilogies, that should be mentioned here is the solitary nature of each narrator. Given the trilogy as a whole, it is appropriate that Nina is an orphan, Jim Latter virtually one. Chester Nimmo's relatives are never mentioned by Nina and seem to play no role (except in his memory) in his adult life. Nina's son dies young and her relation to Sally is distant. Chester Nimmo has no real children. It is a matter of honor for Jim Latter not to acknowledge his. Sara Monday, Tom Wilcher, and Gulley Jimson are each in their own ways alone. The Blake line Jimson quotes—"Go love without the help of anything on earth"—seems to apply universally in Cary's world, and Cary points this up in a variety of ways. In *Prisoner of Grace*, a bitter and complicated novel, we sense failures of communication drowning the successes of Cary's people. The successes are of short duration, frustrated by the real, and based often on the slender support of fictions that are sometimes lies. But Cary never suggests that we can get along without fictions.

Except the Lord

Chester Nimmo's memoir of his childhood and young manhood, which constitutes *Except the Lord*, is the most cunningly constructed of all the statements of the two trilogies. That is to say, Nimmo's handling of his audiences (there are two) is cleverly designed and displays his abilities as a politician and preacher. As we have seen in *Prisoner of Grace*, he has more than one intent in most of his acts, and his trick is to make the acts blend the intents.

Nimmo is writing to posterity to set straight the record of his early career, to reaffirm certain values implicit in his political and religious allegiances, and to confess to a lie and a crime. Michael Echeruo (p. 108) states that *Except the Lord* gives us an aspect of Nimmo, the spiritual, and its background, without which the other two novels would be meaningless. Surely the complaints I have mentioned against *Prisoner of Grace* and the trilogy would be considerably stronger without Nimmo's spiritual history. *Except the Lord* offers grounds for sympathy with its narrator and a new point of view toward *Prisoner of Grace*. The lie to which Nimmo refers is not the lie of parenthood so central to Nina's account; it refers to Nimmo's involvement in planned acts of violence performed during a labor dispute when he was quite young. Nimmo is also writing to his former wife, Nina, though we don't realize this until approximately two-thirds of the way through the book. It is another example of Cary's forcing us back through the preceding action in order to view it from another angle. The situation of Nimmo's writing is that of the conclusion of *Prisoner of Grace*. Nimmo is ensconced in the lower floor of the Latters' home, Palm Cottage, writing his memoirs, indeed, dictating them to his former wife, who is acting as his secretary. The memoir is a lovemaking, an effort to persuade her, as he so often has before, not to abandon him entirely (or, in this case, turn him out). She has, of course, divorced him and married Jim Latter, but Nimmo has "wangled" (to use Latter's term) his way into their house by means of a convenient heart attack on the premises.

The addresses to posterity and to Nina go on simultaneously and are a single text, which is an act of ingratiation, didactic preaching, and piety toward his family, especially his long dead sister Georgina and his preacher father. The memoir has occasionally the gestures of a sermon, and it may even be considered to carry an oblique moral threat against Nina, whose loyalty seems to be compared silently to that of his sister. It is even a sermon preached on a text, the first three verses of Psalm 127:

> Except the Lord build the house, their labour is but lost that build it;
> Except the Lord keep the city, the watchman waketh but in vain.
> Lo, children and the fruit of the womb are an heritage and gift that cometh of the Lord. (*EL*, 284)

This text has a considerable irony if we read the third line and the rest of the psalm in the light of Nimmo's domestic life, but we shall consider that later. Here Nimmo preaches (he tells us he was a preacher for fourteen years after his brief career as a labor agitator) on a text that refers both to the home and the body politic, which are always spiritually connected in his mind, as are religion and political principle.

We respond positively to Nimmo's address to posterity, to the story he tells of his poverty-stricken youth in the family of an Adventist preacher, the devotion of his sister Georgina to the family welfare, his loss of faith, his brief career as a labor agitator, and his reconversion. His style is that of the enthusiast. Nina observes in her book that she found the style difficult at times to respond to, even to take seriously; and there are occasions when Nimmo overdoes it. But for the most part he comes across sincerely. However, Cary will not let us rest on this response. The address to Nina, which only later we learn is occurring, we respond to with ambivalence. Some of Nina's attitudes in *Prisoner of Grace* flow back into our consciousness, and we become uneasy, especially in response to those passages directly describing his wife, but also those more cunning ones which do not mention her but are particularly designed to move her and appeal to her conscience.

There are two formal ways, working together, by which Nimmo constructs the address to posterity. The first is an emergence from his religious upbringing and takes it cue from John Bunyan's *Pilgrim's Progress*. The form is that of the journey of conversion. This journey includes passage through dangerous places, trials, tribulations, and temptations. There is a fall and a redemption. The story is spoken forth in the language of religious evangelical enthusiasm, but not fanaticism. In this Nimmo follows the example of his father: "He was an enthusiast but no fanatic—he acted not from the impulse of passion but from reasons which he was always prepared to defend" (*EL*, 58). In his well-known book, Ronald Knox says, "'[E]nthusiasm' in the religious sense belongs to the seventeenth and eighteenth centuries; it hardly reappears without inverted commas after 1823" (*Enthusiasm* [New York and Oxford: Oxford University Press, 1950], p. 6). Nimmo may be deliberately old-fashioned in referring to his father in this way, but the word persisted in a variety of secular forms and with religious overtones. Susie I. Tucker tells an interesting story: "In November of 1868, Disraeli was trying to dissuade Queen Victoria from appointing Bishop Tait to the throne of Canterbury. 'There is in his idiosyncrasy a strange fund of enthusiasm,' he wrote, 'a quality which ought never to be possessed by an Archbishop of Canterbury or a Prime Minister of England'" (*Enthusiasm: A Study in Semantic Change* [Cambridge: Cambridge University Press, 1972], p. 10). Tucker goes on to note Disraeli's preference for Palmerston over the Liberal leader Gladstone because "in the latter he had to deal with 'an earnest man severely religious and enthusiastic,' and so 'every attempted arrangement ends in an unintelligible correspondence and violated confidence.' He preferred a 'man of the world . . . governed by the principle of honour'." Disraeli found Gladstone's enthusiasm "almost as annoying as his politics." Henry W. Clark notes that it was not unusual at the end of the nineteenth century for complaints to be heard that nonconformist pulpits were proclaiming Liberal politics (*History of English Nonconformity* [London: Chapman and Hall, 1913], II, 424). Something of this complaint may be seen in Disraeli's attitude above, though the situation is reversed: It is the politician who has nonconformist religious attitudes. The Bunyanesque formal structure is natural to Nimmo. It is not an abstract "literary" structure but for him the internal form of his life and that of many other sinners. Disraeli's implied contrast of enthusiasm with honor almost provides a text, though an ironic text, for the trilogy in its politico-religious aspect.

The second formal means that Nimmo employs in his memoir is Wordsworthian, though Wordsworth is never mentioned. Nimmo's device is similar to the Wordsworthian "spot of time." In *The Prelude* Wordsworth speaks passionately of the "renovating virtue" (XII, 210) of the memory of certain clearly defined moments of experience. These moments, recalled in adversity, can, in Wordsworth's view, strengthen the spirit. The remembrances need not be, and usually are not, of happy or light-hearted moments. In the boat-stealing episode of *The Prelude* (I, 357ff.) the emphasis is on conscience and presences in nature that are witness to the event. In another (XII, 287ff.) a gloomy scene is connected with his father's death. Nimmo's are varied in nature and connect to events in his spiritual pilgrimage. Often his remembrance is of a certain character, fixed in a certain pose or representative of a moral state:

> How many of those who knew her, how many who passed only once through her bar, got from her a new impression of the dignity which belongs to the morally fearless—to those who will not bow to the mob, who are not seduced even by the cry of the fashionable rebel. It is such impressions, much more than any exhortation, which turn the soul, that is already half lost between disgust at conventional paths and the bewilderment of the trackless moor, back to the dusty high road of common obligation. (*EL*, 53)

But Nimmo's own experiences of spots of time do not always have the oratorical floweriness of this general treatment of the impressions of others, though they do connect to the theme of journey and they often do have the quality of moral persuasion present here (and they are obviously pointed at the listening Nina in order to get her to consider her "obligation").

Except the Lord's world is that of Devon. Among Cary's notes for the *Second Trilogy* (*OC*, Box 289) is a crudely drawn map of the south Devon coast which equates Lilmouth with Plymouth, Tarbiton with Dartmouth, and Queensport with Kingsbridge. The Longwater is that inlet at the end of which is Queensport, and Palm Cottage is located on the east side of the Longwater, which puts it about ten miles from Tarbiton (Dartmouth). Shagbrook is north of South Brent on the moor; Highfallow farm is not marked but is clearly in that vicinity. Nimmo has two particularly vivid remembrances of events at Highfallow before the family had to move to Shagbrook. The first is that of his mother turning the money box upside down and smiling at his father. The second is that of his father's verbal treatment of a loutish drunkard come to borrow money from him by appealing vulgarly to his Christian charity. The scenes of his young life at Highfallow are also clearly recalled:

> I will not say that I have never known such happiness as belonged to us—every stage in life's pilgrimage has its own sorrow and its own appropriate satisfaction. But there has been none whose scenes are so deeply engraved upon my memory. (*EL*, 7)

This remark is followed by an eloquent description of the moors under snow and his father digging out the sheep. Nimmo's spots of time frequently focus on the family, which is one of the moral themes of the memoir and a vehicle of design on Nina. Detailed description of a prank perpetrated against Georgina is followed by a remembrance of sheer terror at having committed a lie:

> I had committed some fault, and told a lie about it and not been dis-covered, and I had been taught that bad children who do not confess and repent will go to hell.
>
> I do not remember anything but the terror—possibly for a very short time before I was found out, and punished, and so absolved. The fear of hell, the punishment of sin, how the modern parent re-volts from such teaching. Yet I will assert that far from doing us chil-dren harm, it was a sure foundation to the world of our confidence, a master girder in our palace of delight. (*EL*, 8–9)

(The flamboyant metaphors at the end are typical.) Here the spot of time reverses itself and all is absent except the *feeling* of terror and guilt—and the absolution. Nimmo judges that the blankness here is more effective than an effort at description. Buried in the pas-sage is the pattern of Nimmo's memoir as a whole, which is a con-fession of a sin for which he was never punished and forgiven.

Several of the spots of time figure as important steps in the spir-itual journey, and I shall take some of them up in due course. One more ought to be mentioned here, however, for it is clearly in-tended by Nimmo to express how his fundamental political views were formed. It is the scene in which young Chester accompanies his father to an outdoor meeting of striking tin miners. It is a scene of universal poverty and misery. At the end of a preacher's address to the crowd, they strike up the old hymn, "O God our help in ages past":

> I have never forgotten that scene upon the combeside; the sky above full of July sunlight, the stream glittering among the stones, a bird flying over and turning aside in alarm at the sight and sound of hu-manity in this quiet place, and the ragged crowd about the minister, men threatened with the ruin of their lives, raising their voices in chorus, hoarsely indeed, but with earnest appeal in that hymn of prayer. (*EL*, 68)

This passage, which has followed a lengthy description of the un-fortunate miners, leads into a lengthy discussion of his father's im-plying that they, poor as they were, should give to help the miners. Nimmo wants to make clear that this was not the autocratic act of the Victorian father but an expression of conscience and family honor, that if anything he as a child suffered from too much freedom of choice. He and his brother and sisters were constantly faced with the "conflict of duty and inclination" (*EL*, 70). This statement, which summarizes what the spot of time above is all about, has Nimmo's typical multiple design. It describes something formative of the connection between religion and politics in his career. It also defends the past against insensitive contemporary interpreters. Finally, it speaks directly to Nina, who, throughout the marriage with Nimmo and even now when it is ended, must still choose between duty, as Nimmo cleverly establishes it, and inclination. One of the impulses behind Nina's own memoir is to be fair to the past. The effect of the technique of spots of time on us is that it reveals to us a Nimmo far more attractive than the Nimmo of *Prisoner of Grace* or at least the Nimmo Nina sees (for we read through her account to another Nimmo easier to square with the one being revealed to us now). Here we are taken into his own sensibility and are made to recognize aspects of his mind ignored by or unknown to Nina in her account. For one thing, Nimmo has a remarkable capacity to evoke the *spirit* of a scene, to move us by his power to shape particulars into a whole. This ability is a pleasant surprise, and it causes us to think out the possible differences between the inner man we discover in these moments and the outer appearances of the politician. This is not, however, the only side Nimmo reveals to us, as we shall see.

The structure of the journey or pilgrimage is treated principally by reference to specific scenes—spots of time—described in considerable detail. These events are all turning points. Nina remarks, as we have noticed, that everything every day was a turning point to the politician Nimmo. There is no doubt that he looks back on his life and sees things in terms of critical moments. Of these, the most significant early one, and the one Nimmo explores most fully, leading us carefully up to and away from it, is his and Georgina's attendance at the Lilmouth Fair and their seeing the melodrama *Maria Marten*. The episode is foreshadowed by a sudden moment of childish wonder. Chester and his sister, driving their cattle along a country road, suddenly meet a procession led by an elephant! They are stunned by this miraculous appearance which sets the stage for anticipation of greater miracles to come. The elephant belongs to the carnival people. Anticipation is heightened for the children by the question of whether they will be able to attend the fair and the temptation it will present to them if they do go: A play is to be offered, and attendance at plays is strictly forbidden by their religion. There is also the question to be answered: Should they give their fair money to the striking miners? Luckily for them the strike ends before this decision has to be made.

In the process of the children's discussions about going, Richard, the intellectual, utters a remark of interest:

> Georgy doesn't realise how important it might be for us to go to the Fair. Ruth has never seen a lion and has no idea of an elephant. This is her only chance to see the real thing and find out how she feels about them. (*EL*, 65)

Richard, unknown to the others, has lost his religious faith. But he has transposed the idea of pilgrimage over to secular experiential progress with a continued emphasis on feeling and Protestant individual decision. The remark fits Nimmo's theme, and it is not surprising that he uses it.

Lilmouth Fair is Nimmo's version of Vanity Fair in *Pilgrim's Progress*, and Nimmo makes the connection explicit by speculating whether or not Bunyan might have actually used Lilmouth as a model. It was "a sorcerer's world, the world of the great fair where anything was possible and everything was strange, exciting, violent—where there were to be seen at all times [as Bunyan said] 'Juglers, Cheats, Games, Plays, Fools, Apes, and Rogues,' as well as 'False Swearers and that of a Blood Red Colour'" (*EL*, 80). Nimmo remarks that the red Devon dust covered everything and everybody.

Attendance at the play is a "decisive event" of the sort Nimmo likes to dwell on. It produces a troublesome ambivalence in him. He dramatizes it as a fall into forbidden pleasures of primeval seductive power:

> I still feel in my old nerves the vehement tremor of that night. Is it that impersonation by itself has some secret and immemorial power over the growing spirit—some primitive urge older perhaps than humanity itself? (*EL*, 84)

Cary means for us to remember reading in *Prisoner of Grace* of young Tom Nimmo's taking up the profession of clown and mime and doing unconscious broad imitations of Chester himself. These imitations Nina describes as grotesque and fascinating, both a truth and a lie: "I felt that under the horrible nose and absurd whiskers Chester was acting himself" (*PG*, 341–42). Yet at the same time, she says,

> I shall never admit that Tom became an evil person. But I do think that he knew, at least subconsciously, that his mimicry was cruel and false; he simply could not resist that temptation of his "art," which was after all a real art. (*PG*, 348)

This is whistling in the dark. Without the religious impulse or the influence of Bunyan, Nina treats Tom's succumbing to temptation secularly but in much the same way as Chester worries about the feigning that occurs on the stage. The larger irony here is that poor Tom is the product of feigning on the stage of politics. He is not Chester's son, but he does not know this. His Oedipal behavior is a pathetically tragic lie and his life a corruption. His alienation in Germany, where no one can understand his satire, is complete. It is something that neither Nina nor Chester can face directly, and Jim Latter ignores it completely. None of the three mentions that poor Tom has grown up in Vanity Fair and became what the fair required him to be. (One is tempted to play on Nimmo's use of "fair" and Nina's, but I shall resist it.)

In front of the theater tent Chester feels its "evil," but he is drawn into it, "seized by an immense longing to follow the actors and actresses behind the canvas of that mysterious tabernacle, the temple of Satan" (*EL*, 85), which is also the "temple of lies" (*EL*, 87). Chester had been brought up to believe that any kind of pretense was a sin and a trap and that lies corrupt the soul. What particularly shocks him about his decision to see the play that night is that he seemed to be devoid of will, so balanced was he between fear and appetite. He was "beyond reflection . . . all exposed surface" (*EL*, 89). One of the most profound spots of time in *Except the Lord* is Nimmo's recalling the face of Georgina in the crowd. With all her money spent, she had crawled under the tent to gain entrance:

> Georgina's face thrust itself out suddenly between two men in the front row. The men, both large and heavy, were dressed in the dark suits common then to clerks, so that Georgina's pale face, seeming suspended in the air against this background of broadcloth at about the level of a man's elbow, was very conspicuous. The expression was a strange mixture of violent curiosity and alarm. Her eyes enor-

mous, her forehead wrinkled, and her hair even more disordered than usual—long black locks streamed down her forehead and hung below her chin. (*EL*, 89)

United with her in defiance of their religious upbringing at that moment, Chester sees in Georgina's face his own state of mind, except that in *this* mirror the crisis is magnified, as everything is magnified in Georgina's personality. Her love for and struggle with her father is far more intense and tormented than Chester's. It is the suspension of her head in the air, the sort of optical illusion that so fascinated Wordsworth in the boat-stealing and skating episodes of *The Prelude* and the Lucy poems, that dominates this spot of time. Chester sees in it an image of his own suspension between conflicting impulses, his own momentary lack of will, and, as well, a "sin against all her [and, of course, his] father's teaching" (*EL*, 90).

The scene fixes for us the crisis in Chester's mind, which is also a crisis central to the Protestant tradition. It is the crisis of feeling and its role in life, whether it is a true voice, and how to know that it may not be Satanic. He sees in the experience of a play the possibility that this sort of feigning can be more powerful than truth, acting "on the very centers of feeling and passion" (*EL*, 93). He recognizes a close relation between religion, politics, and drama through ritual. Some of those feelings are primitive, and one of them is the lust for power.

The figure that embodies this problem, as it did for some of the romantic poets, was Milton's Satan, against whose splendor Nimmo's father warned his son when he read *Paradise Lost* aloud. Yet Satan carried an "irresistible appeal." Shelley thought that, despite the careful theology of Milton's words, the *image* of Satan persists as that of the grand revolutionary rebel against entrenched and reactionary authority. It is a notion easy enough to read into a text or a performance in an age consumed by struggles against class tyranny. Young Chester reads all that into the defiance of the villainous figure Corder of *Maria Marten*, with little excuse, since Corder is clearly meant to represent class privilege. The reason is that the villainous Corder seems to be a figure of individualized power: "Is it fanciful in me to discover in Corder that cut-throat of a booth drama, some tincture of the Lucifer who took upon himself all guilt and defied the very lightnings of Heaven?" (*EL*, 94). This fascinated admiration for rebellion and power, did it not appear, he asks, in himself, and does it not offer some clue to the crime to which his own memoir confesses?

Let us confess it—power itself has a fascination for the young soul in its weakness and dependence. And when to power is added the guilt of blood, some horror of cruelty, its force can be hypnotic. (*EL*, 94)

The result is that in Chester's deepest being he is moved by the ambivalence of his response to Corder. Is Corder the villain or the hero? Shelley answers that Satan is the hero; but he is not, at least any longer, among the privileged. Blake wonders whether there is a hero at all in *Paradise Lost*.

At this point we are meant to recall, in the presence of Georgina, a remark Nimmo has already made about the strife of love with her father and the gradual shift in their relationship that came about when she deliberately lied to him, did not repent of it, and then against his wishes took work in a pub:

[I]t was unnatural for a child of that age to know such a triumph. Victory is a burden for the strong who alone should win it. Georgina did not want it, and having it, found it a torment—her pride saw my father humiliated—his humility considered only Georgina's special temptations. (*EL*, 59)

This episode has been a "sermon" on the seductive dangers of power and, almost unspoken, the nearness of the actor's power of feigning to the politician's, and the nearness of the power of both to that of the orator and preacher. Because acting was forbidden to him, this power becomes connected in Nimmo's young mind with defiance. For Georgina the play had made her all the more defiant of privilege. While she raged against that enemy, Nimmo unconsciously smiled to himself, though he did not know why, for he had agreed with her views: "Something moved in me that was not yet even an ambition—the mere ghost of aspiration" (*EL*, 100). It is the coming alive of his own ego, a stirring toward a fall, a birth of power that the boy does not yet know how to handle. It is a danger to the soul.

The next major episode follows from this. It is a moment in which a certain frightening freedom is articulated. The scene, or scenes (for there are two of them), are the gatherings of the Adventists for the Second Coming. Nimmo's father disagreed with the generally accepted local date of April 15, 1868, and predicted it for April 30 at a different place. Such predictions were not so unusual as we may now think. Owen Chadwick reports:

The focus and arbiter of instructed evangelical opinion, The Christian Observer, announced in January 1860 that Garibaldi's imminent destruction of the Papacy showed the Second Coming to be near. Dr. William Marsh of St. Thomas in Birmingham was known as Millennial Marsh. Such doctrines did not lessen a congregation. . . . In 1845 Marsh declared in a sermon his expectation that antichrist would be revealed within about twenty-five years and the Second Coming would be at hand. (*The Victorian Church* [London: Adam and Charles Black, 1966], I, p. 451)

The entire Nimmo family attended on April 15, despite the father's dissent. For a moment a stunning sunrise moves the group to prayers and a Wesleyan hymn, but nothing further occurs. April 30 dawns gloomy and wet, and Nimmo's father is also proved to have miscalculated. Richard reveals to Chester at this time his loss of faith; the event removes from Chester his complete trust in his father's wisdom and "opened the way to political agitation." Georgina is brought closer to her father, while Chester is estranged.

The next step Nimmo takes is downward to discover a substitute faith and a new leader. It is the final preparation for the nadir, reached when he becomes implicated in labor violence and subsequently breaks with the communist labor boss Pring. It involves a "false" conversion to Marxism, which begins under the spell of an impressive orator named Lanza. Through Lanza Cary arranges to have Nimmo's career reflect part of the movement of political radicalism in Europe. Lanza was a disciple of Proudhon and later became a lieutenant of Bakunin in the League of Peace and Freedom. But then Lanza broke with the League and adopted a somewhat Tolstoyan position "in the sense that he believed government and property to be the source of all evil and despised organized religion as a branch of the police" (*EL*, 135). The brief treatment of Lanza's career runs parallel to Cary's examination of the history of philosophical anarchism in *Power in Men*, much cut down from an early draft. He traces the tradition from Proudhon through Bakunin to Kropotkin: "Proudhon opposed violence. He thought that education and organization of the workers, certain economic reforms, and above all, the final revelation of the natural laws innate in human affairs would transform society" (*PM*, 55). Cary goes on to remark, "Bakunin, 1814–1876, his chief disciple, was not so logical. He believed in the natural law but preached violence. He hated all government" (*PM*, 55). According to Nimmo, Lanza was a nihilist and anarchist whose one belief was in love, and particularly family

love. The emphasis on family love in Nimmo's "sermon" I shall return to, for it is the one element that remains in the forefront of
Nimmo's account of his fall and redemption, and he is using it as
part of his appeal to Nina's sense of the fair.

Nimmo's discussion of Lanza on the subject of family love is followed by his remembrance of his first meeting with the young
child who was later to be his wife and is now taking his dictation.
Lanza's was a secular appeal to Chester's personal experience of
family love. It had, he says, the force of a "conversion" because it
appealed not to abstract thought but to personal feeling. What he
felt, he thinks, was like that experienced by those impelled to cry
out or groan at his father's services. It was a new form of conversion, because it elevated humanity and the law of brotherhood. But
during this same period Chester experiences a sort of detachment
that makes him unable to feel deeply for the specific problems of
others, particularly Georgina's, and he feels actual contempt for
Richard's interest in family matters. Nimmo's theme here is the isolation of the young man under the pressure of a theory which
views everything in the abstract. He comes to learn, after humiliation and guilt, that his leader Pring "loved power too much and
men not at all" (*EL*, 272). Pring, who appears to take Chester as a
lieutenant into his confidence and leads him into managing a plot
of violence which he must disown by a lie, is the Satan of Nimmo's
story. In appearance he is not the suave Satan of the nineteenth
century. He is "square and short, with rather a plump, pale face
and dark hair cut very short, growing in a widow's peak on his
forehead" (*EL*, 237). He is Blake's kind of Satan, an abstractionist.
He is also a "convinced and doctrinaire Marxist." Nimmo contrasts
him to the old-fashioned local union leader Brobdribb whose union
cards quote Deuteronomy and whom Chester himself views as behind the times and ineffective. As the Lilmouth dockers' strike
drags on, the leaders, with Brobdribb violently dissenting and resigning from the strike committee, decide to apply disciplinary
pressure and private persuasion to those who threaten to break
ranks. These phrases are, of course, euphemisms for violence,
though Chester does not at first realize it. He is implicated by the
appearance of a letter signed by his initial describing a successful
application of "persuasion." He lies to Georgina and evades his father's questions about his involvement. Eventually he lies to a
friend who perjures himself to give Chester an alibi. All this time
he has become increasingly impatient with his brother Richard's

dwelling on family gossip, realizing only later that "if I had admitted the truth of my brother, I should have known that my own life had become a lie" (*EL*, 268).

Nimmo believes he was saved by an accident. It was not quite that. A plan to discipline Brobdribb is adopted without consulting him; in anger he breaks with Pring. His complaint is that he has not been consulted, but it is more than that: Some deep feeling rises in him that makes him see the abstract coldness in Pring's eyes. He refers to this break with Pring as an accident and a sort of miracle. It is an escape from "perdition." Something deeper than the evil in his soul has spoken, and it is traceable to his father's faith in a pacifistic approach, illustrated in his treatment of the excitable Georgina. Nimmo is careful to point out that he had never been a doctrinaire pacifist. Here he takes the opportunity to defend his later decision to join the War Cabinet and set the record straight:

> I believe still that there are occasions of oppression and despair when violence, even war, can be justified. But I know, I think I knew then, that it had no real excuse at Lilmouth. The compromise offered was fair, the victory in sight was reasonable. Pring's motive in the so-called active policy was violence for the sake of violence, cruelty to make hatred, in short, class war and revolution. (*EL*, 252)

The theme of the lie, begun in the memoir with reference to Georgina's struggle with her father, culminates in a picture Nimmo draws of himself as a completely fallen figure. He himself has taken on the characteristics of the inner appearance of Satan. The device used is the characteristic spot of time:

> During my youth in that time before I knew the Dollings, a house fell down in Tarbiton—a house that had a bad name—and with many others I went to see the ruin. The fall was pronounced a judgment, two of the women had been killed. But I was attracted by a different curiosity, to see the inside of a house of pleasure thus exposed to the air.
>
> I do not know what I expected of magnificence, what wicked glory, but I saw only the inside walls and furnishings of half-a-dozen rooms exposed to the afternoon sun in a dirty squalor which was even more pitiful than it was contemptible. As I gazed I felt only a stupid confusion. (*EL*, 279)

It is likely that a Wordsworth would have stopped here and then sent the young man home in a grave and thoughtful mood.

Nimmo the preacher uses the remembrance to point the moral of his fall:

> So I myself was now a ruin with all my secret places laid open, and I was astonished at their mean appearance. My glory had ended in this pitiful rubbish heap, I turned my eyes away from it, it said nothing to me of good or evil, only of sordid failure; I had no meaning even to myself. (*EL,* 279)

The passage reminds one of Blake's description of the interior of Satan in *Milton,* not the Shelleyan hero but the center of stupid unmoving abstraction. Blake's lines are quoted by Gulley Jimson in *The Horse's Mouth,* and I have had reason to mention them before:

> A ruined man, a ruined building of God not made with hands
> Its plains of burning sand, its mountains of marble terrible
> Its pits and declivities flowing with molten ore and fountains
> Of pitch and nitre; its ruined palaces and cities and mighty works
> Its furnaces of affliction, in which his angels and emanations
> Labour with blackened visages among its stupendous ruins.
>
> (*HM,* 220)

The pattern of deceit that is played out in Nimmo's story begins with his father's warning against the external grandness of Milton's Satan. Blake's poem ends with Milton recognizing and facing the Satan in himself: the selfhood or desire for self-aggrandizing power. The vision of power in the villain of *Maria Marten* captivated and yet repelled the young Chester. Revulsion at Pring's abstract hatred, bred in the spirit of his family, saved him from an eternal fall and displayed to him his internal desolation. The memoir now speaks briefly of the dark night of his soul and his eventual rebirth as a preacher of the gospel.

This is the pattern Nimmo does not simply give to his story but sees in it. A successful book for Nimmo must offer a true lesson: "This book would be worthless if it did not show how men, especially young and ardent men as I was then, come to do evil in the name of good, a long and growing evil for a temporary and doubtful advantage" (*EL,* 252).

But, as I have said more than once, Nimmo's acts have more than one intention. If he will tell a story of innocence, fall, and redemption, he will also set the record straight. Biographers, he says, have divided his life into three parts: agitator, preacher, and demagogue. He has been accused in this last phase of offering "something for nothing," of buying the votes of parasites. But, he insists, he advocated old age pensions and insurance because he believed in them as a Christian and a Protestant. He believed also in preserving the family as the responsible spiritual unit. So he sees his own development from preacher to politician as part of a continuum of the spirit.

As he defends his own sincerity, he also defends the record of the Liberal Party, which as he writes lies in ruins:

> I do not stand in a sheet, much less a winding sheet, for our creed—for tolerance, for freedom, for private rights, yea, even for private property—tolerance which is room to learn, freedom which is room to grow, private rights and private property which are the only defence against public wrong and public breach of trust. (*EL*, 276)

Both Nimmo and Tom Wilcher speak of the cruelty bred of impatience and misunderstanding of one age and generation to another. Cary speaks elsewhere about it in his own voice. It is a matter which saddens but does not perplex him. The accomplishments of one generation of politicians are not well understood by the next because they have not lived those changes ("the situation at the time," as Nimmo calls it in *Not Honour More*) and history has not assessed them at an appropriate distance. Cary does not take us through the Liberal accomplishments in any of the books of the trilogy. I have already noted the absence of any real account of political activity of that sort in Nina's memoir. She is not inclined in that direction and assumes conveniently no need to go into such matters. Nimmo's later memoirs remain unwritten. What we do have is an examination of the roots of his political creed in evangelical Christianity and political reformist zeal told as the story of a fallen journey through Vanity Fair and the interior of Satan's bosom. This is quite enough to throw the Nimmo of *Prisoner of Grace* into a new light. If we do not care for him very much, we come to sense his deepest commitments and their source, and we come also to grasp the limitations of Nina's view of him.

But we must still consider the design on Nina. It is not until chapter 47, two-thirds of the way through the book, that Cary has Nimmo reveal quite casually that he is dictating his memoir to Nina. We are astonished at this, though we might have expected it; and the knowledge requires us to think back through the text and see it in a somewhat different or rather additional light. The chapter begins with the following paragraph:

> Last week I had a heart attack, to-day, the ninth of April, is the first on which I have been allowed out of bed. I sit here by the window and look at those fragile buds of spring that may outlive me, yet never have they been more delightful to my eyes, more powerful with the grace of courage and hope. And she who has been my wife, my nobler soul, the close and secret comrade of my darkest hours, who has given to me more than her youth, her life and loyalty—the perpetual knowledge of a truth that is truth's very substance, the faith of the heart—who has sacrificed all to me over thirty years— sits before me, pen in hand, eager to render me that last service of interpretation, anxious, as she says, to dispel through these memoirs a cloud of misunderstanding which has thrown so black a shade upon my last hours. (*EL*, 214)

This is an astonishing paragraph. We are impressed by its boldness. There is certainly nothing subtle about the flattery of the passage. There might once have been, but no longer. It is verbally no more subtle than the physical approaches Nina has told us he had been making to her. We notice also that the passage is oratorical, and we compare it to those remarks Nimmo makes in his political voice in defense of his Liberal creed. It is not that we disbelieve Nimmo's fervor or his sincerity, but we feel that the language is too bombastic and political for its object, even as we recognize that the Liberal creed and his love of Nina are the most important things in his life. There is something sad about the failure of his language any longer to rise to these occasions, and we sense here his declining powers, which are ironically shown forth by Cary as dogged persistence in trying to make old, formerly effective gestures continue to work. We might take the attitude of Jim Latter in *Not Honour More* to these sorts of speeches, if we had not already been told by Nina that Nimmo really was devoted to her and really was a good man. More important, there has been revealed to us already in *Except the Lord* a sensibility of depth, perception, and feeling, as exhibited in the account of Nimmo's youth and the spots of time. We have to conclude that this passage and the flowery defense of his career as a Liberal are expressions in which his anxiety makes him revert to an outworn style out of place in the text.

But not entirely out of place! These passages *are* Nimmo, but a Nimmo like an athlete operating on skill but no longer natural strength. It is important to acknowledge here, however, that on the basis of information we eventually get in *Not Honour More* we shall have to admit that he is still an effective public speaker. Nevertheless, there is something jolting about the passage, because in its context its bold design on Nina, combined with its oratorical clichés, makes it harsh. Yet our response is not Latter's cynicism; ours is a sense of pathos, not pity so much for Nimmo as for the *situation*, and sadness at the exhibit of compulsive behavior that the rhetoric reflects and to which he has been driven in his career. We imagine that the effect on Nina is similar, and then we reflect that in spite of all we have felt, it works! Though not quite on the level Nimmo intended.

But then his treatment of Nina, when it has been thoughtful, has never been received quite in the spirit in which he has offered it, and he has always known of her contempt for his enthusiastic manner of expression. But it has in its way kept her with him, out of her sense of class guilt and her realization that he has needed her. In short, his rhetoric, no matter how hackneyed and seemingly false, is effective. It works on us to some extent. *Except the Lord* as a whole certainly humanizes Nimmo for us, in spite of the design on Nina that reveals an old conniver as well as a desperate spirit.

Chapter 47 is a supreme effort and expresses tension. It breaks into the pattern of the story in a way much more successful than chapter 13 of *The Horse's Mouth* and calls attention to the "present" of narration. It expresses the desperation: "never has she been more lovely in my sight, never has her presence and support been more necessary to this poor atomy" (*EL*, 214). The tension is heightened in our minds by the absence of one important admission: Nimmo nowhere acknowledges that Nina is no longer his wife. The message to her is clear enough: In his mind she still is. The moral is also clear: She should not have left him.

> One flesh, how magic and how terrible is this phrase to those who love—one flesh for good and for evil—one flesh and one soul in which the nerves, the sympathies, speak as across a common heart, with meanings not to be expressed in words.
> She is part of me as I of her—she is my woman's part. (*EL*, 214)

The technique is like that of Nimmo's father (but much cruder), who after saying his piece would leave the child to decide. It is a

repetition of Nimmo's behavior, but much cruder, in the railway
station years before. It, indeed, is fair to say that there is a threat in
all of this—a spiritual threat of damnation for disloyalty. We know
already that Nina is susceptible to this sort of threat; she sometimes even sees one when it is not intended. We know that she has
felt she has been won back to helping him. For Nina there is always
the matter of fairness. Nimmo is playing upon her sense that there
is a need to set the record straight and that her testimony is
needed. Her own memoir, written later than his, can be regarded
as the result of Nimmo's designing speech to her. Of course, it
turns out to be a revelation more than a defense.

In the light of these passages in chapter 47, we look back to preceding remarks and find them also part of Nimmo's design on
Nina. He tries to evoke her sympathy: "But this is a digression.
One must forgive the old war-horse in whose stiffening limbs and
rather shaky heart the 'fire is not yet quenched'" (*EL*, 81). Very important is the passage in chapter 25 where he reviews the phases
into which biographers have divided his career, defends his ad-
vocacy of pensions and insurance, and quotes from a letter which
begins:

> True religion centres . . . in the family—for the Protestant priest-
> hood resides in every parent responsible for a child's upbringing.
> That is why we are bound to stand for any state policy that can se-
> cure the family unit as a unit. (*EL*, 104)

He remarks that this is a letter "so fortunately preserved by the
careful piety of my dear wife" (*EL*, 104). We hardly recognize Nina
in the word "piety," until we acknowledge the Nimmo style and
the Nimmo design.

Cary makes us transpose into another key. True, the passages
to Nina seem sadly excessive—sadly, because of their worn appearance. This excessiveness is, however, partly a matter of our
point of view, which has been affected by Nina's stance and filtered
through her class perception of Nimmo's style. We must therefore
struggle to overcome our suspicion of hypocrisy. For Nimmo, in
spite of this "falseness," is sincere. After the "piety" passage
Nimmo himself sets things straight:

> I can fairly claim that it was not the utterance of a rabble-rouser. The
> picture of my life as a continuous line is quite false—it resembles

rather the iron crook called by shepherds a Hampshire crook; a long strong socket and a long loop ending in a sharp backward curl. The loop begins from my poverty-stricken childhood, and curves naturally, rapidly, into the phase of agitation. But the next turn, the curl, cannot be anticipated, it does not follow. The curve was broken, when I turned back, and I became a preacher not because I had been an agitator, but because I had been brought up to evangelism. (*EL*, 104)

We may not want to accept Nimmo's politico-evangelical style, but Cary forces us to the effort by making Nimmo a perceptive and moving narrator of particular events.

One of these events is apparently a surprise to the listening Nina. She does not mention it in *Prisoner of Grace*, where she states that she did not meet Nimmo until she was seventeen. It is Nimmo's remembrance of her as a beautiful young child; it is meant to touch her vanity. It also works on her sense of class guilt, even though Nimmo denies that at that age she expressed the "arrogance of class": "I perceived then that the candour and confidence of that gaze did not arise from the arrogance of class but from the frankness of childhood, of a soul fearless of man, because innocent of evil" (*EL*, 139). This is not, I think, quite the case, in the light of Nina's memoir. Nimmo is absurdly lavish in his praise of her, but the praise has always apparently encouraged her to live up to it, even against her self-confessed laziness and her passion for Latter. Nimmo is fond of talking about the purity of her soul, as if she were a perpetual Blakean Oothoon, of her "inborn truth," and her "generosity of affection." He treats her as a model of behavior: "Faith, hope—the profound charity which in the truest sense of the word rests in the love of God, and is indeed the very door of His grace—were innate in that spirit" (*EL*, 140). (We are inclined to respond dryly that she is a bit too generous.) Nina hears and takes down all of this. Surely she is embarrassed, as she was when Nimmo prayed for their union on their marriage night. But she is vain, and the excess has its effect on her, no doubt. As we learn from *Not Honour More*, she cannot turn him out. She long ago learned he was sincere, in these flights, even though he worked himself up to deliver them. They come complete with a moral: "What is the purport of all this—that he who founds argument and policy upon our intuition of human goodness will not be disappointed" (*EL*, 140).

There is also a good amount of self-explanation that we imagine directed both to posterity and to her. The remarks speak of matters also taken up defensively by her in *Prisoner of Grace*. He appeals to her sympathy when he speaks of being once again "thrown into the gutter" (*EL*, 274). He designs to touch her when he speaks of himself as condemned to a "double death, of his body and his name" (*EL*, 276). He leads her to forgive what she describes as his excessive sense of insecurity. "I had been made," he says of his early escape from a beating, "to understand the fearful condition of political life, the fundamental want of all security, the appalling risks of those who accept any large responsibility for their fellows" (*EL*, 226). He turns it into a nobility of aim. He confesses ingratiatingly to a fear of conspiracy against him that she has noticed and disliked, explaining it as he does so. It is grounded in his sensitivity to class and his concern for the poor:

> [W]hat enraged me at that time was the idea of conspiracy, the belief that behind all the façade of law and justice, hard enough as it was upon the deprived, there was a secret compact between owners, the rich and their hangers-on, against the dispossessed.
>
> It is this suspicion, I tell you earnestly, this belief that works like madness in the blood. (*EL*, 212)

Surely it is this sort of statement that gains Nina's sympathy when she speaks of it in *Prisoner of Grace*. She hates the notion of class because it makes her feel guilty, and yet it seems to her that people like Nimmo and his friend Goold have used it unfairly to their own ends. But she wants to be fair to Nimmo.

Most important in the design on Nina, and certainly most subtle because it is at the heart of the whole memoir, is the story of Nimmo's sister Georgina. Georgina's behavior is supposed to be a lesson to all of us, as it was to him, and a lesson in particular to Nina. Georgina's spirit is the vehicle of his rebirth. Indeed, the large role Georgina plays in the memoir and the praise she receives must come across to Nina as implying a comparison at her expense. This is but an indication of a certain malicious undercurrent in Nimmo's behavior toward Nina. Nina herself speaks of Nimmo's tendency to strut and swagger after his sexual raids upon her, and this reflects Nimmo's class hatred—submerged as it sometimes is—with her and Latter as its symbolic objects. It is this difference that makes Nimmo—in a quite different way from Latter, who does the same—lay claim to ownership of her, though at the same time he reveres her, as Latter does in quite another way. The story is one of commitment to duty, specifically duty to the family; and it is made all the more meaningful by the fact of Georgina's rebellious spirit. As we have seen, Nimmo states that their childhoods were marked by freedom of choice and thus a constant conflict between duty and inclination. The analogy with the struggle between Nina's inclination to go to Latter and her duty, in Nimmo's eyes, to her earlier marriage is intended to be grasped by Nimmo's auditor. One of the most moving of Nimmo's remembrances is of a scene between Georgina and her father in which he pacifistically exorcises the devil of her rage. The scene contrasts to that between Lucy and her father in *To Be a Pilgrim*, where Lucy is physically beaten.

Georgina's sense of duty to her family and especially her father leads her almost to marry against her inclination and then not to marry the man she loves. Both decisions are crises of duty and inclination, the failure to marry in the first instance becoming all the more reason not to in the second. Nimmo remembers a lie as the critical event in the relation of daughter to father. Her father questions her about whether the storekeeper for whom she works has molested her, and she lies to him. She lies because she knows that if she does not, the father, who always puts morality and truth over the family's best secular interests, will insist that she leave her job. The family needs her income. Also, she has discovered how to deal with the problem. This lie stands between them through their lives, but it also brings them closer together. The father prays that she be saved from the "lie in soul" (*EL*, 51); she ceases to worship him and begins to take care of him in a solicitous way.

The parallel here is the lie of parenthood that Nina and Chester share and Nina's solicitousness, which the present combination of sermon and verbal lovemaking is designed to extend. In the enthusiasm of offering the parallel there is a considerable amount of excitement and tension. Nimmo makes the struggle between Georgina and her father (and his own "struggle" with Nina) a titanic battle: "Do not be deceived by these old-fashioned words, soul and flesh, appetite and brethren—only fools can trifle with the things they mean—in his battle with Georgina my father was fighting for the salvation of a nature, in which there was as great power of evil as good" (*EL*, 58). He convinces us of the issues vis-à-vis Georgina. We are less impressed when they are applied to Nina, because she is not a stark personality in whom things divide so easily. If we are to describe Nina's conflict, apart from what Nimmo makes it into, we should say that she is a rather self-indulgent, spoiled, lazy, beautiful woman who likes pleasure and is faced with the problem of good and evil as her life with Nimmo has presented it to her. This eventually turns into a conflict between inclination and duty similar to that Nimmo sees in Georgina.

There is a kind of incongruity in the parallel Nimmo tries to establish, yet he manages the task. That is part of his hold on Nina—his powerful imagination, even in defeat, even when directed to relatively trivial ends, even when it seems clothed in preposterous or worn-out jargon. Robert Bloom remarks (p. 167) that Nimmo's rhetorical mastery may after a time "come to seem suspect, and the pronouncements, with their spiritual insistence, perhaps a little forced or hollow, or contrived, as if Chester were striking a pose. Chester's nineteenth-century evangelical rhetoric occasionally corroborates this suspicion." But it is not a pose; it is habit that is wearing itself out. It is sincere (Nina was always embarrassed by it), but it has little capacity to convey sincerity. Yet for this very reason Cary intends us to be touched by it, as Nina is, in spite of everything. Jim Latter could never be touched by it, never understand, even though Nimmo's sermon to Nina can be regarded as on the subject of honor, on a notion of duty greater than love. Indeed, Latter would never be able to square the sensitive Nimmo of *Except the Lord* with the Nimmo he knows. He does not have the imagination to do so. Cary challenges us to rise to the occasion.

There are two climaxes in *Except the Lord*. The first is a distant remembrance, a spot of time from Nimmo's young manhood; the second is a moment from only a year previous to writing. The two are connected by the presence, in more ways than one, of Georgina. Defeated and closed in on himself by his experience in labor agitation and his break with Pring, the young Chester one evening hears casually at family prayers his father intoning Psalm 127. Suddenly he is deeply moved. The moment, he believes, accounts for his return to the faith and his decision to take up preaching six months later. He has been tense and annoyed at being thrust back into the family and at the problems of his sister Ruth with her spendthrift husband. He is moved by the psalm, and he steps outside to be alone. He feels, in an eloquent passage, a "strange convulsion" in his soul: "the thoughts which were struggling to be born, the feelings which had not yet taken shape" (*EL*, 285). In a scene that Wordsworth might have established for a Lucy poem, Georgina comes walking toward him in the moonlight.

> She had not seen me yet. As she looked about, the white beam from overhead shockingly revealed her emaciation, the deep hollows of her cheeks, the eyes grown too prominent in the shrinking of her face. The rich and shining abundance of her black hair springing from that pale forehead brought back moor tales of the dead whose hair lives after them, and who walk from tombs to enchant and twine the living in its coils. Georgina then seemed indeed a revenant—her face as she searched, frowning, had the impatient feverish expression of one released only a little while from the grave to do her work on earth. (*EL*, 285)

His first response to her is "annoyance at this typical family interruption," but then there comes on him a different mood engendered by her manner and voice; she had been bringing him his coat: "she smiled at me in that serene and tranquil manner which quite contradicted her tragic looks, 'Why are you so unhappy. Don't you see how proud we are of you?'"

> She was consoling me and it broke my heart—I felt then an indescribable shock of anguish and of exultation. And instantly among the turmoil of my senses a darkness fell away, great presences were revealed, things absolutely known and never again to be obscured. (*EL*, 286)

Conscience plays its role here, as it does in the "presences" that appear to Wordsworth after the boat-stealing. Nimmo is reminded of his deep connection to Georgina, to his family; and his sense of spiritual isolation disappears. This rebirth carried with it, of course, the familiar message to Nina of family fidelity.

It is interesting that Nimmo treats this climax as virtually a chance occurrence. The father is not directing the psalm toward him but toward Ruth's absent husband. It is the psalm entering his idle, detached, and perhaps oddly receptive mind that affects him so profoundly. The second climax has that same chance quality—at least on the surface. It is as if the Wordsworthian memory were working beneath the surface of consciousness, just as Wordsworth implied, the child silently molding the man. About a year before writing *Except the Lord*, by some unconsidered impulse, Nimmo

decided to visit Georgina's unmarked grave in Shagbrook Churchyard. It is here that he discovers something he believes greater
than memory, the *actual presence* of Georgina in the "vast silence of
the moor" (*EL*, 287). He found his own heart beating again in tune
"to a heart that could not know despair because it forgot itself in
duty and love" (*EL*, 287). The message to Nina is clear, but it is also
quite sincerely a message to himself and to his readers. Soon he
will embark on one last political effort, reported to us in *Not Honour
More*. In this climax Nimmo's various purposes all remain at work.

In spite of the moving sincerity of these last pages, we must recognize the fierce irony that Nimmo himself does not express but
that Cary slyly invites us to consider. In the climax of the novel,
Nimmo has occasion to quote the first three lines of Psalm 127; I
have already quoted them near the beginning of this discussion.
The rest of the psalm is instructive:

> It is vain for you to rise up early, to sit up late, to eat the bread of
> sorrows: for so he giveth his beloved sleep.
>
> Lo children are an heritage of the Lord: and the fruit of the womb
> is his reward.
>
> As arrows are in the hand of a mighty man; so are children of the
> youth.
>
> Happy is the man that hath his quiver full of them: they shall not
> be ashamed, but they shall speak with the enemies in the gate.

Chester Nimmo has no children. Fr. Teeling (p. 280) argues that
this is an "authorial comment of the highest moment on the parallel sterility of Nimmo's whole career," but this is mistaken and too
abstract. The sweeping parallel is not characteristic of Cary in any
case. It is the sort of thing, were he to use it, that he would be likely
to undercut with a further complexity. Fr. Teeling is more accurate
when he remarks that Cary emphasizes "the danger in a man like
Nimmo who is supremely skilled in both personal and national
politics . . . he may become the victim of that very skill and degen-
erate into a wicked and conniving old man" (p. 283). Even here,
however, too much attention is given to Latter's reading of Nimmo
and not enough to Nimmo's reading of himself. Fr. Teeling thinks
that Nimmo's death in *Not Honour More* in a water closet is symbolic of his career, but it is symbolic principally to the cynical Lat-

ter. Nina feels Nimmo's body should be removed before others see it there. To her, it is an inappropriate symbolism. The papers do not divulge where he died. Who is correct here? Even Latter confesses that it is "a small point" (*NHM*, 222).

Chester Nimmo's family is founded on a lie, and the denouement of the trilogy seems to bear out his father's admonition that a lie can never be a firm base for anything. But our response is not so simple. Nimmo's memoir raises more complicated issues than his own description of its aim, already quoted, sets forth. A fundamental conflict in Nimmo is between his inclination, both religious and political, always to seek a new beginning and his having to face an intractable *real*. This real is the original condition under which he married and tried to establish a family. It cannot be as easily expunged as his notion of a new beginning suggests. Indeed, it is tragic that Nimmo ritually confesses to an early lie in this memoir but cannot look honestly at his marriage. One notes that here somehow is the limit of the efficacy of fiction-making and the limit of the political regarded as a simply pragmatic art that deals with "the situation at the time," as perhaps it always must. Perhaps this is also the reason that Cary cannot be critical of the Liberal collapse or the collapse of any government that was, for a while at least, effective. The book, regarded as Cary's book, studies these limits constantly, while the book, regarded as Nimmo's book, preaches on the conflict of inclination and duty. Cary's book endorses Nina's sense of a certain goodness in Nimmo. As part of the trilogy, it cooperates in showing how a powerful imagination can struggle with the real. It makes us revise a too easy notion that intentions are either simple and singular or wrong. It offers us also a personal theme. The book is Nimmo's self-expression. However, Nimmo thinks of words as external things. He is—the great orator—more than most of us suspicious of words. At first his remarks about this seem hypocritical, but more reflection makes us feel that they are from the heart. His attitude is that of the enthusiast: Words are complex, feelings are simple. When his own words get closest to particular moments of feeling, they also come closest to simple truth. When he speaks abstractly, our suspicions are fueled and we become wary of being used. Indeed, they are fueled when he speaks of words and their sorcery because we suspect him of being the greatest sorcerer of all Cary's characters—with the self-consciousness Sara Monday lacks, with a finer imagination than Tom Wilcher's, without the irony that is Gulley Jimson's vehicle of sincerity, with a stronger will than Nina's, and greater flexibility than Latter possesses. Words, he argues, are prisons when they become abstract containers. They are like the snake coiled around the falling damned in Blake or the cage around the Orcan child: "To bind man's future in a coil of words is to put an iron cage on the tender limbs of a child" (*EL*, 276):

> But nothing shall persuade me to believe that the generous youth of my country, that these young men who hate and revile me, like those old ones in Lilmouth long ago, practise evil for evil's sake. They are only deceived—they are under a spell of words.
>
> The world itself is young, we are but little removed from the time when writing was a wonder, when any written speech was magic. Words printed in books—Rousseau, Proudhon, Owen, Marx, what power they can wield. But it is the power of sorcerers—the spell they cast is abracadabra. And the fruit of their sorcery is egotism and madness, war and death.
>
> So evil is the brood of the slogans that the most splendid and noble battle cries, Liberty, Equality, Fraternity, bred nothing but new and more cunning, more hypocritical despots. (*EL*, 274)

Words in their old configurations are reactionary and must give way to new. All that is permanent is the life of religious feeling, exemplified by the ministry of his father and countless others. The tragedy of Nimmo's career in politics, beyond the tragedy of his domestic life, is not that he is a bad man but that he cannot any longer make the words of liberal doctrine—tolerance, private rights, freedom, and the like—work. They are themselves changing. All political movements suffer this fate. Nimmo knows this, but he doesn't quite know it about his own words. Yet he has a political instinct that seems to tell him more than his words contain. He associates this instinct, this voice of feeling with his political muse Nina. This is the reason why his memoir is a desperate act to keep her allegiance. Lines from Blake's "Mental Traveller" come to mind here:

> He wanders weeping far away,
> Untill some other take him in;
> Oft blind and age-bent, sore distrest,
> Untill he can a Maiden win.

For Nimmo, not a new maiden but an effort at vision renewed in the same maiden; not a maiden but a woman pregnant by someone else when he won her; not won, because she did not love him. A perilous creation, a miracle that he can sustain it as well as he does, which is in part the reason that one of the newsmen in *Not Honour More* remarks to Jim Latter when Latter asks him what is funny about a crook like Nimmo getting away with his dirty work: "I don't know. . . . But you have to take off your hat to the old bastard" (*NHM*, 33).

Not Honour More

With that remark we have already entered into the bitter, violent world of Jim Latter. Cary describes Latter's book to us as follows:

> It is the statement of a man who believes in authority. He doesn't call himself a fascist and he hates fascism but he has a fascist mind; he has been a soldier, and he asks why a country can't be run like a good regiment by men who believe in duty and discipline and don't grab all the money they can find for themselves. He says, "Why all this rottenness and corruption and lies which you get in a democracy?" He is a perfectly honest man and he is not a cruel man. (quoted by Foster, p. 489)

This is the kind of description that in spite of Cary ought not to be given of a Cary character. It is too abstract. In the novel Latter reveals that he hasn't heard of fascism and has to be given the example of Mussolini before he forms even the vaguest notion of it. If he is not cruel he is certainly violent, and there is at least a question about his honesty. One critic, Malcolm Foster (p. 488), has bluntly called him a liar, but that goes to another abstract extreme. There is little question that, as Jack Wolkenfeld has observed (p. 166) he is rigid and absolutist, but when we have used all these labels, we have oversimplified a complicated particular.

Latter's "statement," as he calls it, he dictates in prison about a month after he has murdered Nina. It is actually his second "statement," the first having been made on the evening of May 1, 1926, when he was under the erroneous impression that he had shot Chester Nimmo to death for "interfering" with his wife. This first statement he quotes verbatim in chapter 4. It is worth placing before us in its entirety, because it establishes the tone of several themes of the whole:

> The reason of my action against Lord Nimmo was because I caught him interfering with my wife. Repugnant as it is to any de-

cent man to make such facts public in the Press, I hereby give them as a public duty. For many years I have considered Nimmo and his gang of a character without the first idea of honourable conduct, public or private, and this proves it. They have been the ruin of our beloved country—have always supported our enemies everywhere and once more in the present terrible danger are only seeking their own advantage to worm their way back into power.

I do not therefore regret anything in my action and would do it again if it called attention to the increasing corruption of everything in the country, the destruction of family life, and the policy of shameless jobbery and double-dealing in high places, only for personal ambition.

It is the same everywhere, decent honest people having no chance against the government. They are just pushed up against the wall. No one will listen to them because the only idea is to get all you can by any dirty trick which pays. And, family life which is the life-blood of an honourable sound-hearted nation mocked at as too much trouble and going down every day. (*NHM*, 26–27)

The reporter who receives this statement from Latter tells him that the first sentence will have to be deleted as libelous, and Latter points out if that were done it would appear that his motive was jealousy and not the defense of honor. The larger statement that constitutes *Not Honour More* is an effort to correct newspaper reports about his motive for murdering Nina. We do not know its fate, of course, but Latter's record of published statements is not encouraging. His first statement, reproduced above, was a failure. In fact, his attempt on Nimmo's life failed. His 1916 book, *The Lugas and British Policy: The Great Betrayal*, did not have the intended result. The effect of the statement that constitutes *Not Honour More* is far from what Latter desires. It is less a clarification and an explanation of motive than an accusation of betrayal and conspiracy. In the end everyone comes off badly.

Latter's avowed style is that of the military report. This one is "dictated at high speed for shorthand" (*NHM*, 27), but it constantly shades off into bitterness and diatribe occasionally spiced with cynical humor, as in Latter's description of the right-wing agitator Brightman's house:

At last young fellow in a white jacket condescended to answer my bell—and asked me to wait some more in the porch. But I didn't see it and walked into ye olde tyme lounge hall, panelled in Elizabethan linen-fold oak made out of chewed paper painted olde shitte colour. Full-length portrait of Brightman at east end, olde shitte, about eight feet high, as olde Englishe good-chappe, with shorts, open shirt and pipe. Slap-up bar underneath with olde chromium fittings. (*NHM*, 73)

Robert Bloom has made the interesting remark that Latter's "sardonic comic exaggerations [are] . . . the only recourse for the antipolitical personality" (p. 191). That is profoundly what Latter is. There is no question that Latter has a certain satirical talent, but it is always expressed in the context of bitter alienation. As R. W. Noble has pointed out (p. 94), Latter is a reliable reporter when he speaks in his military style, but when he lapses into outrage and bitterness he is no longer to be trusted. Among critics, Robert Bloom (pp. 178–79) sees the best in Latter, and argues that we view most of the events of *Not Honour More* with his "sense of outraged honor, and we share, if only tentatively, in his violent denunciations of a corrupt world." He sees Latter as alone trying to "make public and political life over in the image of personal honor. Nina and Chester have long since abandoned such an endeavor" (p. 183). Bloom does not seem to see that Latter's honor is corrupt from the beginning and that he does not really represent private as against public honor, that the two things are not separately definable. Bloom's sense of a certain attractiveness in Latter (p. 194) and his utter dislike of Nina and Chester tend to make Latter in his eyes the closest thing to a tragic figure that the trilogy has. This is a conclusion luckily not shared by many others. Charles Hoffman thinks Latter is "scrupulously honest about the facts he presents, but his facts are almost unconsciously selected to justify his sense of honor and honesty" (p. 151). This is true, but it is worse than this. Malcolm Foster's view is that in addition to being a liar he is a "brute" and an "absolutist run amuck" (p. 487). He elicits (p. 488) as evidence of Latter's lying the several versions that he gives of his seduction of Nina (chapters 2, 12, and 13). I believe that these versions can be resolved with each other easily enough, and that "liar" is perhaps not quite the right word. Latter's problem is emotional inconsistency, governed by his sense of conspiracy against all that he thinks he stands for. In each of the cases Foster mentions he is convinced of the truth he is uttering at the time. Jack Wolkenfeld thinks that Latter comes off the worst of all the characters: Latter accuses Nimmo of hypocrisy but runs out on Nina; he commits adultery with her but accuses Nimmo of "interfering" with her; he fails to understand the situation of the Luga tribesmen; he hates

Brightman but exhibits some of Brightman's own tendencies; he is impatient with rules and law and takes the law into his own hands (pp. 178ff.). Wolkenfeld's view is that any reader ought to see that "no amount of talk of truths and honor can excuse such an action" (p. 180). That Cary explains him "with great sympathy" is not to fail to show how we are to take him. This seems to me quite correct. The residue of sympathetic anger that we share with Latter is part of Cary's design to get us to think the situation through and come to a more mature judgment.

Latter's statement is concerned principally with a period of eleven days from May 1 to May 11, 1926, the period of the general strike in England, and specifically a dockers' strike in Tarbiton. Latter adds to this his selective account of the trial of Special Constable Maufe for assault on the communist strike leader Pincomb. This is followed by an account of Latter's "execution" of Nina and the death by heart attack of Chester Nimmo. These events take place in mid-June, and Latter is dictating some time in July, presumably in advance of his trial for murder. But the statement covers more because of Latter's sense of embattlement. That more is principally Latter's version of his relationship with Nina.

Latter's theme is honor. He does not preach on a text, as Nimmo does, but there is a text that comments ironically on the theme and is used bitterly by Nina in a conversation he reports with her. It is Richard Lovelace's poem "To Lucasta, Going to the Wars." It is Latter's favorite poem since school days when he tried to explain it to Nina. He refers respectfully to its author as "Colonel" Lovelace. He accuses Nina of quoting it from time to time in order to make him feel like a "prig." The irony we see in it is different. It was hardly from "the Nunnery of [Nina's] chaste breast and quiet mind" that Latter went back to the army. Nor was his inconstancy so honorable as that professed by Lovelace:

> Yes, this inconstancy is such
>   As you too shall adore;
> I could not love thee, Dear, so much
>   Loved I not honour more.

R. W. Noble (p. 93) makes the interesting observation that there is a larger, historical irony in the poem's use: Lovelace fought for Charles I against Cromwell, whose "New Model Army . . . was inspired by the Protestant egalitarian vision." Noble sees Latter as "standing in descent from Colonel Lovelace" against the Liberalism of Nimmo that stands in descent from Protestant egalitarianism.

Nina never came to adore Jim's inconstancy. Latter believes that honor is at stake in Nimmo's "interference" with his wife, that the issue is "bigger than politics" (*NHM*, 13), in fact has "nothing to do with politics" (*NHM*, 30), that he has a right to kill Nimmo, and that to do so would "carry out sentence" (*NHM*, 47). The matter becomes greater and greater in Latter's mind. He also feels justified because he thinks Nimmo and his "gang" have destroyed honor in England. The remark is particularly revealing because one of the things he mentions as having been destroyed is the "sanctity of the home and marriage": "No confidence or faith in any man and divorces running at fifty thousand a year" (*NHM*, 9). What he conveniently forgets is that he has helped to bring about one of those divorces, principally because he really refuses to accept Nina's marriage.

Nimmo's responses to Latter's verbal and physical attacks on him are clever improvisations. One of Nimmo's tactics is to accuse him of jealousy and spite and call his honor that of a savage. He never calls Latter a lunatic, but in the novel there is the wry parallel of the woman Brome, who blames Nimmo for the death of her son in the war and periodically attempts to kill him. In Latter's view this woman has a "lunatic grievance" (*NHM*, 23). By contrast, he claims to act in the public interest and decency. The difference is not as great as he would like to make it.

Latter has a very strict sense of truth and a very broad sense of what a lie is. Truth, for him, is simple, absolute, and usually apparent. When it is not, as in political situations, he is disarmed, resentful, and without intellectual resources. He becomes very disturbed over the law of libel as the newspaper reporter describes it, because he learns that it has nothing to do with truth and falseness. The reporter remarks in refusing to accept the first sentence of Latter's statement: "Truth can be the worst kind of libel because doing more damage" (*NHM*, 28). Latter is inconsistent about truth. He claims that truth will always prevail, yet he expresses anxiety that, in fact, it may not:

> I saw at once if Nimmo didn't die, he'd be putting out some lying statement to put me in the wrong or hide the truth. And I'd seen often enough how such men can get their lies received all over the world, so that the truth has no chance against them. Due to their

hook-up with all the other brass wanglers in every department. (*NHM*, 21)

Any statement with which Latter does not agree is a "lie," not a mistake or a misapprehension. All such lies are deliberate and proof of a conspiracy against good men and Latter himself. When someone shouts that Latter is a fascist he calls that a lie at once, though at the time he isn't certain what a fascist is (*NHM*, 35). Yet he accepts and lives the lie of Nimmo's parentage of Tom and Sally, and he does not waver from it after the confrontation with Nimmo in *Prisoner of Grace*, even in his final statement. Obviously, it is a matter of honor for him to do so, but he does not seem to see that here is at least one situation in which honor and the simple, absolute truth collide.

For Latter, rumors are lies, and those who pass them on are conspirators in a lie. In an interesting way Cary contrasts Latter's sense of conspiracy with Nimmo's. In *Prisoner of Grace*, Nina states that early in his career Nimmo acted on a theory of class conspiracy. But Nina, who is irritated by such an idea because she thinks it is an accusation against her class background, also recognizes that Nimmo conquers this idea or at least turns it to productive use. Latter, on the other hand, is captive to his notion, and it finally destroys him, Nina, and Nimmo.

Latter expresses his resentments in the form of diatribe against past conspiracies or shady dealings. Nimmo, he thinks, stole Nina away from him in order to get her money and make a start in politics with it. There is some truth in this interpretation, but Latter fails to acknowledge his own role in this "conspiracy." Nor will he grant to Nimmo that he might also have married her for love. Nimmo is particularly vulnerable to this sort of oversimplification by others because of his multiple motivation: he *did* want her money and her status, but he also loved her, and he made no demands on her funds. She gave them freely to him. Latter also claims that there was a conspiracy to drive him out of England, but he forgets that he had piled up debts of "honor" that required his absence. True, it was convenient for Nimmo that he was in Africa; nevertheless, he brought about his own exile. Latter is suspicious of Nimmo's desire for him to take command of the Specials during the strike, because he claims that Nimmo is protecting himself: It would be dishonorable for Latter to shoot Nimmo while also serving under him. He never imagines that Nimmo's effort is to conciliate him for everyone's sake. He deeply resents what he regards as Nimmo's hold on Nina, but he is unable to imagine Nina's hold on Nimmo. Because he makes Nimmo a scapegoat, his statements fail to reach the absolute truth he believes is so simple: "He'd always worked the religious game on her, prayed over her frivolity and frightened her with the idea she was no better than a social parasite" (*NHM*, 14). He thinks Nimmo held on to her as long as he did by "paying her bills and dressing her up like a London society tart" (*NHM*, 56). Even if this were entirely true in some sense, he disregards Nina's complicity in the crime. The reason is that he thinks of her as entirely passive to Nimmo's evil control; Nimmo could "play on her like a piano" (*NHM*, 103). Latter cannot accept that religion was not used as a "game" by Nimmo instead of a serious matter and that he might have lavished gifts on Nina as an expression of devotion. Finally, Latter is completely unable to understand Nina's sense of the importance of Nimmo's political activity and her belief in his basic goodness. This is the point at issue. When Latter says of the matter of honor that his concern is "something bigger than politics" (*NHM*, 13), we recall Nina's statement at the end of *Prisoner of Grace* that her relation to Nimmo involves "something bigger than love" (*PG*, 402). Nina refers to fairness and to political activity in behalf of the good. Latter refers to personal honor predicated on a fixed notion of right behavior. Nina's is the more humane view because it is simply more realistic and allows for forgiveness. Latter's is the less humane because it has an infirm grasp on the real and turns on accusation.

Latter expends his considerable arsenal of invective on Nimmo, who is at one time or another called "hypocrite," "wangler," "crook," "devil," "liar," "faker," "old swine," and "evil man." He belongs to a species of "politicos" and "talky boys." At one point, Latter as a special constable is prepared to arrest Nimmo for sedition on the basis of a speech only the first paragraph of which he has read (*NHM*, 107). He does not go through with this decision because of intervening events—or perhaps a failure of nerve. As he becomes further embroiled in political events he is increasingly suspicious of everyone except the members of his own unit of Specials, who can do absolutely no wrong and two of whom he nearly canonizes as martyrs. It is, of course, true that they may indeed be good men and wretchedly treated. The point is that Latter's mind is made up with no real attention to the evidence. He is especially quick to respond to insinuations, particularly those which he thinks cast aspersions on his wife (*NHM*, 30–31), but he is also suspicious of the wife whose honor he would defend: "I had to ask myself if she was as tricky as a set of Japanese boxes" (*NHM*, 57). Finally, he is suspicious of words themselves, because the "talky boys" can tie things up in "a lot of big words" (*NHM*, 75). Frequently he reveals himself as helpless and confused by words. This is unlike Nimmo's reservations about words in *Except the Lord*. There Nimmo speaks of words that gain too great a hold on society and frustrate liberty. Here Latter attacks the users of words to mislead the innocent. Latter is, himself, an innocent past the time when innocence is completely attractive.

There is something innocent—and awful—about Latter's devotion to Nina. It is childish or perhaps adolescent. At first, we feel there is something touching in his relation to her, and that he has been much put upon. But there has been something wrong about their relationship from its beginning in their loneliness. We have suspected this from *Prisoner of Grace* when we sense there may be compulsiveness in it more than true love. There is "an old argument" between them that dates back to their first lovemaking and before. The argument is the childish one of whether or not Nina *really* loves Jim. It is the first exhibition of Jim's suspicious nature, and in a form near to hatred. In two places in *Not Honour More*, Latter tells us with unintended pathos of their youthful relationship. In the first instance a bitter argument involves Nina's accusing him of jealousy. In the second, she behaves completely passively in their first lovemaking, so that it seems to be a punishment to both. What comes out is Jim's deep loneliness:

> I am not attempting to hide I was guilty to this woman. I say I behaved like a brute to her, in this respect. Even if due to my great love. For we were brought up together as children, being cousins, and I loved her most passionately from a boy of ten. My mother being dead and my father abroad and not interested, she was all I had in the world. And she being an orphan, she also loved me and gave me all my happiness. (*NHM*, 11)

The lovemaking is a disaster and predicts the disaster that occurs whenever they come together later on.

> So then she said she was not afraid of anything I could do to her, and as for loving me, she loved me much more than I loved her, but if I spoiled this concert [which they were to attend] she would never

forgive me. And there was the Blue Lion Hotel opposite where we were known and we could take two rooms at once and if I really meant what I said, for heaven's sake let us get over the agony and have some peace. So we went in and did what she suggested. But we were angry with each other and I accused her of spite against me and spoiling something that should have crowned our great love, and she said I was cruel and tried to make it a punishment to her. We had a great quarrel and the day was spoilt. And this has always been a cause for anger between us. (*NHM*, 12)

The act of passivity is, Latter believes, a weapon that Nina uses to punish him. As we know, he calls it "going mule," and it involves her adopting a demeanor of indifference and total silence which eventually drives him to shame and apology.

In Latter's version it is not he who goes to Nina's bed when they were children, but Nina who comes to him. He is the naïve, lonely young lad, victimized by a flirtatious child who "hated boys because she could not turn them round her finger," though by his own admission she seems to have had her way with him (*NHM*, 71). Their closeness is characterized by childish strife, a pattern established early.

Cary establishes their aloneness and their insecurity. She thieves from her guardian, perhaps for attention, and she shouts at Jim when he teases her, "You are a fool and nobody loves you" (*NHM*, 71). Their loneliness is what they have in common, but it expresses itself in opposite ways, and that makes their relationship a stormy one. Her response is to be ingratiating; his is to be suspicious of any affection for him that is not, by his measurement, complete. The stage is set for the struggles between them that are key scenes in the novel.

The short space of time covered by the events reported in Latter's "statement" makes *Not Honour More* quite different from any of the novels of either trilogy. The advantage of this to Cary, given the nature of the narrator he chooses and the fact that the novel is a climax, is clear. Latter is a brooder, but not a thinker. Extensive brooding lacks interest and variety. To use Latter as a narrator is to require a reasonably compact action that can be *reported* and a series of events that will themselves contain interest beyond the narrator's self-expression. Finally, the novel is appropriately designed to concentrate more on *events* moving to a conclusion than are its predecessors.

On Saturday, May 1, 1926, Chester Nimmo delivers the second of his three Shagbrook Churchyard addresses. He has taken control of the emergency committee organized to keep peace in the impending labor disputes that become the general strike of Tuesday, May 4. That evening Jim Latter returns to Palm Cottage and through a window sees Nimmo "interfering" with his wife. Incredible as it may seem, Nimmo has managed to remain at Palm Cottage for quite some time after the alleged heart attack of *Prisoner of Grace*. For two years he and Nina have worked together on his papers there while Nina has lived as wife with Latter in the same house. Obviously Latter has been fuming about this for a long time (a year since Nina completed her memoir). We do not know whether to commend the patience exhibited by a naturally impatient man or declare him a fool and maybe even a coward.

Two years does seem preposterous, but then everything seems preposterous in this denouement. The individual events of this trilogy—all imaginable on their own—do add up to the preposterous. One thing particularly emphasized is Nimmo's preposterous ability still to get his way—almost. He has settled for less than marriage with Nina. He knows that is impossible, but he has secured the next best thing, her support and attendance. He spends more of the day with her than Latter does. Cary doesn't tell us all of this; he doesn't have to. We fill in the blanks, our faculties having been roused to act. Another thing that Cary never tells us is the extent of Latter's incompetence. This we gradually put together. Its extent is much greater than we originally might have imagined. It is, indeed, preposterous. Preposterousness is Cary's way of emphasizing the capacities of human imagination, no matter how odd, to construct situations and then to construct solutions, no matter how faulty or provisional.

When Latter finds Nina and Nimmo together, he fires his Winchester 22 rifle at Nimmo, but he misses. The elderly Nimmo reveals his capacity for improvisation even as Latter, a hunter and former soldier, reveals that under severe emotional stress his marksmanship fails him. Nimmo back-somersaults through a glass window and escapes unharmed in a manner that would credit a Western hero. The scene would be entirely comical if it were not so shockingly violent. Latter is then stunned by Nimmo's bodyguard, revives, and escapes with the help of Nina under the illusion that he has actually killed Nimmo. On the way out of the house he meets the "lunatic" woman Mrs. Brome on the way in, who actually assists him through a window. He then issues to newsmen his first statement, which becomes meaningless in the light of Nimmo's miraculous feat of self-preservation and quick denial of any violence. Latter's meeting with reporters and their cynical treatment of him completes the picture of futile incompetence which he tends to interpret as the helplessness of the honest in the face of universal dishonesty.

On Sunday, May 2, Latter returns to Palm Cottage where there is a second triangular scene, culminating in Latter's attempt, out of anger at her mulishness, to shoot Nina; but this too is a failure because the pistol he has taken from Nimmo is unloaded and his own has been taken from him in a scuffle outside the entry. In a rage he throws the pistol at Nina, stunning her and drawing blood, whereupon he has a sudden change of heart and becomes solicitous. This has always been the pattern of their arguments, but here his anger has driven him to unparalleled violence. When Nina leaves, Nimmo in contempt gives him ammunition. This seems to have a relatively calming effect, another of Nimmo's successful and resourceful acts; and Latter is content to fire shots in the floor on either side of him before leaving to visit Brightman, the right-wing agitator. Despite Nimmo's momentary success here, however, his act has courted disaster in a way that seems foolish and excessive. His declaration to all those outside the room that there is nothing to worry about, that it is merely a "demonstration" apparently does calm everyone, but it is hardly believable and has a blatancy that suggests declining powers in spite of persistent desire. Nimmo's motives in all this are complicated. He is concerned about his role in the labor crisis and does not want a sexual scandal to ruin his chance at a political comeback. He does not want to drag Nina's name through the papers. He feels a certain guilt, indeed, always has, toward Latter. And now it may be at its height, given his recent sexual mishandling of Nina. But, too, his act of contempt toward Latter reveals that he likes to strut his superiority, perhaps out of fear that at least sexually Latter is superior to him. Rather than have Latter locked up, as he surely could, he persists in attempting a political solution. His tendencies of a lifetime in politics win out, perhaps compulsively, over what appears to be good sense. Where his politics and good sense had been the same, now in this situation, they are opposed. Latter's tendencies of a lifetime lead him to a violent solution. This reveals the sadness behind the preposterousness of the situation. It is not merely an example of honor gone wrong; it is also politics gone wrong—in both cases through singleminded persistence in keeping to old solutions.

We next see Latter patrolling as a constable of the Specials on Tarbiton dockside. The strike has been called for Monday, May 3. On May 4, he receives a call from Nimmo in London asking him to take over the Specials. He refuses and then finally agrees under pressure from local businessmen. On the 5th he has occasion to warn the communist leader Pincomb about a pamphlet. He has received a letter from Nina asking him to make up with her and start again, but then quite unaccountably she comes to him to say she is leaving him. Apparently Nimmo, always seeking peace by political solution, has influenced her to write the letter, which is quite passionate. Her own response to Latter's violence when she is alone with her thoughts, is different. Her letter has, however, played a part in getting Latter to take on the Specials as Nimmo no doubt intended. On Thursday the 6th, Nimmo gives his third Shagbrook address, which is followed by an incident over buses. Nina comes again to Jim, this time to try to get him to come home. Again we suspect that Nimmo desired this in order to weaken Latter's suspicion of an agreement between Nimmo and Pincomb (with Nina as a go-between) over the buses. Nina stays on in Latter's office, and they sleep together.

Two days of general confusion follow. Sunday is quiet, but on Monday the 10th there is violence caused by the Pincomb group's effort to close down one of the last working boatyards. Late that evening a Special named Maufe attempts to arrest Pincomb for conspiracy to cause a disturbance. In whatever melee occurs, Pincomb suffers a severe head injury. On that day also, several Specials are hospitalized. On the 11th, word comes from Nimmo to suspend Maufe. Latter resigns in disgust and returns to Palm Cottage to discover Nimmo, fully clothed, beneath a cover in his wife's bed. He claims that he had fainted outside and had been carried there. Latter is suspicious again. After a dreadful argument they all proceed to the town hall where Nimmo is to produce proof from his secretary that he had gone to Palm Cottage only to procure important papers. As they enter, Nina turns back and throws herself under the wheels of a lorry. It is some time before it is known that she will live.

When she leaves the hospital, she is reconciled with Latter, and they go into hiding together. They plan to emigrate to Africa. However, she must testify at Maufe's trial. This trial and certain letters between Nina and Nimmo prove, or so Latter thinks, that Maufe, who is convicted, has been deliberately sacrificed by Nimmo with Nina's complicity. Learning this, he chases Nimmo into a water closet where he has a heart attack and dies. Latter then proceeds to cut Nina's throat.

Latter's narration of these events, which I have recounted very sketchily, turns on certain key scenes that are faithfully revealed down to the exact words of the participants. They involve Latter with either Nina or Nimmo or both, and they are characterized by repetition of a special sort. They continually illustrate Latter's inability to deal effectively with either Nina or Nimmo. His only tools to cope with Nimmo's cleverness are anger, rigidity, resentment, and a gun.

It is important to look closely at these scenes. They have that oddly comic quality I have already mentioned. The comedy is not intended by Latter, though he is sometimes deliberately satirical in a bitter way. The first scene I want to discuss occurs on May 2 between Nimmo and Latter (chapters 10–11). Nimmo is still intent on pretending that the previous day's shooting did not occur. He is afraid that the scandal will ruin his attempt at a political comeback, his effectiveness as a strike mediator, and Nina's reputation. When on the next morning he is alone with Latter, he expresses anger and surprise that Latter acted as he did. He accuses him of cowardice and of refusing to face an explanation. Latter describes Nimmo as speaking to him as if he were a meeting. The conversation pits Nimmo's efforts to deal with a problem by discussion against Latter's suspicion of "wangle." Nimmo tries a bewildering number of arguments culminating in his accusation that Latter is prepared to sacrifice Nina for the sake of a "little bit of truth" (*NHM*, 48). Latter replies with typical invective:

> You're always talking about morals and all the time you have the lowest idea of how decent ordinary people act. You are always talking about the noble quality of the people and all the time you despise and wangle them with lies because you think they can't take the truth. You are a man so rotted and soaked in cunning and lies you think everyone is the same. You simply don't know honesty when you see it. You are like a cancer spreading poison everywhere through clean flesh—that's why I say you must be cut out, like a cancer. It's the only way to stop infection spreading. (*NHM*, 49)

After this scathing barrage, Nimmo still attempts a political solution. He has another invention, apparently bolder and more perilous than anything he has done, so perilous as to make us question its good sense. With the remark "Next to men of violence, I detest their paraphernalia" (*NHM*, 49), he offers Latter his own pistol, which has been under his pillow. This Latter sees as a ploy, but for a moment it works, especially when there is added to it Nimmo's remark about Latter's so-called honor. He continues to attack Latter with arguments that his violence will tell on Nina. He surprises Latter by telling him that Nina gave him the pistol for protection—against the woman Brome. Latter is taken aback. Perhaps it was really for protection against him! Latter having made that suggestion, Nimmo denies it, and there follows this exchange, in which Latter is temporarily vanquished:

> He was looking at me all the time, and though he wasn't exactly grinning, he was full of grin. He knew I was puzzled. Then he went on, "Of course you may think that Nina has no right to care whether I get my throat cut by any wandering lunatic. You may think it extremely imprudent for her to show any feeling—especially for the man who was her husband for nearly thirty years."
>
> "She hated you," I said.
>
> "She is incapable of hatred," he said. "That is perhaps her misfortune—but it is something I find possible to forgive. As for the imprudence—I rather call it courage, a true courage, indifference to all but the essential thing—you especially should thank God for it. It was just that high soul, that independence of mind, which brought her back to you. She faced the scandal, the agony of that divorce, to be your wife. She followed the truth of her soul, without fear, without hesitation." (*NHM*, 57)

Latter accepts the truth of this: "I'm not pretending it didn't have a big effect. More than anything he'd thrown at me" (*NHM*, 53). For the moment he is argued down, placated. Later, however, he broods and concludes that Nina doesn't hate because she is afraid to. Her method is ingratiation out of fear, and it has been so from the beginning when she came to him at night. The whole scene shows Latter's susceptibility to words and to emotion and at the same time his suspicion.

The next scene, in which all three are present, occurs shortly thereafter. Latter has discovered two things: first, that when Nimmo "interfered" and Nina apparently resisted him she could have resisted because she had seen Latter's reflection in a picture as he looked in at the window; second, that a discharged maid has threatened to accuse Nina and Nimmo publicly of indecent behavior. When Latter mentions the mirror image, Nina blushes—no doubt at being found out. But being found out at what? It is here that Latter's simplistic way of interpreting things fully plays its role. Her response is to "go mule." Then comes the following curious passage:

> So now I said, "For God's sake Nina, don't play any games but say something. Is there anything to Amelia's story?"
> Nimmo kept babbling, "A pack of lies," but neither of us paid any attention. When Nina had gone mule she did not care for anything or anybody in the world.
> I said to her, "When you helped me get away yesterday, did you know there wasn't going to be any charge? Was all that business . . . just a fake?" She said nothing to this.
> I said to her, "You know what you are doing, Nina, you're trying to drive me mad. You've done it often enough before. But this time you may do it once too often."
> She kept on staring at me, as calm as a dummy with glass eyes. But you could see she was making her eyes like glass.
> I pointed the pistol at her and said, "Tell me, Amelia told the truth?"
> She raised her eyebrows and seemed to think for a moment. Then she nodded her head at me, quite slowly and politely as if saying good morning to the grocer's boy. (*NHM*, 58–59)

Then out of rage both at the revelation and at her mulish manner, he fires the unloaded pistol at her. What we see here is a dreadful intensification of the pattern of accusation, mulish response, violence, and confession that has always characterized their relationship. When finally he throws the pistol at her in an impotent rage, she maintains her mulish demeanor:

> [T]his was always the way she won these fights. Even as a child of seven or eight she would play mule and drive me mad, till I hit her, and drive me to be ashamed of myself and apologize. (*NHM*, 80)

Among the many things that Latter does not understand is that Nina does not intend to win this struggle. Her behavior has shown that she is exhausted and wants only peace. To what has she assented with that polite infuriating nod? Latter interprets it in his absolutist way as admission both of the truth of Amelia's accusation and complicity in Nimmo's plotting. She, on the other hand, seems to be admitting that she can never make Latter understand that the old man's advances mean nothing to her and that her doing his political bidding is out of fairness and loyalty to "something bigger than love." She confesses passively only to be done with it all. She knows that there is no resolution to the conflict, because Latter cannot understand:

> "Damn it," I said, "if you don't get that cut dealt with now, you'll be scarred."
> "Why should you mind?" she said. "You wanted to kill me."
> I said that she was still my wife, though she seemed to forget it.
> "She never forgets," old Nimmo said. "She never forgets it." He was gibbering like a monkey still, and panting like a dog.
> "Then what's been going on in this house?" I said.
> "You wouldn't understand," she said. (*NHM*, 60–61)

Even in a bizarre story it is a sad moment. It expresses her exhausted concession that she can never explain herself to Jim and her acknowledgment that she is committed to helping Nimmo. It expresses anew Nimmo's concession that she loves Jim and not him. But Latter is as confused as ever. He can only answer that whatever their past history, it cannot excuse "the foulest treachery one man can show another" (*NHM*, 61):

> I asked her to forgive me for that cowardly blow. But she made no answer.
> "It's all these lies," I said. "I don't know where I am."
> "You wouldn't understand, it's no good."
> "You don't explain very much." (*NHM*, 62)

We see them going down the road toward another argument. Latter is held back from further violence for the time being, but his attitude has not changed. Nimmo has appealed to him with a genuine attempt at the truth, but infuriates Latter because it is spoken in Nimmo-eze and does not face up to the matter of "treachery." When that effort fails, Nimmo tries something else—frankness combined with flattery. He will risk the truth, but the truth he risks is not the truth Latter is interested in:

> Let us have the courage to face it. You were a brute, you say, to that young girl, and I have loved her, let us say, too much. But aren't we forgetting something—something without which we are merely piling up one falsity on another—throwing words about and getting nowhere. The actual situation *at the time*. . . . We were young, young—that is the big truth. (*NHM*, 63–64)

To remember the situation *at the time* and to *begin again*—those two notions summarize Nimmo's "political" approach, while Latter's sense of "honor" will allow neither. Nimmo's final desperate effort is to attack again that sense of honor, calling it merely spite expressed in an hour of political peril for the nation. The barrage of argument has its effect, but it is a negative one. Latter drives Nimmo from the house with shots on either side of him, claiming that he is now glad he did not kill him. Nimmo is so corrupted that he is not responsible for his own dirt.

This is one of Cary's most brilliant and preposterous scenes. Though I have spoken of Nimmo's resourceful dealing with Latter, one must recognize that it is in the framework of appalling foolishness, as is Nina's. By Latter's standard they *have* conspired, as an exhausted, mulish Nina concedes. She obviously had given up trying to explain her commitment to Nimmo, which seems harmless enough to her. Nimmo's repeated forays against her, however, are stupid and indecent. He seems unable to stop himself. Finally, one feels that values have become hopelessly confused in action by Nimmo's endless efforts to solve every problem by talk and mediation, what Latter calls "wangle." The efforts are clever enough, but the imagination is weak, and Nimmo is in a graceless state of desperation to hold on to his failing inspiration. The business about the pistol is incredibly dangerous, and Nimmo does not seem to realize that he may not be able to talk down Latter; he does not seem to imagine just how dangerous Latter is, that in the end he won't perhaps be talked around. Without knowing it, Nimmo is counting on luck. The powerful old rhetoric is not enough, though we are astonished at how long luck and cleverness manage to stave off the tragedy.

One aspect of the pattern of Nina's behavior is to be ingratiating to Jim after a row, and now she reverts to that pattern, with a push from Nimmo, in a brackety love letter to him. The technique is the same as Jim's: confession of guilt, but she is more successful with Jim than he with her, for he is usually disarmed by it. That is the design of the letter (*NHM*, 96–97). But when she comes to him she has decided that it won't work, she wants only peace, and she is genuinely frightened of him. Yet when they begin to talk, they fall into the old pattern of argument. Nina accuses him:

> . . . you don't know what love means, not proper love. You've never been really in love with anyone. You're afraid of being let down. No,

don't contradict. When just this morning you had that man follow-ing me through the streets. (*NHM*, 102)

Nina speaks almost what we have come to conclude—but only al-most. The charge enrages Latter and he is about to strike her when they are interrupted. Latter believes that she wishes to be struck. Latter does love Nina, but the form of Latter's love has always been corrupted by immature desires for victory and possession. That is all he seems ever to have imagined of love. He has never had to bear the responsibility of it. One would think Nina's words above and Jim's rage would end matters, but the pattern prevails. In a later scene (chapter 25), Nina wants to make up. Again this is Nimmo's desire, for he does not want scandal at a critical political moment. In the scene of reconciliation, matters are made worse be-cause Latter begins to suspect Nina's complicity in an agreement between Nimmo and Pincomb.

The scene on the evening of May 11, after the attempted arrest of Maufe (chapter 34), is critical. Discovering Nimmo returned clan-destinely from London and fully clothed in Nina's bed with Nina present, Latter is prepared to "pass sentence on Nimmo" once again. It is a ridiculous situation. Nimmo is under a cover "fully dressed in white shirt, wing collar, frock-coat and patent leather button-boots" (*NHM*, 164). Again Nimmo's cleverness has been at work, but it is now even more desperate and inconsistent, though it does express a resourcefulness that says: If this doesn't work, I'll begin again with something else! He has offered two different ex-planations for his presence, both of which are untrue, or almost untrue. The first is that he was merely passing by and fainted out-side. Perhaps he did faint (he is not well) but he was not merely passing by. The second is that he had come to settle a misunder-standing about Nina's inheritance. This is possibly true, but it is certainly not his principal motive; in any case, Latter is not buying. Realizing this, exhausted by several days of intense political ac-tivity, and suddenly discovered fully clothed under the blanket, Nimmo loses his temper and takes Latter aback:

> [B]efore I could say this was a funny dress for a sick man to be put to bed in, he jumped up and shouted at me, "What you are is a fool. That's what you are. A fool and a fool and a fool. An everlasting un-limited goddam wooden-headed fool. And I've had enough of your pistol waving. I'm sick of the whole lot of you. For God's sake make a finish. Go away—or shoot. Of course we didn't tell you anything.

Because we knew you'd get it all wrong, because you are our biggest headache. Because you are a kept man. Because you have to be kept by people with some glimmer of common sapience—kept or you'd starve. Now shoot, you kept ass, you hanger-on. Shoot—shoot—shoot." And he actually planted himself in front of me as if I were a firing party. "Go on, get it over and give me a little peace." (*NHM*, 164)

Latter is astonished at this outburst and quotes it to show how Nimmo turns things around. Our response is that Nimmo has finally given way to his own rage and uttered an impolitic "absolute truth." At this moment he is apparently at the end of his tether. We see also, however, that this frankness and anger are to his advantage, that he is usually successful when he employs the tactic of surprise against the rigid Latter, who is usually nonplussed long enough for Nimmo to gain advantage.

It works. But it does not work quite as Nimmo might have expected. Latter is for a moment sorry for Nimmo, "a miserable old wreck fairly coming to bits with his own putrescence" (*NHM*, 164). Nimmo goes on to speak more truth, equally fantastic to Latter: He has had to come down to London to save the situation.

I came here tonight because of your idiotic proceedings in Tarbiton. Because as soon as I turn my back you proceed to murder the only man in the district who knows how to keep the really dangerous elements in hand. I came to save what I can of decency and fair dealing while there may be time to avoid a general crash. (*NHM*, 165)

This is outrageous to Latter, a clear confession of league with evil, and Nimmo's subsequent rant about crises and his willingness to serve does nothing to change his mind. The rant is hollow. However, Nimmo's angry remark is the political truth as he sees it. He is trying to manage the situation, but it must be said that his powers of management have diminished. In his judgment some sort of arrangement with Pincomb has been necessary to maintain a semblance of order. Nina gives Nimmo her assistance because she has trust in his power, a trust that is perhaps now more habitual than rational.

Cary never tires of saying that government is the "art of working on the concrete particular" (*SE*, 219), that every political problem is a "unique problem" (*SE*, 227), and that politics is the science of the possible: "It is from forgetting this hackneyed maxim that the world spends so much time battering its head against stone walls" (*SE*, 102). There is enough evidence in this situation, though we must look *through* Latter's eyes to see it, to decide that Nimmo may not have made the best political decision, may have acted from too abstracted a view, may have lost his old genius. But he was not consciously selling anyone out. His anger at Latter here vouches for his sincerity even as it exemplifies his dramatic cunning. (It may be added, for what it is worth, that Nimmo's actions are taken out of a position on the general strike very close to Cary's in 1926. This has been pointed out by Malcolm Foster, who writes [p. 274] that Cary sympathized with the strikers but feared the strike might lead to a "general breakdown of society." We read the same position in Nimmo's "speeches" in this scene, though it should be clear that Nimmo's motivation for holding the position he does is as a whole different from Cary's, which in any case is more complex. Abstractly, Cary seems to have been in agreement with Nimmo, but he also has sympathy with the attitude of Latter that Nimmo is playing with fire and the strike is dangerous for the nation or at least for law and order. The view that Cary divides his concerns between his depictions of Nimmo and Latter is held by Cornelia Cook [pp. 218–19]. Yet if we detach Nimmo's views from his complex of motivation [impossible, of course, in Cary's view], Nimmo's position seems to contain the balance of Cary's views, as Foster has pointed out.)

There is no doubt that Nimmo has been caught in a half-lie about why he has come to Palm Cottage, in fact, two half-lies. After Nina's attempted suicide we learn from Nimmo's fearful agitation and Latter's coldness that Nimmo really does love Nina in his way and that for Latter there is indeed something bigger than love. Nimmo offers still another reason why he came to Palm Cottage. It is given in his oratorical, evangelical language, so irritating to Latter:

> As I came from that crawling train to-day, I asked how many of us would survive next week—how much of England we love and know. I was at the lowest ebb. And let me admit it—the lights of your house above were too much for my weakness. I told Grant to stop in the lane while I went in for a moment. My dear boy, as God is my witness, I meant only a moment. I went to tell her only that

whatever happened to the country and to me, I could not despair of humanity. For I had known her spirit. My hopes were ashes but I should die in peace. My soul could rest upon the goodness of God, who gave her to the world with her woman's heart. (*NHM*, 177–78)

Latter calls this "bits from speeches." Though Nimmo may not be making an absolutely true report, its sentiment is deeply felt and consistent with his style as reported by Nina. Yet it *does* have a hollow ring, because it is tired out. We understand better by now why it is tired, and this enlivens our sense of Nimmo's deep feeling here, even though we know he has been inexcusably deceitful.

Cary has made us swallow Nimmo's language, which we like not much better than Latter does; but we have to admit that though his love for Nina may be flawed in its way, there is a sense in which it is more profound than Latter's flawed love. Nina knows this. She cannot love him, but she does understand him and with respect for his past and pity for his present state. She is ready to abide his behavior toward her for the sake of what he was and what she, perhaps mistakenly, thinks he is still capable of accomplishing.

Latter's early failures to "execute" Nimmo tell us that something deep in him is preventing him from success. It is not cowardice of the usual sort. It is uneasiness and insecurity, which have always been a part of his character. As events proceed, he seems to need proof even more desperately. His early attempts on Nimmo, as R. W. Noble has pointed out (p. 98), are out of jealousy, his later out of a frame of mind his suspicions have greatly complicated. He must have *absolute* proof in a world where there is a definite real but a real exceedingly difficult to interpret. It is this that finally drives Jim Latter to his mad, violent act—the refusal of evidence to take absolute form, his insistence that it should, and that from such evidence true justice can and must be meted out.

If Latter were merely a maniac, he would be of little use to a novelist. He is of interest in part because he delays, because his self-assurance wilts. On occasion, he tries to do what Nina and Nimmo try to do—begin again. After Nina recovers, they are reconciled. He justifies this on the ground that "this woman was more weak than wicked" (*NHM*, 249), but here something ominous creeps in. The statement is directed to the past. And also we see enacted a repetition of the familiar pattern that their insecurity established: He writes to her asking her pardon. This pattern pathetically persists even in the dreadful last scene of the novel where she kneels before him and asks forgiveness, and he responds, before killing her, that it was for her to forgive him. Robert Bloom (p. 177) says that Cary has Latter "kill the public aspect of [Nina] and ask forgiveness of the private." I don't think Latter any longer makes such a distinction or ever did, and I think that the line about forgiveness sadly refers us back to their childish pattern of fighting and making up, now a monstrous infantilism.

Their last try at reconciliation proves as impossible as all the previous efforts. The trial of Maufe requires her testimony and disclosure of the letters between her and Nimmo. These letters reveal that there had indeed been an agreement between Nimmo and Pincomb with Nina involved. There is nothing criminal about that or about their decision to keep Latter in the dark, though the action is underhanded, considering that Latter commands the Specials. But it appears to Latter that Maufe has been sold.

In fact, we do not know whether or not Maufe used undue force, and the disagreement between Nimmo and Latter on this point cannot be resolved. As Jack Wolkenfeld points out (p. 115), the papers have the facts wrong, the trial has the case at least partially wrong, Latter's version may or may not be right, Maufe may or may not be guilty: "It would be quite false to assume that Jim has learned through the letters that Maufe was not guilty" (p. 182). This is quite correct. Charles Hoffman is inaccurate in trying to establish the simple irony that "Jim Latter is right about what the truth is but wrong about the absoluteness of truth and justice" (p. 154). Both Nimmo and Latter have their reasons. Nimmo's are stated with all due attention to political implications in one of his letters to Nina. Latter's reasons are offered in his account of events. Neither was an eyewitness, and the eyewitnesses do not agree. Nimmo's argument that it must be proved, "that this is not yet a police state where a constable can beat up a citizen merely because he disapproves of his political opinions" (*NHM*, 217), may be self-serving, but it also may be read as a perfectly reasonable reaction to events. It may or may not be relevant to the facts in the Maufe case. It appears that Nimmo may have tried to suppress evidence in the Maufe case. We do not know for certain. In any event, the evidence came forth and was not sufficient before a jury.

Latter's argument that Maufe has been sold is also self-serving; we know that his interpretation endorses and is not the cause of his sense of conspiracy everywhere. This does not mean he is wrong about Maufe. As for us, we are affected by what seems a cruel blow. It is a classic case of the sort we see reported in the newspapers over and over again. One recognizes the terrible difficulty of justice in such cases. It is this, in the end, that we must express our anger at, but not really anger—*recognition*.

At the end, there is nothing very admirable about the behavior of any of the members of this triangle. Each one exhibits childishness that contributes to the dreadful ending. Our sympathy with Latter, despite the fact that he is the narrator, has been severely diminished and yet we still cannot endorse the behavior of Nina or Nimmo. Yet, as Jack Wolkenfeld has observed (p. 185), the moral questions Latter introduces, in no matter how corrupt a way, are valid questions; but so are the questions of fairness introduced by Nina's behavior, and the questions of political decision-making raised by Nimmo's. We ask ourselves as the novel proceeds, why one of them has not said, "That's enough. I want some peace away from this madness." But then we must look again; each of the three protagonists does say this or as much as says it at some point. But what would such a peace be but escape from the real? It is a bitter conclusion—to be imprisoned in our own freedom and in our own conceptions of honor, truth, and love. This is why Cary sees education as the best hope for human civilization, though he is wise enough to recognize that education increases tension as it increases freedom from narrowness and rigidity in one's language. Like Chester Nimmo, Jim Latter is suspicious of words, but for a different reason. Nimmo does not like words that become fixed in outworn definitions (though some of his own have done this). Latter is confused by the dynamism of verbal change and resents it. Much as we may dislike Nimmo and what he has become, we must side with him on this important point.

I have said that Cary takes greater chances with us in the *Second* than in the *First Trilogy*. I think also that inside each trilogy, as it moves along, he takes ever greater chances. We discover an increasingly bizarre or burlesque element. In *The Horse's Mouth* one thinks of the sack of the Beeders' flat and the preposterous gesture of the wall painting at the end. In *Not Honour More* we recognize something bizarre in the very persistence of the love triangle, which is in so many ways not a *love* triangle at all. Then, too, we recognize that persistence is one of the characteristics of a Cary narrator, though different in each case. Each persists in his folly, but not necessarily to become wise, as Blake would have the fool do. Instead each persists in order to survive intact or nearly so, in the terms, no matter how desperate, he creates for himself. In the *Second Trilogy*, Cary holds to this pattern to the bitter end, where the cycle of struggle and reconciliation is so dreadfully played out. Cary says much in his speculative writings about freedom, but it is to express how truly condemned his people are. Freedom is a constant necessity to choose in the situation *as it is at the time*, in all its particularity. It is not surprising as he matured as a novelist that he discovered more and more of the preposterousness of this situation. His denouements become more bizarre, his characters in certain ways less attractive, his own chances with our patience greater. I have quoted a critic (Garrett, p. 252) who senses in the *Second Trilogy* less patience with fiction. I should say that what has really happened is a deeper realization of the preposterousness of human situations and of the human condition itself. Not a loss of faith in human power or freedom, but a more intense discovery of how it can go wrong.

Cary wrote *Not Honour More* when he was already ill. R. W. Noble has pointed to certain discrepancies in the chronology of the novel, but even he does not see how confused the dates Cary uses are. The dates mentioned by Bell in his testimony at the Maufe trial (chapter 43) cannot possibly be correct, and it is not Cary's intent to have Bell lie or be inaccurate. The dates of the letters between Nina and Nimmo of 9/5/26, 10/5/26, and 11/5/26 cannot possibly be correct. Each would have to be dated at least two days later. But even if we make this relatively simple correction, it is impossible that the letters could have been written to Nina on those dates and read by her, because she is in critical condition in Tarbiton Hospital at this time. She cannot have interviewed Bell, as she says she did (and Cary wants her to have done), at any time after the attempted arrest of Pincomb because she was recuperating. These are Cary's oversights, and they mar the conclusion of a novel otherwise a genuine tour de force. It is here that Cary's world for a moment becomes indeterminate, and it is probably a result of his final illness.*

---

*There are some other inaccuracies about dates in the trilogies. They have mainly to do with the ages of some of the women—Sara, Rozzie, and Nina. These may have been intended by Cary and the narrators, who thus make themselves appear to be younger than other dates make it possible for them to be. See Appendices A and B.

Beyond this, it is clear enough that Cary's *Second Trilogy* is a *particular* expression. We as readers moralize on a fictive political world very carefully constructed to express the ways in which human beings struggle individually to establish referents for words like "honor," "truth," and "love." It seems to me that Robert Bloom is quite mistaken to argue: "Cary . . . would maintain . . . that political life is muddled because the people engaged in it seek their own subjective ends guided only by their own subjective values" (p. 107). Like so many remarks that have been made about Cary's work, this one is too abstract and exclusive in its explanation. If we are going to speak abstractly, we must seek a broader explanation: Politics is muddled because individual life and the real are complicated and exceedingly difficult to manage. Thus people make mistakes. This is not to say that Cary believes there is only error and no evil.

The difficulty of the struggle in life to make something that a word like "honor" can refer to is not better shown than in Latter's remark about Nina, which echoes but does not have the same content as her final remark in *Prisoner of Grace*. She there recognizes "something bigger than love" in her relation to Nimmo. Latter says:

> She couldn't understand she was up against something bigger than either of us or anyone's happiness. The truth. And nothing could change it. She didn't want to understand. It was too big. (*NHM*, 221)

She says of Latter that *he* can't understand. The big thing in each case is a different sense of how to act out honor. Neither has been sufficient to deal with the intractable real, which includes for each the other's sense, the dreadful real that Cary provides for these unfortunate people. We don't like any of this very much; we want to rush away from the preposterous. But the preposterous has its own persistence, and Cary is not yet through with us. The murder itself has a terrible deliberateness about it, after all. Nina does not die as she thought she would, shot in an outburst of passion. Rather, Latter cuts her throat in an act that is both more personal and yet colder and more ritualistically a passing of sentence, the work of a man possessed. Even in this, however, something goes wrong. Latter tells us that when the papers reported the murder, after his first statement, there was no mention of honor at all. Latter has to admit, and does, that *on his own terms* he killed his "darling" for nothing. Thus, even his final act, so efficiently performed, involves an incompetence. Only the novel as a whole, the authority of Cary, present yet silent, gives us space to consider what honor might be were each of us to run the preposterous risk of trying to find its referent in our own lives.

6

From Particular Real to the Abstract of Theory

As I have tried to show, the problems frequently befogging the critical appraisal of Cary's trilogies have been those of construing the ethical implications of his work. I began to deal with these problems as problems in criticism in chapter 3. I return to them here, presenting in abstract form the theoretical structure into which I would like you to put everything I have said. To read the books on Cary by Andrew Wright, Robert Bloom, Michael Echeruo, Barbara Fisher, and Cornelia Cook is to see demonstrated a variety of searches and askings. Wright's book, though still an excellent introduction, tends to generalize Cary's characters into types and risks losing the particular. Bloom attacks the modern novel through Cary for its moral flaccidity. (One suspects that he thinks all novels ought to be *romans à thèse*.) Echeruo tends to read Cary's novel through philosophy and Cary's own philosophical assertions. Fisher's book is a jumble of approaches that offers no clear perspective. Cook is interested in showing that all Cary's work conforms to and confirms a liberal stance. A reading of these critics (and many others on Cary) raises theoretical issues not addressed systematically in their texts. As a theoretical container for what I have said about the trilogies, I propose here a conspectus of perspectives ranging from "author" to "reader" *in* which I believe we critically constitute the text. You will note that from the beginning I place these terms in quotation marks. There has been so much discussion in recent years about readers in texts, readers outside of texts, narration in general, and all the rest, and so much terminological confusion as a result, that to use these terms or any others with respect to Cary or anyone else requires clarification. All of this is especially necessary because, as we have seen, past efforts to constitute a meaning for Cary's trilogies in the general, the ethical, the philosophical, the political, or to seek meaning strictly *in* the text, unless accompanied by many reservations, does not work very well with the trilogies. These reservations have rarely been made, partly because a set of terms such as I shall offer has not been systematically employed to distinguish elements of the interpretive problem.

I begin with some preliminary remarks about how we might best consider the notion of *meaning* with respect to Cary's trilogies. Cary's work does not have *closure of meaning* in the usual sense we might apply to this phrase. Instead we find what I shall call a process or what Cary calls a "total symbol." In his very interesting phenomenologically oriented collection of lectures, J. Hillis Miller remarks:

> The silence after the last word of a novel, like the silence after the last note of a piece of music, is by no means the silence of triumphantly perfected form. It is rather a stillness in which the reader experiences a poignant sense of loss, the vanishing of the formative energy of the work. This secret source of form was never reached while the novel continued but was held open as a possibility toward which each page separately reached, as each note in a musical composition reaches out toward the whole. When the novel is over the sense of that possibility is lost, and this generates a feeling of nostalgia, of regret for having lost the last glimpse of a marvelous country which can be seen afar not when the music or novel is over, but only while it is still going on in its continuous failure to be perfect or perfectible. (*The Form of Victorian Fiction* [Notre Dame and London: University of Notre Dame, 1968], p. 48)

For many reasons, this is a provocative statement. It is clearly an attack on so-called modernist formalism, and particularly certain spatializing aspects of it. It brings the "reader" into the novel as a participant. It attacks the notion of closure. But, for all its interest, it is not quite right when we look at the trilogies (or at ourselves just having completed reading them). The trilogies do not leave me with nostalgia as for a lost country. They remain, instead, a world opened to continued exploration. Rereading is part of this, but what is mainly opened up is the act of speculation leading to new discoveries in the text. Now, "discoveries" is not quite the word, nor the only word, I want here; because strictly speaking one could well argue (as Stanley Fish seems to do in *Is There a Text in This Class?* [Cambridge, Mass., and London: Harvard University Press, 1980]) that these discoveries are really constitutive acts. (One notices here a displacement of Eliseo Vivas's conflation of "creation" and "discovery" from the text to the act of reading itself.) However, I am going to insist that there is a text *there*, that it contains the potentiality for a reading that I am going to make of it, and that it (as it exists in the culture) makes certain readings preposterous, others (though interesting) not as good as mine, and an always as yet unconstituted reading better. This last is, of course, a fiction that has not taken and cannot take shape beyond the ideal (impossible) form I give it here.

I am further going to claim that, in my role as critic, I constitute a reading of Cary's trilogies sanctioned by them as they exist in a cultural context which they take into themselves by the very fact of their existence. The paradox of a context that is taken *inside* is deliberate on my part. Even as I claim the sanction, I recognize that the constitutive reading I make does not and could never fulfill the potentiality of the text, but I claim that one reading can be determined to be better than another.

You may ask, as many critical theorists now ask, "What is this text that is *there* but must be constituted as a reading?" I reply that I believe there is one there and that it is the same one you or anyone else reads. Common sense tells me that, but I constitute it *as read*. And in order to make my constitution of it as sophisticated as I can, and in order to avoid recourse to an "allegorical" meaning produced without any sense of the ironic position of critical discourse vis-à-vis a text, I constitute it as spread *a priori* among all but items 1, 2, 9 and 11 on the elevenfold conspectus of perspectives that follows.* I characterize these perspectives as *a priori*, despite grumblings I hear from the spirit of Kant and all philosophy, because I am willing to hold that these eleven, and no doubt others, are categories that shape all narratives or, to be specific, shape critical readings of narratives.

With respect to my reading of Cary's trilogies, I am fictively returning it to the text in a way that is analogous to Kant's fictive attribution of beauty to the "object." And so I speak of my reading as *in* the text, as it is in the sense of potentiality. I further fictively claim that I have become something other than my *self* in this crit-

---

*For the significance I give to the notion of the text as there and the terms "allegorical" and "ironic," as well as the notion of "potentiality," see my *Philosophy of the Literary Symbolic* (Gainesville: University Presses of Florida, 1983), which provides a ground for my procedures here.

ical act; that is, I claim (by analogy to Kant's claim for subjective universality and disinterest in any apprehension of the beautiful) that my reading is a *critical* act with the right to claim assent from others, though I recognize at the same time that this cannot be the complete assent required in Kant's apprehension of the beautiful, only an assent that recognizes lack of finality in the reading. You will recognize that I am talking not about beauty but about interpretation, and am thus displacing the move of Kant to which I refer.

In reading Cary's trilogies I could, I suppose, indulge in the regret Miller mentions when I contemplate the unavailability of Alabaster's book on Jimson or Sally and Bootham's study of Nimmo. But a little thought convinces me that these lacunae—and many more subtle ones—are appropriately just that. They are what Wolfgang Iser calls "blanks"; they are, then, part of the text as such rather than absences. When John Keats wrote of Benjamin West's painting *Death on a Pale Horse* and declared that it did not bring about any "momentous depth of speculation," he was not thinking of nostalgia, though he does go on to imply that a successful work conjures images of desire that, one supposes, threaten nostalgia. A "momentous depth of speculation" would be, then, for me an activity based not on loss but on something positive in the painting that generates critical activity. We can call this something a "blank," as Iser does (I have done so once in this book), or a "negation," or an "absence"; but these words bear an unintended irony. They seem to be written from a point of view toward language that allows only what is indubitably "said" to be present. Yet the language of literary art offers in a positive way a great deal more than that. It always offers the potentiality for critical speculation. I would want to revise Miller's remark, then, to say that the novel does perform a sort of closure unlike the closure of an argument or even of a *roman à thèse*. It is a structural closure that performs an opening of speculation. It does not generate nostalgia so much as a challenge to thought and to the revision of one's perspective. This is a mundane enough suggestion, but I submit that it has, as Wilcher says of Sara's maxims, the force of a platitude, by which Wilcher meant true power. Indeed, it is not far from a remark that Cary makes in *Art and Reality* and that I have quoted on page 30. There he speaks of the book as a "total symbol." This does not mean the book is not a process from beginning to end, but that its process closes itself in order to open up speculation.

The range of perspectives I offer is to be regarded as a range of *critical* perspectives. By this I mean that the perspectives are those generated as a necessity by the speculative activity of criticism it-self as a form of thought. They are called perspectives in order to distinguish them from properties of literary works themselves. In this they are, as I have suggested, like what Kant called categories, though in this case categories of a specific cultural activity—criticism itself, by which I mean the kind of reading it would be better if we could all do. I shall take them up in order and of neces-sity briefly and incompletely, focusing on issues relevant to dealing with the text of Cary: (1) our notion of an author, (2) historical au-thors, (3) authority, including the arranger, (4) narrators and foci of narration, (5) the fictive story, (6) heroes, heroines, protagonists, (7) fictive internal readers, (8) fictive external readers, (9) em-pirically or ideologically constructed readers, (10) the authoritively projected reader, (11) our notion of ourselves. For the sake of clarity I italicize these terms in the rest of the book. This schema multi-plies both author and reader, and various of the elements that make it up shade into their neighbors in the study of many texts. Criticism needs a language that distinguishes these categories at the outset, though I do not insist that as applied to any specific work all categories are distinct from each other. Criticism may con-flate some of these categories when faced with certain works. But they must be available to be conflated so that the range of pos-sibility is present to critical discourse.

1. *Our notion of an author.* This notion is always present, but even when we expend quite a lot of imagination on it, it is in itself of hardly any use to criticism. It is only a ground—a necessary ground—for the possibility of criticism. It is a notion dictated by common sense. In practice it is constituted by a jumble of facts or reveries over a text, and the fact that it has to be constituted apart from the text seems to remove it to a great extent as a *necessary* cate-gory of criticism. When imagination is *systematically* employed to develop it, it quickly becomes one or both of two quite sophisti-cated fictions, the first of which is certainly helpful, the second ab-solutely necessary. These follow as items 2 and 3 below.

2. *Historical authors.* The first of these are the authors constituted by scholarship, biography, memoirs, interviews, and the like. I borrow a page from William Blake here. He contrasts an historical Jesus we imagine referred to by the Bible to the Jesus who is pres-ent to us in, that is, constituted by, our reading of the Bible. This

presentness is apparently what Blake thought the so-called second coming of Jesus was. The Jesus referred to by and, in this sense, outside the Bible is for Blake (though this Jesus is always a *was*) an historical construct inevitably thrust back into and alien from us in an irretrievable past that can't be located except in its present construction as a past. He is (was) for Blake, therefore, the anti-Christ. Borrowing from this notion, we might think of historical authors (obviously several authors can be constructed for one text even though we think of all these constructions as referring to one person) as anti-authors, fictive constructs always to some extent separate from another author we recognize as the shaping force in the text. The information developed about these anti-authors can be immensely valuable as a help to interpretation, but the information can theoretically have no *direct* relation to the text and must always be tested skeptically against what I name *authority*. I have called on and attempted to order such information for skeptical use in the first three chapters of this book.

3. *Authority* (including the *arranger*). Many critics have attempted to formulate an adequate term for this second fiction. Wayne Booth called it both an "ideal author" and an "implied author." Wolfgang Iser adopted the term "implied author" (*The Act of Reading* [Baltimore and London: Johns Hopkins University Press, 1978], p. 207) as a counterpart of his "implied reader." The movement known as the New Criticism tended to conflate it with the attitude of the text conveyed by its formal order. Thus Cleanth Brooks and Robert Penn Warren in the first edition of *Understanding Fiction* (New York: Appleton-Century-Crofts, 1943) called it the "point of view" of the story, using the term differently from their Jamesian predecessor Percy Lubbock, who meant by the same term the consciousness through whom the events of the story are perceived (if a third-person narration) or told (if a first-person). In *Fiction As Process* (New York: Dodd, Mead, 1968), Carl Hartman and I treated this same figure as the "authority" or "voice" of the text, distinguishing it from such voices speaking in the text. However, the word "voice" is more appropriately identified with these various possible internal *narrators* or speakers, as Hugh Kenner does in his *Joyce's Voices* (Berkeley: University of California Press, 1978). "Authority" seems to me now the preferable word, and I have employed it for this book. It is preferable to Booth's "ideal author" because there is no hint in it of Platonizing the author out of, behind, or above the text (though this is not what Booth had in mind). It is

preferable to Booth's and Iser's "implied author" because it cannot as easily be confused with a fictive narrator or an historical author. It is to be located only in or as the text.

The danger in reading here is to try to constitute *authority* by reduction to some discursive statement about ethics. This would mean emphasizing abstractable content as meaning without attention to the process of the text (which some would call the process of reading);* or, it would be as in the case of Robert Bloom's reading of Cary, to seek an abstractable content as authoritative meaning and, failing to find it as such, convert it in its absence into a principle of flaccid moral indeterminacy. Thus it is important to study this matter of *authority* in Cary and determine how or where it is located.

Authority may be principally invested in the way things are presented. But when we get into this matter there is a tricky problem, because *authority*, as has frequently been observed, seems to be fully masked by a *narrator's* role. Miller considers the position of the typical Victorian novelist and concludes that he or she is an immanent omniscient god of the text, rather than a transcendent one. A transcendent one would be, I suppose, the author mentioned by Stephen Dedalus in *A Portrait of the Artist As a Young Man* who withdraws to pare his fingernails. The problem with these various *authorities* is that, once identified, they become roles behind which *authority* seems to recede once more. We notice this in Miller's following remark: "The sympathetic participation of the narrator in the subtle movement of thought in the individual character takes place within a consciousness as wide as all mankind, and this justifies the narrator in claiming he has the angelic omniscience" (p. 113). An angel, of course, is not a god, but at best a messenger, and most modern fiction seems to recognize that narration is always angelic, not godlike. This suggests that authority comes from without as well as within, the "without" being called "reader competence," "the informed reader," and the like. I am going to hold that these "withouts" are finally best regarded as "withins," but the argument must go on for a while before I do that, and clarify what I mean by it.

---

*I do not call it the process of reading, because in my critical language the process of a *critical* reading is always fictively returned to the text, from which it then emerges as the process potentially *there*. The reason for this will become clear when I come to declare that certain readers are included in the categories of the text, which I admit freely are the categories of criticism that constitute its *ex*istence.

Much effort has been expended to define the nature of the *authority* in Joyce's *Ulysses*. The term "arranger" has been happily offered by David Hayman (*Ulysses: The Mechanics of Meaning* [Englewood Cliffs, N.J.: Prentice-Hall, 1970]) and others, and adopted by Hugh Kenner in his later work on that book. The effort has been to find a word free of the many voices in the text, some of which are nameless *narrators*. Even the apparently objective *narrator* who intrudes into Bloom's and Stephen's monologues looks less objective to us after we have traversed the text. There is an *authority* behind or, perhaps better, enclosing that *narrator* as there clearly is behind all the many voices of *Finnegans Wake*. *Arranger* is an excellent term to convey an *authority* that does not speak in its own voice but is the construction of the text as a system of relations in process as well as the invention of the voices and what they say. To this *authority* we can attribute certain attitudes, but not too hastily, for if we do we may return to the place where Robert Bloom left Cary criticism.

Arranger itself as a word suggests certain techniques and reticences that we must take into account in any interpretation. We are impressed by what Joyce's arrangement does not do as well as by what it does. But *arranger* does not serve for all sorts of *authority*. It will not do as well for the *authority* of Henry James, because his narrated texts usually possess a single focus ordained and manipulated by the *authority*. This would be true of Cary's novels, taken individually, but they belong to larger arranged units. When we accept the trilogy as the unit, we see that Cary's *authority* is more rigidly restrictive than Joyce's (and in certain respects than James's), yet Cary's is an "arranging" *authority*, like Joyce's, though this *arranger* is more reticent about displaying himself as the mover of the text than is Joyce's. (Note that even here in my language an unsuspected, new *authority* begins to recede behind the *arranger*.) I have to confess now that in this book I have called this *authority* "Cary," even as I have called my *historical author* "Cary." Yet as you see, I must insist theoretically on a difference between the two, without imposing my barbaric terminology wholesale in the foregoing chapters.

4. *Narrators and foci of narration*. The idea of an *arranger* as *authority* is particularly useful in order to draw a line between *authority* and any conceivable *narrator*. It appears that the mere presence of criticism *itself* threatens any authorial voice. Criticism teases itself with the possibility of an *authority*, once constructed from the text,

slipping to the status of still another *narrator*. This offers a number of interesting problems (including an infinite regress) which I shall avoid here, to observe only two things: 1) that for awhile we must ignore the infinite regress even as we are aware of it as indicating a flaw in a reasonably workable set of categories, perhaps a reminder of the fragility of system, and 2) that narration as such is never quite equivalent to *authority*, even in the most Victorian of novels discussed by Miller. Or, to put it more accurately, narration ought never to be regarded critically as categorically identical to *authority*, even though in some cases it may turn out practically to be so. Gerard Genette makes this point with an illustration from *Père Goriot*: "the narrator of *Père Goriot* 'is' not Balzac, even if here and there he expresses Balzac's opinions, for this author-narrator is someone who 'knows' the Vauquer boardinghouse, its landlady and its lodgers, whereas all Balzac himself does is imagine them; and in this sense, of course, the narrative situation of a fictional account is never reduced to its situation of writing" (*Narrative Discourse* [Ithaca: Cornell University Press, 1980], p. 214). This is clearly seen in an extreme instance such as Byron's *Don Juan*, where the situation of writing or of expressivism (to use the word in M. H. Abrams's sense) seems to be present, but it is still best regarded as a projection of the activity of the *narrator*, who is dramatized in the act of writing by an *authority*. By their structures Cary's trilogies seem to acknowledge the inevitability of this. I have taken this whole matter up and tried to create a theoretical context for it because in a radical treatment such as Cary's, where the *narrators* seem to have usurped the authorial role, the problem of interpreting *authority* is at its extreme.

Also at the extreme is the problem of an inner *authority* which belongs to each of the *narrators*, because if all I have said so far is correct, then each of Cary's *narrators* in his or her book has receded behind a first person narration, projecting a fictive narrating self as well as a self as *hero* or *heroine*, and we must take this removal into account when we read. As an "author" Jimson is particularly interesting because of his awareness of this situation, which he deliberately projects in the tone. The other "authors" project fictive narrating selves and heroic selves but with lesser awareness of their fictiveness—in varying degrees. As a matter of theoretical principle, my elevenfold conspectus does not allow us any necessary connection among Cary *our notion of the author*, Cary *the historical author*, and Cary's *authority*, though in practice we frequently make such connections, even conflations. However, this stricture cannot apply to Gulley Jimson or any of the other of the trilogies' *narrators*, conceived of as "authors" of their texts. They are created in the text, and the text is concerned *with* the relation between the "real" authors Jimson et al., the "historical" Jimson et al. (as created by Cary's *authority* via the other two "authors" and the relation between their views), and the "authority" of Jimson et al. All, of course, are fictions in the text; they do not exist at the authorial level of the trilogies, at which I have been discoursing.

If one were to adopt Plato's distinction between pure narrative, or what James calls "telling," and mimesis, or James's "showing," we would have to conclude that Cary's trilogies are entirely mimeses, but mimeses of telling. His *authority* never tells us anything. His *authority* lies in the arrangement of these tellings ("narrations") and their natures. However, Genette (p. 166) observes that showing can only be a way of telling; by this remark he seems to be acknowledging the notion of an *authority*, though he does not develop it. Each of Cary's *narrators*, of course, employs both pure narrative and mimesis in various mixtures. Genette collects questions of narration under the terms "perspective" and "focalization." He laments (p. 186) what he regards as "regrettable confusion between . . . *mood* and *voice*, a confusion between the question *who is the character whose point of view orients the narrative perspective?* and the very different question *who is the narrator?—*or more simply, the question *who sees?* and the question *who speaks?*" He seems to think that Brooks and Warren coined their phrase "focus of narration" as an equivalent for "point of view" and that he is establishing a distinction based upon his two questions for the first time. However, Brooks and Warren's two terms are not equivalent. They were drawing a distinction between what Genette calls "focalization" and what I call *authority*. (Unaccountably they retreated from this distinction in their second edition [1958, p. 196] which may explain Genette's confusion, though he cites the first edition.) *Focus of narration* or "focalization," is not limited to whether the narration is first person or third person but involves various possibilities, including the variety of projected voices and *narrators* in *Ulysses* and, of course, the six *narrators* of Cary's trilogies, two of whom (Jimson and Latter) are actually "speaking" voices and another of whom (Nimmo) is at least partly so. But there are also projections within these projections, including earlier versions of the *narrators'* selves.

5. *The fictive story.* There is a commonsense notion that a story

lies behind a fictive narration and that the author is trying to tell it.
Genette calls the story the events themselves as they happened,
the signified or the narrative content. It is frequently said, "No tale
can be told in its entirety." However, a little reflection shows that
this zero-degree of narration is a critical fiction and that one might
say that every fictive tale is *always* told in its entirety since there is
nothing but what is told. This book has two appendices which are
chronologies of the two trilogies; they are constructed *from* the text
and do not have any status *previous to* or *behind* the text. If one were
to continue with this argument, would one next have to say that
neither is there any story lying *behind* the narrations of Cary's six
narrators? No, because a historical narrative always posits a story
behind it, all of which it can never tell. There is thus an important
difference between Cary's story and that of the *narrators*. Cary is
arranging a literary fiction. The *narrators* within this structure are
writing or speaking what they regard as memoirs—a sort of history. They are referring to events which the fiction declares to have
happened; they are sometimes referring to events that external history also declares to have happened. In both cases the events are
declared "real." The *narrators* must be imagined to select, order,
and emphasize, whereas Cary's *authority* never does. They agree
on some matters, disagree on others, and interpret according to
their stances. In recent years, theoretical writing emerging from literary criticism has taught us quite a lot about historical writing. As
a result we are more alert to the so-called "literary" aspects of historical narration. In confronting Cary's *narrators*, we quickly become aware of the problematic nature of historical "fact." Before a
lot of the recent reflection on the writing of history occurred,
Cary's *narrators* were already demonstrating the "literary" nature of
historical narration; for Cary's *arranger* forces us to dwell on just
those aspects that would seem least important from an empirical
point of view. He does this in part by making certain "facts" impossible to ascertain. As I have suggested, in the *Second Trilogy* the arrangement seems deliberately to force us away from a consideration of what the facts were, partly by teasing us about them. The
matter of Maufe remains undecidable. That does not mean that everything is undecidable, but it may well mean that other sorts of
decisions—moral judgments in the face of the undecidable—are of
basic importance and that the chance of moral failure for the *narrators* is, in spite of good intentions, greater and more dangerous
than we had imagined. Finally, we cannot leap from the factual in-

determinacy of certain alleged events to assume the moral indeterminacy of what the *authority* projects.

Cary's *narrators* are trying to reconstruct situations that have left for the *narrators'* use only traces in the memory and documents, letters, and previous histories. They themselves are contributing their own documents based on their materials, and we must employ these (it is all we can know about them in addition to Cary's juxtaposition of the texts) to project a satisfactory "history." This act has its own moral challenge. An interesting question here is to what extent Cary's novels as fictive documents ought to be considered in the light of the history of the period as we know it. A second question is to what extent Cary's work contributes to a better historical grasp of the age in which it is set. But the prior theoretical problem is to determine the nature of the text offered to us, and it is not a history, though it contains a "mimesis" of history. Complaints have been made against Cary's work that he has misread some of the events of the times, that he is politically naïve about them, etc. (One of the reasons for these complaints is that critics often assume that in a literary fiction a character stands for a political position or a concept of some sort or even some historical personage and must be judged for what he or she represents, not as an individual being in a particular situation. I shall say more about this with respect to Cary shortly.) Some of the complaints have themselves been politically simplistic; some have been misdirected at Cary instead of at one of his *narrators*. Often the problem has been an inability or unwillingness to assume that Cary can have sympathy for a character with whom he disagrees. Like any novelist who sets things in a recognizably historical situation, Cary has constructed his characters and events to fit into a containing "historical" world, often with a good amount of agility. But to fit things in is in this case also to make and interpret the container. It is not simply to grasp it as an unchanging external fact or even as an already made historical abstraction. Therefore, there is always in such cases a reasonable question to ask: What about Cary's constitutive "mimesis" of history? It is, I think, a fair question to ask, though it needs to be asked in a way that recognizes there are many prior questions belonging to literary criticism, including what part of the history is Cary's and what part his *narrators'*. This book stops short of asking these questions. There are two reasons for this: I have not discovered how to ask them in an interesting way; and my task of getting the critical questions clear is taking long enough. I am content to claim that Cary's text's role as a symbol is different and contrary to that of a work of history, though I know that historical works look more and more like literary texts the older they get.

Nor can criticism, as criticism, read Cary's text as if it seeks the abstract universal, the type, the archetype, or the allegorical figure. As I have already said (despite Cornelia Cook's evidence for the model), Chester Nimmo must not be read as a substitutive allegory of Lloyd George, a generalized allegorical image of Lloyd George's cabinet, the politician, or the like. (In spite of this, Cook's work goes some distance toward answering questions I have avoided previously.) Cary's characters are particulars on the way to being imaginative universals in a Viconian sense. We may now—as we do—speak of Gulley Jimsons we have met. His particularity established, his imaginative universality follows in a situation where the nature we constitute treats art as a sort of paradigm, but, as Oscar Wilde said, never quite succeeds in living up to the particular image. Each trilogy offers the materials for the reading of a world within an historical world that is partly (or in one sense) provided outside the text, partly (or in another sense) constituted in it. In order for that smaller world to sit easily and successfully in the larger, the smaller must be a synecdoche for the larger, but the reverse of synecdoche must occur as well. Each must evoke and invoke the other. As a whole, neither trilogy has anything that can be said to be unequivocally *behind* it. It evokes and invokes. It requires projection from world to world, but it is idle to speculate on matters that *as literarily fictive projections* (rather than historical projections) cannot be decided on. In both cases, literary and historical, there is a constitutive act, but these acts are constitutive in different ways, with history always requiring an empirical element. The point of some projections in Cary is that they are constituted as undecidable, like the birthdate of Rosina Balmforth. (This is never true of historical constitutions, since the assumption is that more might become known.) A speculation about the girlhood of Shakespeare's heroines will always seem like idle talk and is probably pointless, but my chronological appendices can be regarded as projections from the text of the trilogies, because their *narrators* constitute a history behind their texts, more of which might be known (inside the fiction), though there is, strictly speaking, no story behind Cary's purely fictive text, except, of course, the historical "age" that the trilogies as a whole invoke. (An interesting text for its tendency to violate the line between idle speculation and projection from the text is John Raleigh's *Chronicle of Leopold and Molly Bloom* [Berkeley: University of California Press, 1977], where occasionally Raleigh tries to decide on a matter that Joyce has clearly left undecidable. The critical speculation in such cases is why it is undecidable, not what the "truth" may be.)

6. *Heroes, heroines, protagonists.* (I use the term "hero" here in a way less systematic and expansive than Michael Bakhtin's notion of *hero* as anything about which the discourse is concerned that is treated as animate.) Many novels distinguish their *heroes* from their *narrators*, if only by making the *heroes* earlier versions of the *narrators*. In Cary's texts the narrative presence frequently dominates the earlier self, and the narrative act itself becomes heroic. Jimson's narration is the best example of this. His narrative presence dominates the telling. It is not until very late in his story that the conditions of the act of telling are revealed, and then only in an offhand way. This delay casts a harsh light, forcing us back through the whole text to rethink its implications. In *To Be a Pilgrim*, the journal form of Wilcher makes the presence of writing dominant; all of the recalled past is subservient to the *narrator's* present state and is recalled so that Wilcher can clarify that state to himself. Nimmo's telling is deeply motivated by one of his audiences, Nina. So what we have is often a conflation of *narrator* and *hero*, though another *hero* is told about. Indeed, the conditions under which each of Cary's *narrators* tells his or her story become more important the more we think about the matter. Unlike Proust's *À la Recherche du temps perdu*, the narrating place is always indicated by Cary, though not always at the beginning; and it plays an important role. In *To Be a Pilgrim*, the duration of the narrative act also plays a significant role, and in the other novels the temporal situation is a factor though not the actual duration of the narrative act. Latter's style is affected by the time allotted to him to get his story dictated. All of this is not contrary to Genette's notion that "a fictional account is never reduced to a situation of writing" (p. 214), because what we have here is not the real situation of writing, which would be Cary's, but a fictive one that does play a part in the structure of the text. We have, in other words, what we might roughly call a "mimesis" of something Genette declares cannot exist, which suggests that "mimesis" can be radically constitutive.

Some fictive *heroes*, when the *narrator* (or an earlier self) is not the *hero*, and sometimes when he is, as in *Don Juan*, are alter egos

for the *narrator*. Cary employs no alter egos in spite of a few connections pointed out by scholars between his own career and Latter's (and in any case, Cary is not the *narrator*, only the *arranger*;
and this *arranger* remains theoretically separate from the historical
Cary). One of the tendencies that some readers have had with *Not
Honour More* is to assume that Latter is more sympathetically
treated than he is. Even with a clear connection like that between
the young Joyce and Stephen Dedalus, we must be wary of simplistic equations, even more so perhaps when *authority* is invested
wholly in an *arranger*. But one might better say that vigilance is
more necessary the more we are tempted to equate *authority* with
historical author on the one hand or *narrator* on the other. Clearly
Cary refuses to embody truth in a character. Indeed, it appears that
Cary regards such embodiment, or the embodiment of *authority* in
a *narrator* as a mistake, both technical and ethical, or perhaps an
impossibility. He may even think the effort a kind of *hubris*. But it is
also a mistake for the critic to assume that because *authority* and
truth are not present there, the *narrator* is necessarily wrong or totally unreliable. Cary's own worry about how his novels were being
read may have led him to remarks that are helpful only when they
are seen as efforts to balance extremes of interpretation. Thus outside the novels he felt compelled at one time or another to emphasize Nimmo's goodness, Nina's justness, and Latter's paranoia
against the interpretations of others.

7. *Fictive internal readers.** I come now farther along the scale to
the interesting but vexing and vexed question of readers. For every
narrator there are fictive readers, and Cary's trilogies are notable for
the variety of them. I have discussed already in this book the *fictive*

*Just as I had completed this book, W. Daniel Wilson's "Readers in Texts" ap-
peared in *PMLA* 96 (October 1981): 848–63. It is a useful attempt to bring order out
of the mass of competing systems of terms surrounding the notion of what I collect
under the two terms *fictive internal* and *fictive external readers*. He opts for "characterized fictive reader" to cover both and "implied or intended reader" for my *authoritively projected reader*, and he would probably criticize my term *external* (as he
criticizes Arthur Sherbo's "outer") for implying that these readers are somehow not
in the text, and that is why I call it fictive. I mean it to be thought of as fictively
projected by a *narrator* as the object of his or her art. My criticism of Wilson's "implied or intended reader" (which he adopts with certain reservations from Wolfgang
Iser and Erwin Wolff) is that the notion of intention is thereby too baldly implied,
although I recognize that my *authoritively projected reader* seems to require an author
who intends to project. However, as I make clear, my *authority* is the structure of the
text, as is this reader. The phrase is a deliberate redundancy.

internal readers (or in some cases auditors) to whom the six *narrators* address their work: Sara to readers of a popular newspaper; Wilcher to himself and slyly to Ann and perhaps the relatives who will survive him; Jimson to posterity, but also to the "honorary secretary" who takes it all down and provides an immediate audience. In the *Second Trilogy*, things are more complicated. Nina declares that she writes to set the historical record straight. Her readers are posterity; but a curious quality of recklessness pervades the book, as if there were some other unnameable reader to whom she is exhibiting herself. (What I have just called a "reader" here may be merely a tendency of presentation in her that we might assume present in all her acts—part of her character.) Nimmo, as a self-consciously historical figure, also writes to posterity, but also to Nina, to whom he dictates at least part of his memoir. Nimmo's design on Nina as auditor is very different from Jimson's on his "honorary secretary." Nimmo is trying to influence Nina to action. Jimson is "performing" before his auditor, and his relation is intended to be one of a certain distance with no involvement of purpose to cause immediate action. Latter dictates a confession to a court, but it is more an explanation to a vaguely conceived larger audience in order to set the moral record straight and to save a society that he believes must be shocked out of its corruption. The policewoman auditor, whom he formally thanks, has very little existence for Latter other than as a functionary. The relation between the *narrators* and these immediate auditors is a means by which the *arranger* projects his *narrators'* characters.

There is much irony in the way we respond to these narratives, for we are not in the position of the reader internally addressed, even though we are tempted into the position from time to time in all the narratives, and especially in Jimson's. This is part of the characterization and part of the process of the text as it requires us constantly to make judgments about our own stance with respect to each *narrator* and *fictive internal reader* at any given time. (But now I must confess that when I have spoken of "us" in this book, I have referred to the *authoritively projected reader*, number 10 in my schema, for reasons I shall soon advance.)

8. *Fictive external readers.* Of Cary's *narrators* it is Jimson who most clearly projects what I call with some trepidation a *fictive external reader*. Of course, it is not really an external reader because that would have to be Cary's, but it is different from the readers I have so far offered as *internal*, and it appears as the product of Jim-

son's artistic drive. One can symbolize it by referring to his playing before his "honorary secretary." For all his suspicious nature, Jimson makes a pact with this reader, whom he tacitly regards as the ultimate critic and trusts to understand his exuberances and his ironies. This reader is not quite the posterity to whom he writes internally. It transcends this, and here we may have the reason that many of Cary's readers have thought Jimson to be an *authority*, and in praising or criticizing him have thought they were discussing Cary, whereas what they had discovered was considerable sophistication in a *narrator* who is not the *authority*. To some extent there is a *fictive external reader* in each of the novels, evident to the degree that each *narrator* posits a sort of ideal critical reader beyond the *fictive internal* one. This audience becomes discussable, however, only in terms of the text as a result of the *narrator's* artifice, and is never mentioned by the *narrator* as an audience. In any case, such *fictive external readers* belong to *narrators*, and not directly to authors; and they can be regarded as identical to the presence in the text of artifice and making, the text's commitment to being something, the *narrators'* commitment to making it something. I claim that this element is present to a greater degree in Jimson's memoir. Jimson is made by the *authority* of the text to present a memoir written to fulfill a more sophisticated notion of artistry.

9. *Empirically or ideologically constructed readers.* If the *narrators* have *fictive readers*, so also does Cary's *authority*. We might say that these are merely "us" (and I have used the term), but "us," strictly conceived, is no more a theoretical concept than *our notion of an author*. Numerous readers have been constructed for literature that fall into this category. A counterpart to the *historical author* is the historical reader, created by scholarship as a contemporary of the author or, conceivably, as representative of any given era or place. This construct is sometimes conflated with the intended reader, an idea promulgated in different ways by E. D. Hirsch, Jr., Erwin Wolff, and others. This reader turns up in some form in most reader-oriented criticism. Extreme efforts to eradicate it or simply to disregard it (as in the case of the early Empson) have ended in curiosities where word-meanings impossible for the author to have known are employed in interpretation. (At least one text, Joyce's *Finnegans Wake*, may actually have as part of its design the admission of such future meanings, however; but here one notes that to consider this matter is to introduce the question of what the "meaning" of a word means with respect to *Finnegans Wake*.)

Various other readers have recently been suggested. There is the "superreader" of Michael Riffaterre, the "informed reader" of Stanley Fish, the "subjective reader" of David Bleich, and the notion of reader competence borrowed from linguistics and philosophy by Jonathan Culler and others. Some are constructs based on a certain amount of empirical evidence of a rather shaky sort. Some are perhaps best describable as metaphysical objects. And others, I think, are what I call *authoritively projected readers* masquerading as *empirically constructed readers*. In addition to these we have readers constructed on psychoanalytical or some other principle—the Freudian reader being the one most often in evidence in recent times. We also have a popular distinction made much of recently between a first reader (or reading) and a second (or third, or fourth, etc.). Too much has been made of this distinction. It is not, I think, a critical concept of much use either on psychological or philosophical grounds. All criticism, if we must talk of it in this way, is at least second-reading criticism, not the least when it tries to reconstruct a first reading, and any reader of the least bit of sophistication is capable in a later reading of a distance suspending knowledge that what I am about to call the *authoritively projected reader* is not yet to know. In any case there is a good amount of role-playing in a first reading, and there might as well be a little more in a second. It does not make sense to me to regard the new understanding gathered in a second reading as somehow illicit, if one makes some obvious distinctions.

Finally, one does not have to believe in the possibility of an objective reading in order to view with suspicion a purely subjective criticism that posits a sort of majority rule or a negotiated settlement. Both objective and subjective interpretation belong to the same party without seeming to know it. Both offer an *empirically constructed reader* as the only real reader, sometimes without recognizing it as a construct appropriate to sociology or psychology, but not to literary criticism, which can never use such empirically derived constructs as its fictions without taking on more problems than are solved.

10. *The authoritively projected reader*. None of the above is the reader addressed by the *authority* of the text. When we consider a reader so addressed, we note with surprise its tendency to recede like *authority* behind any term we are likely to posit for it. For example, let us take the cases of Byron and Wordsworth in *Don Juan* and *The Prelude* respectively. Byron's *fictive internal readers* are the "dear

reader" addressed from time to time (once addressed as "grim reader"), the English people who are made readers only to be castigated in the text, and Robert Southey, to whom the poem is ironically dedicated. Southey is also, of course, an *historical reader*, but one we are unlikely to wish to posit as a critical standard. There is also in *Don Juan* an external fictive reader like Jimson's, who is not quite anyone addressed but someone for whom the *narrator* really narrates—someone the *narrator* takes into his confidence, whom he respects to the extent that he believes this reader will understand and appreciate his many ironic gestures. This appears also to be an *authoritively projected reader* if one conflates Byron's *narrator* with the poem's *authority*, as has been the tendency of romantic-period scholarship and criticism; but I have already suggested that this conflation can never be theoretically regarded as complete. Wordsworth's *internal readers* are his sister Dorothy and Coleridge. (There are also *historical readers* called Dorothy and Coleridge.) Wordsworth has also another reader, whom the *narrator* takes into his confidence, though a confidence quite different from Byron's. He has a message for this reader and hopes to teach him something. (This is not to say that *Don Juan* does not teach something, only that Byron's gesture is not didactic.) Again the temptation is to conflate *narrator* and *authority*. Also, we tend to think of this reader as ourselves. I am going to claim that "we" is not a theoretical notion, so there is required a term for a reader nearly ourselves yet never quite mentioned in the text. Iser, whose work in this field is well known, offers the term "implied reader" to us. His own argument eventually drives him to claim only fictive status for it and no status apart from the text itself. It is, he says, "a textual structure anticipating the presence of a recipient without necessarily defining him: this concept prestructures the role to be assumed by each recipient" (p. 29). It is a "network of response-inviting structures which impel the reader [us] to grasp the text." Everything about this "implied reader" is traced back to "predispositions . . . laid down by the text itself" (p. 34). In spite of Iser's careful effort to include a real reader or "us" in the situation of the text, his notion of the "implied reader" as a real reader is very shaky and at last collapses in his recognition that this reader is both *in* the text and a fiction, not "us." (As such it can, of course, have little to do with notions of actual first and second readings.) I remind you of my confession that when I have spoken of the "reader" or "us" in this book, I have actually been referring to this *authoritively projected reader*.

But this *authoritively projected reader* is also the reader constituted by the critic, or rather by anyone reading. It is a necessary fiction that criticism creates, and many critics who seem to be establishing *empirically constructed readers* are actually creating their versions of it instead. *Empirically constructed readers* I view as anxious attempts to bolster a critical category with belief, which I regard as a mistake generated out of a false assumption that all thought and most belief must have an empirical methodology in order to be socially acceptable in our age. The categories I have named here can never be based on empirically derived belief. That would be like asking Kant to derive his categories from empirical evidence, when the empirical act is governed *a priori* by the categories. In my view both Culler's "reader competence" and Fish's "informed reader" are terms for the *authoritively projected reader* masquerading with no more than a mustache and nose of empiricism.

I have said that this reader is constituted by anyone playing the role of critic. I mean also that in actual practice you and I constitute ourselves as critics, that reading, as critical theory constitutes it, is always criticism, that in the act we are not ourselves, and that this is a good thing. This brings me to the final category.

11. *Our notion of ourselves.* This, like *our notion of an author*, with which I began, is not a theoretical notion of use to us; but it is a valuable and necessary ground for establishing the important difference I have just insisted on. If we resist for a moment the inevitable conclusion that this self is itself constituted by us (thus apart) and that we are never "really" it, we can (for just the moment I need to complete my theory) claim that the *authoritively projected* (and critically constituted) *reader* is always better than we are. This reader is always the reader that in actual reading we try to become. Such an effort is finally, I should say, an ethical one and is the ground for reading at all. Through the history of criticism there has been a tendency to declare it as such. This ethical element is what is living and not dead in the much maligned Kantian notion of disinterest in the apprehension of the beautiful (displaced from questions of beauty to those of meaning) and in the notion of play that Schiller tried to build on it, transforming aesthetics back into the ethics from which it seemed to have been divorced. In the notion of the *authoritively projected* (and critically constituted) *reader* is the notion of the ethical blindness of self-interest and a larger and wiser sense of the real than self-interest will allow. It is a matter, to put it too simply, of a vantage from which the larger picture can be seen. If one could ever *actually* succeed in fully constituting this reader in

one's life, then one would look back on the self, declaring what one saw unreal and the fiction real.

One may look at this set of categories and ask, "Where is the text?" My answer is that any text as we can know it in criticism is constituted by negation, after some possible use, of categories 1, 2, 9, and 11 and by and in the remaining seven categories. Analysis of these remaining categories leads us in a circle from *authority* to *authoritively projected reader* and back to *authority*. It is no surprise, then, that terms for *authority* have developed their authorial and readerly counterparts. Interesting examples of this are Keats's authoritive "negative capability" and Edward Bullough's readerly "psychical distance." Perhaps a better image of this circular situation is a set of concentric circles in which *authority* is itself a Blakean circumference containing all the others (except 1, 2, 9, and 11). To talk about the reader is always to talk about *authority* under a particular critical aspect.

At this point, a question arises, because it seems that this system does not allow a *critical* rejection of any text without stepping out of the system into self-interest. Many years ago Walker Gibson, in a well-known essay (*College English* 11, February 1950), remarked that there are many situations in which as readers we refuse with good reasons to become what he calls the "mock reader," a term which looks like my *authoritively projected reader*. It is not. In my system, Gibson's "mock reader" must be a reader intended by *our notion of an author*. We often refuse to accept what we constitute as this author's intention, as Wayne Booth does with Céline. My claim is that when such a situation occurs, the *authority* of the text itself reveals both the intention and the ground for such a rejection. That is, it reveals its own "fault," so to speak; and as *authoritively projected readers* in such cases we apprehend the *authority's* undermining of the authorial intention. *Authority*, then, transcends intention. There is no question in my mind that many, indeed most, texts, and maybe all are what William Blake though of as consolidations of error, in which the error is actually revealed, and that the text's authority has ways of telling us this, confounding the best efforts of the so-called real author. Blake was trying to point out a situation of this sort in his criticism of *Paradise Lost*. He did this imperfectly, trying to show that *Paradise Lost* was a consolidation, therefore a perfectly clear embodiment, of error, therefore in his view prophetic to a *critical* reading.

When we look at Cary's trilogies, we discover that he has arranged a "mimesis" of this situation in the narrations seen as texts in themselves. The most obvious example of this is, of course, Jim Latter's narration in *Not Honour More*, where Latter's *authority* is constantly betraying the "real" author, Latter. (There can be a "real" author whom we can take into account in this fictive "historical" situation.) The *authoritively projected reader* of Cary's whole text is constantly invited to exercise the whole text's *authority* in judgment on the "real" authors of the individual texts. They are made available as "real" in a way that Cary *our notion of an author* can never be to *critical* reading. Thus Cary's arranging makes possible the insertion into the fictive situation of a "mimesis" of category 1 (in the form of a Latter et al. perceived by others). It becomes available *because* it is a fiction and not a pretense of the real.

Given all of this, it is simpler—and perhaps of some practical pedagogical use—to talk naïvely, as I have in this book, of "us" or a "reader" when we consider these matters, as long as we see that it is a reader projected by that *authority* and thus residing in the "text." The *arranger* of the trilogies requires the *authoritively projected reader* periodically to rethink all that has gone before and then to order those thoughts upon completing the whole. In the previous chapters I have given examples of this occurring. Not only do the six *narrators* tend to leave things unsaid that when finally said cast events in a new light; but the *arranger* of the trilogy also does the same with his radical shifts of perspective from novel to novel. These shifts are orchestrated so as to elicit greater understanding in the process, rousing (as Blake says) the faculties to act in judgment on the *narrators*. The movement in the *First Trilogy* is toward greater sophistication of narrative self-consciousness from Sara through Wilcher to Jimson. The movement in the *Second Trilogy* gradually reveals irony on irony. We have there a piling up of moral confusion which we find increasingly difficult to sort out on any general principle brought in from outside the text. Inside this structure (which we may want to call a process) are the narrations, which are built in various ways on a principle requiring that the *authoritively projected reader* (as well as some early version of the *narrator*) be confronted and, in a sense, tested periodically by the unique and unexpected. Sara's surprise is a motif illustrating this sort of movement. Her and Nina's tendency to assert periodically that the public interpretation of something was *not the way it really was* is another. Jimson constantly demonstrates his own (and in his view everyone's) need to respond to the unexpected with imagination and resilience. Wilcher's whole didactic approach culminates after many wanderings in a message that warns against applying outworn categories to unique new events, in spite of another voice in him that hates change. The tragedy of the *narrators* of the *Second Trilogy* is surely in part their failure to respond in new ways to new situations. Nina's behavior tends toward repetition. Nimmo's earlier capacities to improvise are merely parodied by him in his later relations with Nina. Latter's combination of inconsistency and moral rigidity has the most appalling results.

It is in the techniques and motifs at the level of both *arranger* and *narrator* that one must look to find the ethical stance of Cary's *authority*. That *authority* emphasizes in the process of the trilogies the need for the ethical imagination of both the characters and the *authoritively projected reader* to confront without binding predispositions a *particular* real. The trilogies show the necessity and risks of doing so. In order to keep the emphasis where he wants it, Cary's *authority* never allows his characters to be labeled simply good or bad. Rather, they are particular, facing the particular real and trying to cope with it. The ethical element is present, therefore, not so much in content or meaning as we usually think of it, but in process culminating in the symbol, both at the *narrator's* and the *authoritively projected reader's* level. The didactic is no longer something being taught *at* us, but something happening in and *as* the text, and we (and I am again asking for a moment in which we don't constitute ourselves as an other) come to know the *authoritively projected reader*, and discover thereby a better *us* for us to become, an *us* we have perhaps for a time had the fortunate illusion of inhabiting and to whom perhaps we can return.

In the movement of both trilogies a process occurs in which always new particular reals assert themselves as new grounds for new judgments and frustrate the desire for general laws of moral and social life that fail to take into account the unique and unforeseen. This process is for Cary the "total symbol." It seems to me a process that on the face of it might be capable of projecting the depth of ethical speculation that characterizes a great work. And it has done so.

Appendixes

In these appendixes the dates are in many cases approximate. One cannot count absolutely on the accuracy or consistency of any of the narrators, and in some cases on the accuracy or consistency of Cary. However, it is possible to say, I think, that some narrators are more accurate than others. Except for Cary's own errors, Jim Latter's account seems scrupulously accurate with dates. Gulley Jimson tends to make his reader a confidant, and I have accepted most of his datings. It is clear, however, that if we do this we must assume that he was not always honest with Sara about his past. Both Sara and Nina are inaccurate about their own ages, or at least inconsistent, and Nina is not accurate about Nimmo's age. These inconsistencies are very likely deliberate on Cary's part, since both women express a certain vanity. I have had to make certain choices about other dates, and I have taken into account the likely dependability of each narrator in doing so. However, in a couple of cases I have noted an inconsistency. There may well be others I have not noticed.

Appendix A
A Chronology of the *First Trilogy*

1839	Tom Wilcher's mother is born.
1848	Gulley Jimson's father "became famous for about five years" as a painter.
1857	Edward Wilcher is born.
1858	Gulley Jimson's father finds his painting out of style. The Pre-Raphaelites flourish. Jimson's father is ousted from the Academy, attacks "modern art" in the *Times*.
1860	Bill Wilcher is born.
1863c.	Lucy Wilcher is born.

1867	Tom Wilcher is born.
1869	Rosina Balmforth is born in this year, if Sara is right about Rosina's being two years older than she is. However, this conflicts with the date on Rosina's tombstone, which puts her birth in 1881, a date more likely, since she gives birth to Jimson's son in 1920. Neither date is certain.
1871	Sara Monday may have been born. However, there are conflicting statements by Sara in *HS* 11, 167, 262 about this; and Wilcher apparently believes her to have been born circa 1878. Clearly her birthdate is for us undecidable.
	Gulley Jimson is born.
	Amy, who marries Bill Wilcher, is born on April 14.
1885	Tom Wilcher goes to Oxford.
	Lucy Wilcher runs away with the Benjamite preacher Brown and marries him three months later.
	Edward, age twenty-eight, wins his first election at Queensport.
	Julie Eeles, an actress, becomes Edward's mistress.
1886	Gulley Jimson goes to London as a clerk.
	Tom Wilcher seduces a maid at Tolbrook.
1887	Jubilee year. Queen Victoria on the throne fifty years.
	Sara is working as a cook.
	Tom Wilcher meets Julie Eeles.
1889	Bill Wilcher, age twenty-nine, comes home from the army, marries Amy, age seventeen.
1890	Bill and Amy's first child, William, is born.
1892	Sara marries Matt Monday.
1893	Sara meets Hickson.
	Sara and Matt's first child, Belle, is born.
1894	Sara and Matt's second child, Edith, is born.
1896	Gulley Jimson begins painting; his wife leaves him; his mother dies.
1897	Sara and Matt's third child, Nancy, is born.
1899	Tom Wilcher starts managing the family business.
	Gulley Jimson goes to London.
1900	Bill and Amy Wilcher's son, John, is born.
	Edward Wilcher's "most ferocious" election takes place.
1902	Julie Eeles returns from U.S.A. after a three-year tour.

Edward Wilcher wins another election.

The Wilchers' father dies. Tom Wilcher takes over the estate.

Lucy Wilcher comes home, but there is an argument and she leaves until 1910.

Bill and Amy Wilcher return to India.

1903   Edward Wilcher is bankrupt.

Julie Eeles attempts suicide.

1904   Bill and Amy Wilcher's son, Loftus, is born.

Gulley Jimson's exhibition.

1906   Tom Wilcher becomes Julie Eeles's lover.

Edward Wilcher marries Mrs. Tirrit.

Death of Mrs. Tirrit.

1908   Critics mention Gulley Jimson for the first time. "A nasty young man who didn't even know what art was."

1910   Sara Monday meets Gulley Jimson and Nina.

Lucy and Brown's son, Robert, is born.

Edward Wilcher loses an election by 15 votes, goes to France, marries Lottie.

1912   Edward and Lottie Wilcher's daughter Ann is born.

Lucy Brown brings Robert, age 2, to Tolbrook.

Amy Wilcher brings John, age 12, and Loftus, age 8, to Tolbrook. All stay at Tolbrook until the war begins in 1914.

1913   Julie Eeles's estranged husband dies.

Edward Wilcher returns from France and prophesies war.

1914   Lucy returns to Brown.

War begins.

1916   Tom Wilcher goes to France as a stretcher-bearer.

Matt Monday takes ill.

Gulley Jimson reappears in Sara's life.

1917   Tom Wilcher returns injured from the war.

John Wilcher, age 17, is drafted.

1918   John Wilcher is wounded and taken prisoner.

William Wilcher dies in action.

1919   John Wilcher returns from the war.

Bill Wilcher dies.

Edward Wilcher returns, retired, to Tolbrook without Lottie.

	Matt Monday dies.
	Sara Monday lives with Rosina Balmforth at Brighton.
	Gulley Jimson and Rosina Balmforth have an affair while Sara is selling her house.
	Sara and Gulley Jimson have a "honeymoon" at Bournemouth, then go to Miss Slaughter's; Jimson is to paint a mural there.
1920	Rosina Balmforth has a child, Tom, fathered by Gulley Jimson.
	Hickson puts on an exhibition of Jimson's work, attacked by critics.
	Lottie sends for Ann, seeks a divorce from Edward Wilcher.
	The Wilchers' old mother dies.
	John Wilcher marries Gladys.
	Edward Wilcher dies, age 63, of pneumonia.
1922	John Wilcher dies.
	Lucy Brown comes to Tolbrook, dies.
1924	Gulley Jimson finishes picture for Miss Slaughter.
	After assaulting Sara, Gulley disappears. Sara is imprisoned for passing bad checks. She implies that at this time she is 46 years old. She is perhaps 53.
1925	Sara goes as cook to Tolbrook, meets Tom Wilcher, accompanies him to Craven Gardens, London, in the winter.
	Sara meets Robert Brown, Jr., said to be age 16 but actually 15 if he was indeed born in 1910, at Tolbrook.
	Loftus Wilcher is married to Blanche Hipper.
1926	Tom Wilcher puts Sara in charge of both of his houses.
	Hickson acquires some Jimson canvasses from Sara.
1927	Robert Brown graduates from school and goes to Canada for ten years.
1928	Rosina Balmforth dies in a railway accident, age 59 by Sara's reckoning, but 47 according to her tombstone.
	Gulley Jimson, now with Lizzie, appears with Tom, said to be age 10 but actually age 8 if he was indeed born in 1920, at Craven Gardens.
1929	Tom Wilcher leaves Tolbrook "for good."
1932	Sara's affair with Tom Wilcher begins.
1936	Blanche Wilcher fires Sara.

Fire destroys Craven Gardens.

Tom Wilcher acquires the Ranns Park house, proposes marriage to Sara.

Sara goes to jail for eighteen months, during which time she writes her "confession" for the newspaper.

Tom Wilcher is sent to Tolbrook under the care of Ann Wilcher, who is a physician.

Tom Wilcher begins to keep his journal.

Robert Brown, Lucy's son, returns to Tolbrook, marries Ann Wilcher.

Gulley Jimson, working on *The Living God*, goes to jail.

Lizzie takes the two children to her parents.

1937   Sara is released from jail, begins living with Fred Robins.

Edward John Wilcher Brown ("Jan") is born to Robert and Ann Brown.

1938   Tom Wilcher goes to London to find Sara. Robert and Ann return him to Tolbrook. Tom Wilcher's diary ends in the autumn of this year.

Gulley Jimson is released from jail. (The action of *HM* begins at this point. Gulley has not seen Sara for three years. They meet again through Miss Coker at Sara's home with Fred Robins. Jimson states that Sara has been living with him for about four years, but this is not possible.)

Jimson is returned to jail for harassing Hickson.

1939   Jimson, released from prison in the spring, meets Alabaster, who writes to him on February 2.

Sara is now living with Byles.

Jimson and Sara meet at Rosina Balmforth's grave in June.

Jimson, painting *The Raising of Lazarus* on the Beeders' wall, ransacks the Beeders' flat, ends up in the hospital.

Later in June, Jimson pushes Sara downstairs, causing her death in hospital in July.

Jimson begins *The Creation* with £50 from the Beeders.

The wall on which Jimson is painting *The Creation* is torn down.

Jimson bursts a blood vessel and is hospitalized.

1939–40   Jimson dictates his memoir in hospital.
1940   Jimson dies, age 69.
           Alabaster's *Life and Works of Gulley Jimson* is published.

Appendix B
A Chronology of the *Second Trilogy*

1844–45c. Aunt Latter is born.
1853   Richard Nimmo is born.
1855   Georgina Nimmo is born.
1857   Chester Nimmo is born.
1858c.   Ruth Nimmo is born.
1865   The Nimmo's mother dies.
1868   The prediction by the Nimmos' father of the second coming fails (April 30).
           Richard Nimmo goes to grammar school.
1869ff.   Chester Nimmo is working at the farm, Georgina Nimmo at the dairy.
1870   Chester Nimmo reads the socialist pamphlet "The Grand Design."
           Jim Latter is born.
1871   Chester Nimmo hears a lecture by Lanza, lieutenant of Bakunin in the League of Peace and Freedom.
1873ff.   Nina Woodville is born. The exact year is uncertain, for dates Nina gives create an ambiguity.
1875   January 19: The "Shagbrook Splash."
           Chester Nimmo becomes a union organizer.
1877   Chester Nimmo with Georgina Nimmo visits Richard, now a clerk in London, meets Pring.
           Nina Woodville's parents die. She goes to live with Aunt Latter.
           The Lilmouth Strike.
1878   Chester Nimmo meets the child Nina Woodville.
1880   Death of Fred Coyte.
1881   Georgina Nimmo dies.
1883   Jim Latter and Nina Woodville's dangerous swim.
1887   Jim Latter and Nina Woodville's dangerous sail.
1889   The London Dockers' Strike.
1890   Nina Woodville as a young woman meets Chester Nimmo.
1894   Marriage of Chester Nimmo and Nina Woodville.

Appendix B: A Chronology of the *Second Trilogy*

1895	Birth of Tom to Nina Nimmo; he is actually the son of Jim Latter.
1899ff.	The Boer War.
	The Chorlock Riot.
	The Lilmouth Riot.
1902	Death of Jim Latter's father.
1902c.	Jim Latter invalided out of the army. Sent to Africa in the colonial service.
	Birth of Sally to Nina Nimmo; she is actually Jim Latter's daughter.
1905	The election which makes Chester Nimmo Undersecretary for Mines. (Nina is mistaken. The election occurred in January 1906.)
1908	Nimmo joins cabinet as Secretary for Mines.
1909	The "Fight against the Lords." Nimmo supports Lloyd George's land bill.
	Jim Latter returns on his second leave from Nigeria.
1912	Tom Nimmo's preparations for "Puss in Boots" at the Tribes.
	The "Contract Case," two months previous to the Marconi Case.
1913	Chester Nimmo preaches pacifism in his "move to the left."
	(Nina states that Chester Nimmo is 53 in 1913, but he is probably 56.)
	Engagement of Tom Nimmo to Julie Tribe.
	Tom Nimmo expelled from Eastborough, later enters Oxford.
1914	Chester Nimmo's "tour of the west" preaching pacifism.
	Chester Nimmo turns around, joins the war cabinet.
1915	The Brome case.
1917	Jim Latter returns from Nigeria on sick leave.
1918	Tom Nimmo is awarded the Military Cross.
	Death of Robert Latter, Jim's brother.
1922	Chester Nimmo defeated for election.
	Tom Nimmo, jailed in police raid on his club, is exiled to Germany, where he commits suicide.
	Jim Latter puts the Luga case before the League of Nations.
1924	Divorce of Nina and Chester Nimmo.

	Marriage of Nina and Jim Latter.
	Chester Nimmo again defeated in election.
	In early April, Chester Nimmo's "heart attack." He writes *Except the Lord*. Nina writes *Prisoner of Grace* after Sally and Bootham walk out on Chester.
1926	April 24: Chester Nimmo's second speech at Shagbrook.
	May 4: Jim Latter appointed special constable.
	May 4: First day of the general strike.
	May 6: Chester Nimmo's third speech at Shagbrook graveyard.
	The East Tarbiton bus incident.
	May 9: Injury to Pincomb and arrest of deputy Maufe.
	May 20: Trial of Maufe.
	Death of Chester Nimmo.
	Jim Latter murders Nina.
	July: Jim Latter makes his "statement," *Not Honour More*.

Index

Library of Congress Cataloging in Publication Data

Adams, Hazard, 1926–
  Joyce Cary's trilogies.

  "A Florida State University book."
  Bibliography: p.
  Includes index.
    1. Cary, Joyce, 1888–1957—Criticism and interpreta-
  tion.   I. Title.
  PR6005.A77Z58   1983   823'.912   83–3461
  ISBN 0–8130–0759–3

University Presses of Florida is the central agency for scholarly publishing of the State of Florida's university system. Its offices are located at 15 Northwest 15th Street, Gainesville, FL 32603. Works published by University Presses of Florida are evaluated and selected by the faculty editorial committees of Florida's nine public universities: Florida A & M University (Tallahassee), Florida Atlantic University (Boca Raton), Florida International University (Miami), Florida State University (Tallahassee), University of Central Florida (Orlando), University of Florida (Gainesville), University of North Florida (Jacksonville), University of South Florida (Tampa), University of West Florida (Pensacola).

280